Discourse and Digital Pract

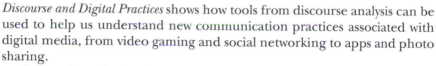

Discourse and Digital Practices shows how tools from discourse analysis can be used to help us understand new communication practices associated with digital media, from video gaming and social networking to apps and photo sharing.

This cutting-edge book:

- draws together fourteen eminent scholars in the field including James Paul Gee, David Barton, Ilana Snyder, Phil Benson, Victoria Carrington, Guy Merchant, Camilla Vásquez, Neil Selwyn and Rodney Jones
- addresses the central question: "How does discourse analysis enable us to understand digital practices?"
- demonstrates how digital practices and the associated new technologies challenge discourse analysts to adapt traditional analytic tools and formulate new theories and methodologies
- analyses a different type of digital media in each chapter
- examines digital practices from a wide variety of approaches including textual analysis, conversation analysis, interactional sociolinguistics, multimodal discourse analysis, object ethnography, geosemiotics, and critical discourse analysis.

Discourse and Digital Practices will be of interest to advanced students studying courses on digital literacies or language and digital practices.

Rodney H. Jones is Professor of English at City University of Hong Kong.

Alice Chik is Senior Lecturer in The School of Education at Macquarie University.

Christoph A. Hafner is Assistant Professor in the Department of English, City University of Hong Kong.

Discourse and Digital Practices

Doing discourse analysis in the digital age

Edited by
Rodney H. Jones, Alice Chik and
Christoph A. Hafner

Routledge
Taylor & Francis Group

LONDON AND NEW YORK

First published 2015
by Routledge
2 Park Square, Milton Park, Abingdon, Oxon OX14 4RN

and by Routledge
711 Third Avenue, New York, NY 10017

Routledge is an imprint of the Taylor & Francis Group, an informa business

British Library Cataloguing-in-Publication Data
A catalogue record for this book is available from the British Library

Library of Congress Cataloging-in-Publication Data
A catalog record for this book has been requested

ISBN: 978-1-138-02232-4 (hbk)
ISBN: 978-1-138-02233-1 (pbk)
ISBN: 978-1-315-72646-5 (ebk)

Typeset in Baskerville
by Swales & Willis Ltd, Exeter, Devon

Printed and bound in the United States of America by Publishers Graphics, LLC on sustainably sourced paper.

Contents

Illustrations

Figures

Tables

Contributors

David Barton is Professor of Language and Literacy in the Department of Linguistics at Lancaster University. His research is concerned with: carrying out detailed studies of everyday literacies and rethinking the nature of literacy, especially in the online world. He is co-author (with Carmen Lee) of *Language Online* (Routledge, 2013) and (with others) of *Researching Language and Social Media* (Routledge, 2014).

Phil Benson is Professor of Applied Linguistics at Macquarie University. His main research interests are in informal language learning and language learning and new media, and he is currently especially interested in YouTube as a space for language and intercultural learning. He is co-editor, with Alice Chik, of *Popular Culture, Pedagogy and Teacher Education: international perspectives* (Routledge, 2003).

Victoria Carrington holds a Chair in Education in the School of Education and Lifelong Learning at the University of East Anglia. She researches and writes extensively in the areas of new technologies, youth and literacies with a particular interest in the impact of new digital media on literacy practices. She is co-author (with Muriel Robinson) of *Digital Literacies: social learning and classroom practices* (Sage, 2012).

Alice Chik is Senior Lecturer in The School of Education at Macquarie University. Her main research areas include narrative inquiry, literacy and popular culture in language education. She is the co-editor of *Popular Culture, Pedagogy and Teacher Education: international perspectives* (Routledge, 2014).

James Paul Gee is the Mary Lou Fulton Presidential Professor of Literacy Studies at Arizona State University and a member of the National Academy of Education. His most recent books include: *Unified Discourse Analysis: language, reality, virtual worlds and video games* (Routledge, 2014); *Sociolinguistics and Literacies*, Fourth Edition (Routledge, 2011), *How to Do Discourse Analysis* (Routledge, 2011); and *Language and Learning in the Digital World* (with Elizabeth Hayes, Routledge, 2011).

Christoph A. Hafner is Assistant Professor in the Department of English, City University of Hong Kong. His research interests include specialized discourse, digital literacies and language learning and technology. He is co-author of *Understanding Digital Literacies: a practical introduction* (Routledge, 2012) and co-editor of *Transparency, Power and Control: perspectives on legal communication* (Ashgate, 2012).

Rodney H. Jones is Professor of English at City University of Hong Kong. His main research interests include discourse analysis, health communication and language and sexuality. His books include *Discourse in Action: introducing mediated discourse analysis* (edited with Sigrid Norris, Routledge, 2005), *Understanding Digital Literacies: a practical introduction* (with Christoph Hafner, Routledge, 2012) and *Health and Risk Communication: an applied linguistic perspective* (Routledge, 2013).

Brian W. King is an Assistant Professor in the Department of English at City University of Hong Kong. His work on corpus-assisted discourse analysis and language and sexuality has appeared in international journals such as *Language in Society, Sexualities, Journal of Language and Sexuality* and *Gender and Language,* as well as in numerous edited volumes, including *Contemporary Corpus Linguistics* (Continuum, 2009).

Carmen Lee is Associate Professor in the Department of English at the Chinese University of Hong Kong. She has published and carried out projects on social aspects of language and literacy, linguistic practices on the internet, and multilingual literacy practices. She is co-author (with David Barton) of the book *Language Online* (Routledge, 2013).

Jackie Marsh is Professor of Education at the University of Sheffield, UK. Her research focuses on popular culture, media and digital technologies in young children's literacy development. Her latest book (with Julia Bishop) is *Changing Play: play, media and commercial culture from the 1950s to the present day* (Open University Press, 2013).

Guy Merchant is Professor of Literacy in Education in the Faculty of Development and Society, Sheffield Hallam University. His research focuses on the relationship between children, young people, new technology and literacy. His books include *Web 2.0 for Schools: learning and social participation* (Peter Lang International Academic Publishers, 2009), co-written with Julia Davies.

Neil Selwyn is Professor at the Faculty of Education, Monash University. His writing and research focus on education, technology and sociology. Recent books include *Distrusting Educational Technology* (Routledge, 2014) and *Digital Technology and the Contemporary University* (Routledge, 2014).

Ilana Snyder is a Professor in the Faculty of Education, Monash University. Her research has focused on the changes to literacy practices associated with the use of digital technologies and the implications for literacy education. Her books include *Hypertext* (Melbourne University Press, 1996), *Page to Screen* (Routledge, 1997) and *Silicon Literacies* (Routledge, 2002) and *The Literacy Wars* (Allen & Unwin, 2008).

Camilla Vásquez is an Associate Professor of Applied Linguistics at the University of South Florida, where she teaches graduate courses on discourse analysis, pragmatics and qualitative research methods. Her research has appeared in such journals as *Journal of Pragmatics, Narrative Inquiry, Text and Talk* and *Discourse Studies.*

Acknowledgments

The editors would like to thank the Department of English of City University of Hong Kong for providing the fuding for *The Fifth International Roundtable on Discourse Analysis: Discourse and Digital Practices*, where the ideas in many of these chapters were discussed and debated. They would also like to thank Ms. Yaxin Zheng for her invaluable adminstrative and editorial assistance and Ms. Yan Dou for her assistance in copyediting the manuscript.

The editors and publishers would like to thank the following individuals and companies for permission to reproduce the following material:

Screen shots from iDrate reproduced with kind permission from Locassa.

Screen shots from Withings Health Mate App reproduced with kind permission from Withings Inc.

Screenshots from Moshi Monsters reproduced with kind permission from Mind Candy Ltd.

Photographs on Flickr by Nadia Gradecky, Julia Davies, and Jody Jay reproduced with kind permission from the photographers.

Chapter 1

Introduction

Discourse analysis and digital practices

Rodney H. Jones, Alice Chik and Christoph A. Hafner

Digital technologies have given rise to a host of new ways for people to communicate, manage social relationships, and get things done, which are challenging how we think about love and friendship, work and play, health and fitness, learning and literacy, and politics and citizenship. These new practices are also challenging the ways discourse analysts think about texts, social interactions, and even the nature of language itself. The affordances digital media provide for the production of multimodal texts, for example, call into question analytical paradigms that focus only on written or spoken language. Interactive writing spaces such as blogs and social network sites make possible very different forms of social interaction than those found in face-to-face conversation and traditional written texts. And practices of remixing and 'curating' raise questions about the status of authorship. Even analytical tools designed to examine the ideological dimensions of discourse need to be adapted to contend with discursive environments in which the loci of power are much more diffuse and the instruments of ideological control and discipline are more subtle and complex.

Although there have been numerous attempts in discourse analysis (see for example Herring 2007), and sociolinguistics more broadly (see for example Androutsopoulos 2011), to formulate new analytical frameworks especially designed for the study of digital communication, the range of social practices associated with digitally mediated discourse, and the rapid pace at which new technologies are being introduced, make it difficult for any single framework to meet the challenge of understanding all of the complex relationships between discourse and digital practices. In order to cope with the fast-changing landscape of digital media, discourse analysts need to both draw upon the rich store of theories and methods developed over the years for the analysis of 'analogue' discourse, and to formulate new concepts and new methodologies to address the unique combinations of affordances and constraints introduced by digital media.

This book brings together fourteen eminent scholars in linguistics and literacy studies to consider how various practices people engage in using digital media can be understood using tools from discourse analysis.

The methods adopted represent a range of approaches to discourse, from more traditional analyses of textual coherence and interactional turn-taking to newer approaches such as corpus-assisted discourse analysis, mediated discourse analysis, and multimodal discourse analysis. Each chapter focuses on a particular social practice associated with digital technology and shows how tools from a particular approach to discourse, or combination of approaches, can help us to understand that practice.

What are digital practices?

The focus of this volume on digital *practices* is in line with recent approaches in applied linguistics (Pennycook 2010), literacy studies (Gee 2012), and discourse analysis (Norris and Jones 2005) which take as their starting point not discourse per se, but, rather, the situated social practices that people use discourse to perform.

The orientation towards social practice taken by contributors has its roots in a number of intellectual traditions, including the critical sociology of Bourdieu (1977), who sees practice in terms of the way social conventions become submerged into people's habitual dispositions, and the cultural critique of Foucault (1972) and his followers, who see it in terms of the regimes of knowledge which define what sorts of behaviours, identities and relationships are considered normal. But it is most closely informed by the understanding of practice articulated in the new literacy studies (Barton 2006; Gee 2012) and mediated discourse analysis (Norris and Jones 2005; Scollon 2001), in which practice is seen less as a matter of dispositions or regimes of knowledge and more as a matter of the concrete, situated actions people perform with particular mediational means (such as written texts, computers, mobile phones) in order to enact membership in particular social groups. In these approaches, practice is nearly always used as a countable noun ('practices') and refers to 'observable, collectable and/or documentable . . . events, involving real people, relationships, purposes, actions, places, times, circumstances, feelings, tools, (and) resources' (Tusting, Ivanic and Wilson 2000: 213). It is difficult, from this perspective, to speak of the 'practice' of social networking, or the 'practice' of 'video gaming' without considering the ways these practices are performed by real people in real situations. Indeed, as many of the chapters in this volume dramatically illustrate, practices (such as 'tagging') can have very different meanings and very different social purposes, and, in fact, involve very different actions, in different contexts (for example Twitter vs Flickr) (see Barton this volume). Practices are, in this way, often hard to 'pin down', always changing to meet the demands of new circumstances or to respond to the affordances and constraints of new cultural tools. Complicating this is the fact that practices are almost never engaged in in isolation, but are always mixed in complex ways with other practices. Practices such as purchasing animals to decorate one's language learning garden on Busuu (described by Chik), keeping track of one's calories with *MyFitnessPal* (described by Jones), reading to children with an iPad (described by Merchant), or attending online parties held by 'elite' Club Penguin Music Video production teams (described by Marsh) all involve multiple overlapping practices such as shopping, gardening, dieting, story-sharing and socialising, which have long histories independent of the digital practices into which they have been recruited. Digital practices are always 'nestled' or 'nested' (Marsh this volume) with other cultural practices, some new and some old, to form what Scollon (2001) has referred to as a 'nexus of practice', a configuration of tools and actions with various conventions and histories associated with them which come together to form recognisable sequences of actions and to make available to actors recognisable social identities.

What we mean by 'digital practices', then, are these 'assemblages' of actions involving tools associated with digital technologies, which have come to be recognised by specific groups of people as ways of attaining particular social goals, enacting particular social identities, and reproducing particular sets of social relationships. The assumption is that digital technologies, because of the different configurations of modes and materialities they make available, both make possible new kinds of social practices and alter the way people engage in old ones. The practices dealt with in this volume include the tagging of pictures by users of Flickr, the use of iPhone apps by 'self-quantifiers', and the creation of music videos by participants in an online virtual world. Our definition of 'tools associated with digital technologies', however, is not limited to software or websites, but includes hardware (physical objects) and semiotic tools (such as conventional ways of talking or writing that have grown up around digital media). Therefore, the practices considered are not limited to those that occur 'online' or within the borders of the screen, but also include practices that have developed around the handling of physical artefacts like iPhones and iPads, and even practices of urban signage which appropriate linguistic features of computer-mediated communication. In fact, none of the practices described in this book can be said to reside in strictly defined 'online' or 'offline' spaces. Digital practices always transverse boundaries between the physical and the virtual, and between technological systems and social systems.

What is discourse analysis?

What, then, do we mean by 'discourse analysis', and what is its utility in helping us to understand digital practices? 'Discourse' is a term that is used in a variety of different fields and can mean a variety of different things. It can refer to the formal properties of semiotic artefacts that make them 'hold together' as certain types of 'texts', it can refer to the ways people use language and other semiotic systems to accomplish particular social actions, or it can refer to broader systems of knowledge which act to regulate what people can say, write or think. For the purposes of this volume, we will define discourse broadly as the ways people build and manage their social worlds using various semiotic systems. This definition, of course, places discourse in an intimate relationship with social practices. On the one hand, all social practices are to some extent mediated through discourse – that is, discourse is used as a tool for performing social practices. And on the other hand, discourse plays an important role in maintaining, reproducing and transmitting social practices. 'Discourse analysis', then, is the study of the ways different 'technologies of entextualisation' (Jones 2009) (including semiotic systems like languages, as well as media like televisions and computers) affect the kinds of meanings people can make in different situations, the kinds of actions they can perform, the kinds of relationships they can form, and the kinds of people they can be. In order to engage in such study, discourse analysts usually pay attention to four things:

- *Texts*: How different technologies of entextualisation allow us to combine semiotic elements to form socially recognisable texts that can be used to perform different kinds of socially recognised actions.
- *Contexts*: The social and material situations in which texts are constructed, consumed, exchanged and appropriated.
- *Actions and interactions*: What people do with texts, especially what they do with and to each other.
- *Power and ideology*: How people use texts to dominate and control others and to create certain 'versions of reality'.

Different approaches to discourse, of course, emphasise these aspects of discourse to different degrees, but all of them, in one way or another, take into account all four of these elements, and strive to understand how they work together: how, for example, contexts influence the form and meaning of texts, how different kinds of texts make possible different kinds of actions and interactions, and how the ways people use texts to act and interact in specific contexts both reflect and help to reproduce certain ideologies and power relationships. In other words, all approaches to discourse seek in some way to understand the relationship between the 'micro' level of discourse (having to do with the way texts are put together and used to take specific actions in specific situations), and the 'macro' level of discourse (having to do with the way texts reflect and help perpetuate certain social orders).

As we mentioned above, the particular configurations of modes and materialities that digital media make available present considerable challenges to the way analysts approach each of these four aspects of discourse. In some cases, the tools that have been developed for face-to-face conversation and writing in print media can be easily adapted to analyse online conversations and texts. In other cases, new concepts and new methods need to be developed. The real issue, however, goes beyond just the applicability of particular analytical tools to the analysis of digitally mediated communication to the fact that digital media in some ways force us to rethink our very definitions of terms such as text, context, interaction, and power.

Texts

By texts, of course, we do not just mean written texts in the traditional sense, but include conversations – both written and spoken – videos, photographs, drawings, paintings, street signs, websites, software interfaces, video games, and any other aggregate of semiotic elements that can function as a tool for people to take social action. Despite the breadth of this definition, discourse analysts do have some fairly strong opinions about what constitutes a text and what does not. Most agree that for a collection of semiotic elements (words, sentences, images, sounds, etc.) to be considered a text, it must have what is known as 'texture'. Texture is a property of connectedness that is created through *cohesion*, that is, the way different parts of the text are held together using the syntactic and semantic resources of whatever semiotic system is being used, and *coherence*, the way different parts of the text are ordered sequentially so that it can be recognised by readers as logical and meaningful (Halliday and Hasan 1976; Schegloff and Sacks 1973).

Although texts like video games, social networking sites, and iPhone apps are in many ways very different from the written texts and face-to-face conversations from which these principles were developed, they are also characterised by texture. This is one of the main points Gee makes in the chapter immediately following this introduction, that to be amenable to discourse analysis, a semiotic aggregate must exhibit properties of what he calls 'packaging' and 'flow' – the combination of different elements using principles of syntax and semantics, and the arrangement of these elements in some kind of temporal patterning. He illustrates this by analysing how the various elements in a video game fit together and are arranged in meaningful sequences. Another important point Gee makes is that texture is there for players to *use*. It is not just about abstract meaning or form. The way players approach games (and the way people approach written texts and conversations, for that matter) is in terms of how they can use these principles of combination and sequencing in order to enable certain kinds of actions. And so, for discourse analysts, syntax and semantics are not just about rules and structures – they provide the basic textual resources people use to enact social practices.

The way texture is manifested in different kinds of texts, of course, varies considerably. Halliday and Hasan (1976) for example, distinguish between texts that have a 'tight' texture, that is, most of the connections between the parts are explicit, and those that have a loose texture, that is, the connections between parts are less explicit, depending more on the active efforts of readers to hold them together. Much of the early discourse analytical work on computer-mediated communication focused on the relatively loose texture of computer-mediated texts. In her classic article on coherence in text only chat, for example, Herring (1999) discusses how phenomena such as disrupted adjacency, overlapping exchanges and topic decay give to some forms of computer-mediated communication a much looser texture than found in face-to-face conversations or print-based written texts, but she also argues that this apparent incoherence can actually facilitate increased interactivity and creativity. A similar point is made by Barton in his chapter on the practices of tagging on Flickr: even though they might at first appear to be loose collections of words, lists of tags associated with pictures often exploit properties of syntax and semantics in ways that allow users to transform a form of discourse originally intended for simple classification into a tool for communication and storytelling. A similar kind of loose texture seems to characterise the YouTube comments analysed by Benson, but, as he shows so convincingly, an underlying coherence of the comments can be revealed through attention to 'sequential implicativeness' (Schegloff and Sacks 1973).

While many digitally mediated texts are loosely textured, many others are rather tightly textured, giving users little choice as to how elements can be connected up or sequenced. Many choices about 'packaging' and 'flow' in computer-mediated discourse, in fact, as Jones points out in his chapter, are not made by people, but by computer programs. Sometimes the texture imposed on discourse by algorithms can amplify users' abilities to perform certain actions, form certain relationships, and construct certain identities, but at the same time, these 'algorithmically imposed' textures can also create constraints on people's ability to take action, interact with others, or be the kinds of people they want to be. In addition, sometimes the texture imposed on discourse by a particular set of algorithms can create confusion as to how users are supposed to read texts. One of the most interesting points Benson makes about YouTube comments, for instance, is that, despite the fact that they are produced through sequential implicativeness, the site's algorithm displays them (by default) in descending order based on the number of 'likes' they have received, imposing an entirely different pattern of texture on them.

Another important property of texts that discourse analysts are interested in is the way they create connections with other texts. Of course, intertextuality and interdiscursivity are properties of all texts. Digital media, however, because of its technological affordances for hypertextual linking, embedding, copying and pasting, combining and curating, make it much easier to connect texts with other texts and to mix and mash texts together. The fundamental intertextual and herteroglossic (Androutsopoulos 2011; Bakhtin 1981) nature of new media texts doesn't only change practices of reading and writing (Jones and Hafner 2012), but also has the effect of disturbing comfortable notions of textual boundaries and authorship. In marvelling at these new forms of linking, mixing and mashing made possible by new media, however, it is sometimes easy to ignore the more conventional ways people create intertextuality in digitally mediated texts using purely linguistic resources. In the only chapter in this volume which focuses exclusively on intertextuality, Vásquez demonstrates some of the more 'low tech' ways participants in the digital practice of online reviewing use to create linkages with other texts and creatively mix the conventions of different genres. The most important point about intertextuality that Vásquez makes, a point that can just as strongly apply to the examples given by Marsh and Snyder, is that intertextuality is essentially a *social* process through which people not only create linkages between texts, but also create relationships between themselves and other users of texts, showing themselves to be competent members of particular communities by using the conventions of intertextuality of those communities.

A third important quality of digitally mediated texts that the contributors to this volume take up is their dialogic character. Again, just as all texts are to some extent intertextual, they are also to some extent dialogic, in that they respond to previous texts and create the conditions for subsequent texts (Bakhtin 1981). The difference with new media texts is that this dialogism is much more dynamic than it is with conventional written texts. Reading and writing have become much more like having a conversation, with readers being able to 'write back' to writers, and writers shaping their texts in anticipation of an almost immediate response from readers. The responsiveness of digital texts, however, not only involves the interaction between writers and readers, but also involves interaction between human users and machine algorithms which automatically alter texts based on the ways users use them or on certain characteristics of users such as location or pre-defined user settings. This is what Jones means when he points out that, more and more, texts are able to 'read' us and, in many ways, to 'write' us as certain kinds of people. This, of course, has important implications for issues like human agency and the status of texts as socially shared objects. It also calls into question what it actually means to read and write a text, when our media have acquired the ability to read texts without us and to take actions on our behalf, and when physical actions like eating at a restaurant, making a purchase or going for a run automatically become acts of writing.

Finally, one of the most conspicuous characteristics of digital texts that present challenges to discourse analysts is the fact that they are almost always multimodal, consisting of rich combinations of semiotic modes like writing, visuals and sound. This has consequences for the way discourse analysts approach issues like cohesion and coherence, intertextuality and dialogicality, since the affordances and constraints of different modes affect how they fit together, how they connect to other texts, and how readers can interact with texts. The most important thing about multimodality is that, because of the inherent dynamism of digital texts, meanings are rarely expressed in stable configurations of modes, but rather travel across modes and combinations of modes in ways that alter them, sometimes subtly, sometimes dramatically, a process Jones (this volume, after Iedema 2001) refers to as resemiotisation. Through processes of resemiotisation, actions like walking or drinking water are transformed into graphs and images, photos on Flickr are transformed into lists of tags which combine to form narratives, and videos on YouTube become the initiating moves in written conversations.

Related to multimodality are the dramatic ways digital technologies have changed how we relate to texts as material objects. Web pages are different from newspapers not just textually, but also physically. iPads are very different kinds of material objects from books. The new forms of materiality texts take has important consequences for things like the kinds of access people have to texts, the physical and social contexts into which they can be appropriated, and the ways we physically manipulate texts. Merchant, for example, points out how tablet computers have made reading into a much more *haptic* activity, requiring readers to master actions like tapping, dragging, swiping and pinching. Similarly, Carrington shows how teenagers use their mobile phones not just as tools to access texts, but as texts themselves, objects through which they communicate things like their identities, their affiliations, and their orientations towards others.

Contexts

The second important component of discourse analysis is an attention to the material and social *contexts* in which texts are produced, consumed, and used to take social actions. The meaning and utility of texts reside not just in their textual elements, but also in how these elements are 'situated' within actual contexts of communication. In fact, an analysis of texts that 'gets stuck' in the examination of formal textual elements like syntax, semantics, and sequentiality does not really count as discourse analysis, since discourse is all about how texts and conversations 'fit into' the real world.

Understanding the effect of context on language and other semiotic systems is complex enough when dealing with more traditional spoken and written texts, since such an understanding must take into account multiple aspects of context including spatial and temporal aspects, as well as those aspects of context (both material and cognitive) that are 'brought along' by social actors (van Dijk 2008), and those aspects that are 'brought about' (Auer 1992) by people's actions and interactions. Furthermore, a consideration of context must also take into account what Malinowski (1923) calls 'the context of culture', the wider sets of expectations about how people are supposed to behave in different situations.

Digital technologies have made all of these aspects of context much more complicated. They have altered our experience of the spatial and temporal aspects of context by creating complex 'layerings' of online and offline spaces. They have altered our experience of social contexts, allowing us to participate in a wide range of different kinds of synchronous and asynchronous social gatherings with different configurations of participants (Jones 2004). And they have altered our experience of the 'context of culture' by enabling new and complex global flows of cultural products and ideas.

Much of the early work on computer-mediated discourse made a clear differentiation between online and offline contexts; however, more recent work (see for example Jones 2010), including many of the chapters in this volume, recognise that in considering the contexts of digital practices we must come to terms with the ways physical and virtual spaces, times, interaction orders and cultures interact. As the children described in Hafner's chapter travel through different online spaces and engage in different activities with other players of Moshi Monsters, they also inhabit the material spaces of their home, where they must negotiate different activities with other co-present individuals, including their researcher-father. As the joggers described in Jones's chapter move across physical spaces, the routes that they transverse appear on the computer and smartphone screens of their *Nike+* followers situated in other physical spaces. And as the characters in the digital children's stories described in Merchant's chapter appear and move across the screens of iPads, they affect the configuration of spaces and bodies in the physical environments in which they are read.

Under these circumstances, one of the most important issues facing discourse analysts is developing methods to trace the way texts (and the meanings, social relationships, and identities associated with them) change as they travel from context to context, moving across virtual and physical spaces, being (sometimes automatically) 'synced' across multiple devices, and being appropriated into situations which their producers may never have anticipated. Just as intertextuality and multimodality are defining features of digitally mediated discourse, so is recontextualisation (Bauman and Briggs 1990). Much of the way we craft our texts and utterances depends on how we take into account the contexts in which they will be interpreted – that is, much of our meaning making is based upon some expectation of what Nissenbaum (2009) calls 'contextual integrity'. The complex overlapping and internested networks of contexts that digital technologies have created makes it much more difficult to maintain contextual integrity.

For analysts this is not just a theoretical issue, it can also be an ethical one as well, as King points out in his chapter on analysing the conversations of gay men in a 'public' chat room. Just because these conversations are available to the public, King argues, does not necessarily make them 'public'. Most online communication in contexts like chat rooms and social networking sites, he argues, 'is neither inherently public nor private; rather it depends on how each participant sees the context of communication'. Seeking informed consent is, for him, a way to discover how participants feel about that context. This argument should give all researchers of digital practices pause to consider their relationships with and responsibilities towards the people they are studying. It should also serve to remind us that contexts are not simply pre-fabricated, but rather are to a large degree 'brought about' through the practices that people engage in.

Finally, this discussion of decontextualisation and recontextualisation reminds us that any study of digital practices must, as Merchant puts it, not just 'reach down' into embodied, material and situated contexts of digital practice, but also 'reach up' to consider the broader global contexts in which technologies and information are produced, circulated, and valued. There is, for example, something fundamental, not just in the technology of the internet but also in the *economy* of the internet, that works against contextual integrity (Lanier 2013), making it more difficult for participants in gay chat rooms, users of commercial self-tracking apps, learners in online language learning sites, and children in virtual worlds to maintain control over the texts they produce.

Actions and interactions

Perhaps the most important thing that distinguishes discourse analysts from other kinds of linguists is their focus not just on the structure and meaning of texts, but also on how people use texts to perform concrete social actions. From their early concern with how people 'do things with words' (Austin 1976) to their more recent interest in language as a 'mediational means' (Norris and Jones 2005), discourse analysts have long been preoccupied not just with language but with 'language in use'. In turning their attention to digital media and the forms of discourse it makes possible, then, a central question for contributors to this book is how these new 'technologies of entextualisation' and the kinds of texts they result in allow people to *do* different things, or to do old things in different ways.

In nearly every chapter of this volume you will find the word 'affordances' used to refer to the particular ways digital media make certain kinds of actions possible. The term comes from the work of the perceptual psychologist James J. Gibson, who used it to describe the potential that environments, substances, places, events, other creatures, and artefacts (such as technologies and texts) have for serving as tools to perform certain actions. One of the problems with the way people often speak of the affordances of digital media is that they talk about them as if they are properties of technologies, downplaying the agency of users and encouraging a kind of technological determinism. Gibson, however, is quite clear that affordances have as much to do with users as with technologies. In his classic work, *The Ecological Approach to Visual Perception* (1986: 127) he writes of the term 'affordance': 'I mean by it something that refers to both the environment and the animal in a way that no existing term does. It implies the complementarity of the animal and the environment.' This complimentarity between technologies and users is a theme emphasised in many of the chapters, starting with Gee's explanation of how, in playing video games, players search for affordances in the rules of the game or in the various tools the game provides that align with their own 'effective abilities' (or those of their avatars) (see also Gee 2014), a phenomenon which is further illustrated in the chapters by Hafner and Marsh. Similarly, Jones describes how the effectiveness of smartphone apps for diet and exercise depends upon how users interact with them at various stages of inputting data and interpreting output, so that users themselves become fused with technologies to form what he refers to as 'servomechanisms'. One of the best examples of the negotiated character of affordances can be seen in Barton's description of the affordances users of Flickr have found in the tagging function of the website that allow them to do things the designers of the site 'probably never dreamed of'. 'It is this creative space between the designer and the user,' writes Barton, 'where the unexpected can happen which constitutes the affordances.'

The key point of these observations is that digital technologies (like all cultural tools) are not determinative of their use. Although they influence what we can do in many important ways, amplifying or diminishing different aspects of our perception and action, people also regularly adapt technologies to different circumstances or different goals, appropriate them into different contexts, modify them, and mix them with other tools in ways that alter the affordances we can find in them (Jones and Hafner 2012). Lee, for example, shows how the affordances of linguistic forms associated with texting and instant messaging change when they are appropriated into the new contexts of urban signs, and Snyder shows how the affordances the web introduces for gathering and 'curating' information are exploited differently by marketers and educators. The way people use digital technologies, and the different social practices that come to be associated with these uses, are the result of an active process of matching the kinds of things people want to do with the kinds of things that technologies allow them to do.

When people take actions using technologies and texts, they rarely do so alone. They are almost always acting with and/or on other people. And so a subclass of action that is of crucial interest to discourse analysts is *interaction*, which discourse analysts define as the 'joint action' (Clark 1996) people engage in to create their social worlds. From the earliest forms of computer-mediated communication, however, digital technologies have challenged the ways discourse analysts approach the analysis of interaction. There are three main reasons for this: first, the differences in the way computer interactions are synchronised alter the way analysts must deal with issues like turn-taking, adjacency, and topic management. Second, the different material and semiotic tools that digital technologies make available both change the ways people manage things like mutual monitoring and contextualisation and make available a range of new forms of 'low friction' instrumental and phatic communication like text messaging and 'liking' (Jones and Hafner 2012). Finally, digital technologies facilitate a range of new participation frameworks (Goffman 1981) for interaction, allowing people to inhabit different sorts of roles and responsibilities vis-à-vis their interlocutors and providing new ways to accomplish things like 'audience segregation' (Goffman 1959) and 'ambient intimacy' (Carrington this volume).

The chapter that takes up these issues most explicitly is that by Benson, which explores how tools developed for the analysis of face-to-face interaction can be adapted to understanding interactions on YouTube, but they are also relevant to Barton's argument regarding the interactive function of tags on Flickr, Hafner's discussion of how participants in virtual worlds for children interact with each other and with their avatars, Marsh's exploration of the interaction between producers of Club Penguin Music Videos and their fans, and Jones's discussion of how self-tracking apps convert things like exercise and diet into forms of social interaction. Meanwhile, both Carrington and Merchant demonstrate how digital technologies do not just alter the ways people interact online, but also the ways they interact in the physical spaces in which these technologies are used.

One important question that emerges in these discussions is what actually constitutes an interaction in digitally mediated environments. Benson, citing Rafaeli and Ariel (2007), distinguishes between two kinds of interactivity, one, which Rafaeli and Ariel refer to as 'responsiveness', having to do with the ways technologies interact with humans, and the other having to do with the ways technologies facilitate human-to-human interaction. In other chapters, however, this distinction appears much less cut and dried. When the self-trackers described by Jones interact with apps which respond based on the aggregated behaviour of all of their other users, does this constitute interaction with the app or with these other users? And when the children described by Hafner interact with their own or other players' monsters in the virtual world of Moshi Monsters, who exactly are these interactions taking place with – people, monsters, or the software that is controlling them? In fact, often when we are using digital technologies, we are involved in multiple interactions with other humans, with avatars, with algorithms, and with institutions. One important point that Hafner makes is that any interaction with technologies also constitutes a conversation with the designers of these technologies (see also Gee), a point which reinforces the observation about 'affordances' we made above – affordances are not just a matter of what technologies allow us to do – they are a form of *communication* between the designers and the users of technologies (de Souza 2005).

Another important question raised by contributors has to do with how technological tools act to shape the ways people interact, and the kinds of social relationships and social identities they can produce through their interactions. Hafner presents one of the most dramatic illustrations of this question in his exploration of the different 'positions' (Davies and Harré 1990) participants in Moshi Monsters can take in relation to their monsters, sometimes treating them as versions of themselves, sometimes treating them as pets, and sometimes treating them as tools for accomplishing actions in the game world. Chik also uses positioning theory in her discussion of the different kinds of identities and relationships online language learning sites make available for their users. Both of these chapters show how the kinds of relationships and identities websites encourage contribute to creating and maintaining certain social practices by reinforcing what Davies and Harré call 'storylines'. Similarly, Marsh shows how interactions in the peer-to-peer networks that form around Club Penguin Music Videos serve to reproduce storylines of recognition, status and competition that replicate the celebrity–fan relationships in more mainstream media. Perhaps the most important observation that can be made about actions and interactions, then, is how they serve as the building blocks for social practices and for the formation of maintenance of communities associated with these practices (see also the chapters by Carrington, King, and Vásquez).

Ideology and power

The last important component of discourse analysis is a concern with the way discourse helps to construct certain 'versions of reality' (ideologies) and certain relationships of power between individuals and groups. This concern is not just a feature of critical discourse analysis, as discussed in the chapters by Snyder and Selwyn, or Foucauldian discourse analysis, as practiced by Marsh in her chapter, but is also evident in, for example, Chik and Hafner's application of positioning theory, Jones's application of mediated discourse analysis, Benson's analysis of the organisation of online interactions, and Barton's consideration of tagging. In fact, all of the chapters in this volume, in one way or another, shed light on the ways digital technologies affect how people understand the world and treat one another, and how this affects how social goods (both material and symbolic) get distributed.

One place where we can see the workings of power and ideology is in ideological agendas and biases expressed in the discourse that circulates through digital media. Numerous scholars over the years (see for example Herring 1993; Nakamura 2002) have demonstrated how, despite their 'newness' and the promises of 'democracy' and 'equality' associated with them, new media often reflect and reinforce many of the same biases and ideological assumptions as 'old media'. And so, as Marsh points out, despite the new and creative opportunities peer-to-peer social networks provide for young people to produce and share their own creative products, these processes often serve to reproduce old media values of fandom and celebrity. And despite the promises of free learning on the language learning sites analysed by Chik, learners are constantly 'sorted' based on whether or not they have paid for a 'premium membership'. Virtual worlds like Moshi Monsters do not just provide spaces for children to have fun, but also teach them how to value certain forms of consumption, social relationships and notions of privacy and safety (Hafner this volume; Jones and Hafner 2012), and apps like *Nike+* do not just encourage users to exercise, but also turn them into virtual advertisements for Nike products (Jones 2014, this volume). As much as the digital practices discussed in this book facilitate things like creating, learning, and self-improvement, what many of them seem to facilitate best are commercial practices and the promotion of dominant values of competition and conspicuous consumption.

Often these values and relationships are not so much expressed in texts, as they are in the more subtle ways that software and web interfaces channel users into certain kinds of actions and interactions. Small incremental actions, like clicking one thing rather than another, filling in a text field in a certain way, agreeing to 'terms and conditions', creating a hashtag that will make content (and people) searchable, or 'liking' a photo or video, are, as we mentioned above, the building blocks of social practices and social identities, and they often come with consequences that users may not be entirely aware of. One way in which the analysis of the workings of power and ideology is complicated when it comes to digital technologies is the fact that ideological assumptions and social relationships are not just inscribed in texts, but often submerged in algorithms that operate beneath the surface of texts and fundamentally affect the way we experience the world (i.e. what kind of information we have access to, what kind of behaviour is rewarded and reinforced, and what sort of people are considered normal), a point made by Jones in his discussion of health and fitness apps, but also hinted at in other chapters (for example, those by Barton, Benson, Chik, Gee, Marsh, and Snyder).

Another important place discourse analysts can look for ideologies and power relationships associated with digital practices is in the ways digital technologies and practices are represented in public discourse, a topic taken up by Lee, Snyder and Selwyn. Lee, for example, discusses how the appropriation of 'netspeak' in offline commercial discourses represents a shift from a 'language ideology' in which the textual practices of (mostly young) internet users were marginalised, to one in which these same practices are being 'enregistered' (Agha 2003) and commodified. Snyder examines the different ways the digital practice of 'curation' is represented in the fields of digital marketing, online communication, online education and digital literacy studies, revealing how the ideological biases of these different fields can lead to very different understandings of what it means to create a text, own a text, and distribute a text. Curation, she argues, is 'always ideological, always rhetorical and often political'. Finally, Selwyn analyses what he calls the 'discourse of disruption' that dominates media and policy discussions of the impact of digital technologies on education. While much of the public discourse about technology focuses on its power to disrupt 'old-fashioned practices' and introduce new and better ways to do things, what this promise often masks, says Selwyn, is the promotion of the same old free market values and neo-liberal agendas that have dominated education in the past several decades. These chapters serve as a reminder that, despite the promises that digital technologies will level the discursive playing field by putting into the hands of ordinary people the power to create and broadcast texts, the rules of the game are still set by a relatively small group of powerful players (see also Lanier 2013).

Conclusion: discourse analysis as a digital practice

As much as the chapters in this volume shed light on all of the various digital practices discussed, they also shed light on the practice of discourse analysis itself, and the affordances and constraints of the different analytical and theoretical tools we make use of to engage in this practice. In this regard, a number of important themes emerge. One of the most consistent themes is the inadequacy of approaches that focus solely on textual data removed from the context of its use. It is not surprising, then, that many of the contributors opt for more ethnographic approaches to data gathering, combining the collection of texts with interviews and sustained observations of users. Different contributors go about this in different ways, using such techniques as in-depth face-to-face interviews (Carrington), online interviews (Barton, Marsh), focus groups (Jones), stimulated recall sessions (Hafner), video observations (Merchant), the gathering of photographic data (Lee), auto-ethnography (Jones and Chik), and object ethnography (Carrington). Another important theme that emerges is the role of digital technology not just as an object of research but also as a research tool. For some of the contributors, such as King in his use of corpus tools, Lee in her use of Flickr, and Merchant in his use of digital video, the appropriation of digital technologies as research tools is quite conscious, but, in fact, all of the studies in this volume are conducted through the researchers themselves engaging in digital practices (including searching for and curating web content, trying out different kinds of applications, and interacting with participants through social network sites, email or chat programmes). And just as we must ask how practices like digital self-tracking, tagging photos on Flickr, conversing in gay chat rooms, caring for virtual monsters, and all of the other practices described in this book are affected by the affordances and constraints of digital technologies, and how these practices contribute to the formation of certain kinds of social relationships, social identities and social realities, we must also contemplate how these same technologies affect the kinds of data we can collect, the kinds of relationships we can develop with those whom we are studying, the kinds of identities we can cultivate as researchers, and the 'versions of reality' our studies end up promoting.

While, as we have tried to argue in this introduction, many of the social practices made possible by digital technologies force us to re-evaluate our analytical tools and theoretical assumptions, we do not wish to frame these studies in a 'discourse of disruption' of the type described by Selwyn. As much as these chapters demonstrate how sometimes we need to alter and adapt our tools to new circumstances, they also demonstrate the reliable potency of the tools of discourse analysis – tools for the analysis of texts, contexts, actions, interactions, power and ideology – to increase our understanding of the practices people engage in with digital technologies in ways that other analytical frameworks cannot.

References

Agha, A. (2003) 'The social life of cultural value', *Language and Communication*, 23: 231–274.

Androutsopoulos, J. (2011) 'From variation to heteroglossia in the study of computer-mediated discourse', in C. Thurlow and K. Mroczek (eds) *Digital Discourse: language in the new media*, 277–297, Oxford: Oxford University Press.

Auer, P. (1992) 'Introduction: John Gumperz's approach to contextualisation', in P. Auer and A. Di Luzio (eds) *The Contextualization of Language*, 1–37, Amsterdam: John Benjamins.

Austin, J. L. (1976) *How to Do Things with Words*, Oxford: Oxford University Press.

Bakhtin, M. M. (1981) *The Dialogic Imagination: four essays*, trans. C. Emerson and M. Holquist, M. Holquist (ed.) Austin, TX: University of Texas Press.

Barton, D. (2006) *Literacy: an introduction to the ecology of written language*, 2nd edn, Malden, MA: Blackwell Publishing.

Bauman, R. and Briggs, C. L. (1990) 'Poetics and performance as critical perspectives on language and social life', *Annual Review of Anthropology*, 19: 59–88.

Bourdieu, P. (1977) *Outline of a Theory of Practice*, trans. R. Nice, Cambridge: Cambridge University Press.

Clark, H. H. (1996) *Using Language*, Cambridge: Cambridge University Press.

Davies, B. and Harré, R. (1990) 'Positioning: the discursive production of selves', *Journal for the Theory of Social Behaviour*, 20(1): 43–63.

de Souza, C. S. (2005) *The Semiotic Engineering of Human-Computer Interaction*, Cambridge, MA: The MIT Press.

Foucault, M. (1972) *The Archaeology of Knowledge*, New York: Pantheon.

Gee, J. P. (2012) *Social Linguistics and Literacies: ideology in discourses*, 4th edn, London: Routledge.

Gee, J. P. (2014) *Unified Discourse Analysis: language, reality, virtual worlds and video games*, London: Routledge.

Gibson, J. J. (1986) *The Ecological Approach To Visual Perception*, Boston, MA: Psychology Press.

Goffman, E. (1959) *The Presentation of Self in Everyday Life*, New York: Doubleday.

Goffman, E. (1981) *Forms of Talk*, Oxford: Blackwell.

Halliday, M. A. K. and Hasan, R. (1976) *Cohesion in English*, London: Longman.

Herring, S. (1993) 'Gender and democracy in computer-mediated communication', *Electronic Journal of Communication*, 3(2), Online. Available HTTP: <http://www.cios.org/EJCPUBLIC/003/2/00328.HTML> (accessed 12 May 2014).

Herring, S. (1999) 'Interactional coherence in CMC', *Journal of Computer-Mediated Communication*, 4(4).

Herring, S. C. (2007) 'A faceted classification scheme for computer-mediated discourse', *Language@Internet*, 4, Online. Available HTTP: <http://www.languageatinternet.org/articles/2007/761> (accessed 15 June 2014).

Iedema, R. (2001) 'Resemiotization', *Semiotica*, 137(1-4): 23–39.

Jones, R. H. (2004) 'The problem of context in computer-mediated communication', in P. LeVine and R. Scollon (eds) *Discourse and Technology: multimodal discourse analysis*, 20–133, Washington, DC: Georgetown University Press.

Jones, R. H. (2009) 'Dancing, skating and sex: action and text in the digital age', *Journal of Applied Linguistics*, 6(3): 283–302.

Jones, R. H. (2010) 'Cyberspace and physical space: attention structures in computer-mediated communication', in A. Jaworski and C. Thurlow (eds) *Semiotic Landscapes: text, space and globalization*, 151–167, London: Continuum.

Jones, R. H. (2014) 'Advertising culture: new challenges for stylistics', in P. Stockwell and S. Whiteley (eds) *The Cambridge Handbook of Stylistics*, 522–537, Cambridge: Cambridge University Press.

Jones, R. H. and Hafner, C. A. (2012) *Understanding Digital Literacies: a practical introduction*, London: Routledge.

Lanier, J. (2013) *Who Owns the Future*, New York: Simon & Schuster.

Malinowski, B. (1923) 'The problem of meaning in primitive languages', in C. K. Ogden and I. A. Richards (eds) *The Meaning of Meaning*, 296–336, London: Routledge.

Nakamura, L. (2002) *Cybertypes: race, ethnicity, and identity on the internet*, New York: Routledge.

Nissenbaum, H. (2009) *Privacy in Context: technology, policy, and the integrity of social life*, Palo Alto, CA: Stanford University Press.

Norris, S. and Jones, R. H. (2005) *Discourse in Action: introducing mediated discourse analysis*, London: Routledge.

Pennycook, A. (2010) *Language as a Local Practice*, London: Routledge.

Rafaeli, S. and Ariel, Y. (2007) 'Assessing interactivity in computer-mediated research', in A. N. Johnson, K. Y. A. McKenna, T. Postmes and U. D. Rieps (eds) *The Oxford Handbook of Internet Psychology*, 71–88, Oxford: Oxford University Press.

Schegloff, A. E. and Sacks, H. (1973) 'Opening up closings', *Semiotica*, 8(4): 289–327.

Scollon, R. (2001) *Mediated Discourse: the nexus of practice*, London: Routledge.

Tusting, K. R., Ivanic, R. and Wilson, A. (2000) 'New literacy studies at the interchange', in D. Barton, M. Hamilton and R. Ivanic (eds) *Situated Literacies*, 210–218, London: Routledge.

van Dijk, T. A. (2008) *Discourse and Context: a sociocognitive approach*, Cambridge: Cambridge University Press.

Chapter 2

Discourse analysis of games

James Paul Gee

Can there be a field of discourse analysis for games?

A field of discourse analysis applied to video games does not yet really exist. But could there be such a thing? If there was such a thing, what would it teach us about discourse analysis for language?

The question about whether there could be a field devoted to the discourse analysis of games does not ask whether we can analyse games. We can analyse any semiotic system. However, to linguists, discourse analysis builds on syntax and semantics (Gee 2014a). That is, discourse analysis takes as its beginning point 'sentences' or 'utterances' that have already been assigned a structure (syntax) in terms of basic units and their combinations and a semantics in terms of the basic ('literal') meanings of these units and their combinations.

Discourse analysis analyses language in use and it deals with meanings that go beyond semantics and involve context and inference. In my view, discourse analysis studies two closely related things (Gee 2014a). We can call these 'packaging' and 'flow'. First, discourse analysis studies how things are said and written and how they could have been said or written differently and what difference it makes that they were said or written the way they were. For example, why does someone say or write 'It took only an hour for my house to burn down in the fire' versus 'My house took only an hour to burn down in the fire'. In these two sentences information is packaged (combined) in different ways, using the syntactic resources of language with different intentions and expected effects. And, of course, this information could have been packaged into more than one sentence, for example: 'My house burned down in the fire. It took only an hour.'

By the way, it is sometimes argued that there are no sentences in speech (see Gee 2014a for further discussion of this issue). This is, as far as I am concerned, not true. The basic rules of syntax determine what counts as a sentence. Of course, in speech, sentences are often more loosely organised and often more fragmented. Furthermore, intonation plays a major role in what count as units on the order of clauses and sentences.

Second, discourse analysis studies how sentences connect, combine, and pattern across the sequence and flow of time in written or spoken language used in different contexts and situations. For example, why does someone say or write 'My house took only an hour to burn down in the fire' (one sentence) versus 'My house burned down in the fire. It took only an hour' (two sentences) versus 'There was a fire. My house burned down. It took only an hour' (three sentences).

Both in the case of packaging and of sequencing discourse analysis concerns itself not with the sorts of meaning semantics deals with, but with 'situated meaning' (sometimes called 'utterance token meaning'). Situated meanings (Gee 2004, 2014a) are the meanings words, phrases, sentences, and sequences of sentences take on in actual contexts of use. Semantics deals with meaning, or, better put, the meaning ranges (possibilities) of words, phrases, and sentences (this is sometimes called 'utterance type meaning'). For example, at the semantic level, the word 'coffee' means anything to do with the substance coffee. In actual contexts of use the word can have different situated meanings. For example: 'The coffee spilled. Go get a mop' (liquid); 'The coffee spilled. Go get a broom' (grains or beans); 'The coffee spilled. Stack it again' (tins); 'I'll have coffee ice-cream' (a flavour); 'Big Coffee is as bad as Big Oil' (an industry).

Situated meanings are determined by what speakers/writers and listeners/readers take as relevant aspects of context. Situated meanings are also determined by shared cultural knowledge. Such knowledge has been studied under umbrella terms like 'folk theories', 'cultural models', 'figured worlds', 'schemes', 'frames', and others (Gee 2004, 2014a; Holland et al. 1998). Thus, discourse is also related to the study of cultures and social groups that share knowledge and practices with each other.

Thus, the question 'Can there be a discourse analysis of video games?', taken literally, asks whether games have a syntax (a grammar), semantics, packaging, sequence/flow, situated meanings, and associated social and cultural knowledge. If they do, they are in that sense 'like language' and open to discourse analysis.

Before we proceed, let's be clear that to demand that a system have a 'syntax' is to demand that it have basic units that combine in predictable ways into larger units. It is to demand, as well, that the meanings of the larger units be computable in some fashion from the meanings of the smaller units. To demand that a system have a 'semantics' is to demand that its basic units and their combinations have basic meanings or meaning ranges fixed by conventions. While these conventional meanings can vary across different contexts (and new contexts can extend or change their meaning ranges), there must be a conventional core that sets some limits on contextual variation and shapes how contextual variation in meaning operates.

While this chapter presents the view that there could be a discourse analysis for games, the proof would be in the doing, not just the suggesting. We would actually have to attempt to build the field to see if it could exist and would have any interesting impact. We need to start by considering if and how games have syntax, semantics, packaging, sequence/flow, situated meanings determined (reflectively) by context and social and cultural knowledge

The world has a syntax and semantics for us humans thanks to how human vision works (Marr 1991, 2010). The eye sees the world in vaguely bounded 2D (upside down) images. The eye and brain then process these images in order to construct 3D images with bounded edges and clear shapes. These edges, angles, and bounded surfaces and the way they are combined into spaces and objects (and actions across the flow of time) constitute the syntax of the world for us humans. We then assign names and conceptual labels to the spaces and objects and actions, based on context, cultural knowledge, and social conventions. This is the semantics of the world for us humans.

Scientists have special tools that allow them to see the world in a different way from 'everyday people'. With their telescopes and microscopes, they see different units (like atoms, cells, and stars) that combine in different ways (into molecules, organs, and galaxies). For them, the world has a different syntax and semantics.

Games are made out of a flow of visual images. So they share the syntax and semantics of the human visual world. But, like scientists, gamers have special tools that allow them to see the game world in a different way. Gamers have controllers and avatars through which they can manipulate the game world to accomplish goals and solve problems. Thus, they see the game world not just in terms of spaces, objects, and actions, but in terms of what these things in the game world are good for in terms of accomplishing their goals for winning the game and solving its problems (Gee 2007, 2014b).

Gamers see the game world in terms of what we can call 'game mechanics' (Gee 2007, 2009, 2014b). Game mechanics are what you can do with things in a game. So gamers see the game world in terms of verbs (actions): crates are good for breaking, ledges are good for jumping, shadows are good for hiding, and so forth. Additionally, things in game worlds can combine in various ways to enable certain actions. For example, a ledge, gap, rope, and wall can in some games combine to enable a deft set of moves to get across the game world (as in Tomb Raider games, for example, games in which the famous character Lara Croft dexterously explores caves, ruins, and other mysterious sites).

Though games are built on the syntax and semantics of human vision, their distinctive syntax is composed of the objects and spaces relevant to action in the game. The semantics of a game is a conceptual labelling of these spaces and things not just in terms of their real world identity (e.g. a crate) but in terms of what they are functionally good for in the game (e.g. breakable to get a power-up).

We might say that games have a second-order syntax and semantics based on top of the first-order syntax and semantics of human vision. It is worthy of note, however, that the syntax and semantics of games, based as they are on 'what actions things are good for' is very much the way we humans look at the 'real' world when we have goals and must take actions we care about to carry them out. There is a real sense in which games 'mimic' our human ways with the world when we are engaged actors (Gee 2014c).

While little work has been done on the discourse of games from the perspective developed here and in Gee (2014c), there are some important related sources. These include: Bogost (2007, 2011); Wolf (2012); Petersen (2012); Paul (2012) and Squire (2011) among others. But, keep in mind, we are not here talking about the language in games or the language gamers use in and out of games. We are talking about games as multimodal forms of digital–human interaction within a system with syntax and semantics and open to discourse analysis in a linguistic sense.

Given that games have a syntax and semantics, we now can ask: Do the ways video games package things, the ways they sequence things, what things mean in actual contexts (situated meaning), and how situated meanings relate to context and culture work, in any significant way, like they do in language? To get at these questions in the small space I have here, I will discuss but one game, *Thomas Was Alone* (*TWA*).

Thomas Was Alone

TWA is a game that uses very simple 2D images. It is about as minimal as a game can get, but for that very reason exposes the basic structure and function of game worlds quite well. Figure 2.1 is an image from *TWA*. Note that while this image is static, the placement of the characters in it was determined by the player. The image is a result of action. Further, the very

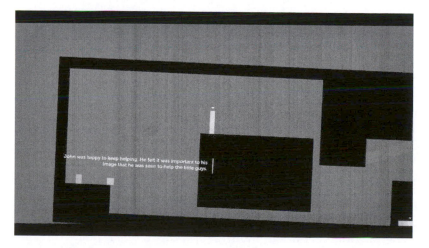

Figure 2.1 A screenshot from *Thomas Was Alone*

next screen will be created by the player's actions, as well, based on his or her assessment of the problems to be solved. Each sequence created by the player will reflect, too, the player's interactions with the story and with the emotions of the characters (even though they are shapes!).

If you play the game *TWA*, you immediately see that the small coloured rectangles in the game are like words that can be combined together (like a phrase). For example, players can stack the rectangles on top of each other in certain orders (e.g. red on orange on yellow on blue). Order matters in a minimal way. Each shape has a characteristic movement of its own and each can be moved independently, but when they are combined, the bottom one determines the movement. The bottom one functions like a predicate in language. In the game, the player must get all the shapes to the end of each level, using their different actions and combinations.

So we have a clear, albeit simple, syntax and semantics here. For example, 'red on orange on yellow on blue' means 'stack can move over water' (because that is the blue rectangle's basic action). The order of the stack matters in terms of what subsequent actions are possible, since the shapes can jump off only from the top down.

So how do situated meanings work in *TWA*? Do the shapes and their actions take on specific and extended meanings in actual contexts of use (play)?

TWA has a story. The story is narrated by a narrator whose narration is heard and whose words are printed on the screens. Within the story each shape has a name and something of a backstory as an artificially intelligent agent inside a computer whose programming has gone awry. The shapes are trying to escape the system. In an interesting twist, each shape has certain unique abilities and limitations (determined by the game's game mechanics/semantics) that fit with the character's personality trait and role in the story.

For example, Thomas, the red rectangle, has an up-beat attitude and can do an average jump. John, the yellow rectangle, is arrogant and eager to show off and can jump quite high. Claire, the blue square, who starts off feeling bad about herself but comes to see herself as a superhero, cannot jump well or move fast, but she can float and move in water and thereby save others by giving them rides across water.

The game's story allows us to assign meanings far beyond 'short jumping yellow rectangle'. They allow us to assign emotional and narrative meanings to the rectangles as they act alone and together. The story – and our cultural knowledge about escape stories and about computers – give us cultural models or frames within which we can give richer interpretations to what is happening.

In *TWA* the game's oral narration is also printed on the screen. Since *TWA* prints the words of the narration on the screen, this, in a way, subtracts the words from the oral narration and means that the oral narration mainly functions to carry the intonation of the narrator's voice, the musical and affective part of speech. This affect is created in part because we can read much more quickly than we can hear, so the player has often read all the (short) material on the screen before the narrator has finished saying it. The player has the 'meaning' but still must pay attention to the intonation contours. The narration in *TWA* is in a British accent that is amazingly good at indicating the emotions of the characters (rectangles though they be), emotions like fear, self-loathing, loneliness, liking and love, caring, arrogance, humility, and trust.

We attribute these emotions and attitudes as deeper meanings for each character by considering the contexts they are in. Consider the image from *TWA* above. Given the words on the screen, the positions of the characters, and the situation we are in in the game at this point, as well as our earlier play in the game, we can attribute to John (the tall yellow rectangle) a situated meaning or inference like: John wants to help, though not necessarily for altruistic reasons, but because he likes to show off and look good to others.

Let's turn now to the ways meanings and inferences are built up in the context of the order, sequence, and flow of screens in the game. Let's assume, for the sake of argument, that a screen prior to the image above had John, the yellow triangle, down on the same level as Thomas (the red rectangle) and Chris (the orange square). Assume further the player has then jumped John – a very good jumper – up to where we see him in the image, up above Thomas and Chris. From this vantage point, a player can clearly see that he or she could move John to the right, down the little alley, and then again further to the right and away from Thomas and Chris.

But the player can also readily see that moving John to the right will not get Thomas and Chris up the ledge so they can move on in the game as well. They cannot alone or together jump high enough to get up the ledge. John must come back down and allow Chris to jump on top of Thomas and then to jump from Thomas to John and, finally, to jump up to the ledge. Thomas can then jump on John and then up to the ledge. And only then can John jump back up by himself. This creates a sequence in the player's mind, a sequence that he or she can then create.

In the image we see that John is higher than Thomas and Chris and that he can easily go on without them. We see, too, that if the game (and its story) is to continue, he must go back down, place himself again on the same level as Thomas and Chris, help them, and then move on last (not first) himself. All these meanings derived from sequence reinforce the sorts of situated meanings we have drawn from the story and contexts of play. John thinks more highly of himself than he does of the others. Forced to go back and help, he has to rationalise this as not a weakness, but as a strength. This strength is not only that his help is essential to mitigate Thomas's and Chris's weaknesses. It is also that John will look good in the act and others will see how special he is.

It is clear from even this simple analysis that how game designer and players (through their choices and actions) create context is a crucial way in which games take on meanings beyond their game mechanics (semantics). Note that in the case of language, context is a co-creation of the world and of how humans construe things in certain ways. As in the case of language, gamers have to know what is relevant (and how it is relevant) in the contexts of their play, which often involve games that are much more graphically complex and rich than *TWA*. Games and players co-create contextual relevance and meaning, as does the world and speakers and writers.

Conversation and affordances

The discussion so far has been meant to be just a mile high overview of a language-like analysis of the structure and meaning of video games. Nonetheless, one very important variable has been left out. Language is used in interactions. We can interact with other people or we can interact with a written text. In either case, there is a sort of conversation going on. So, too, when a player plays a game, the player is having a conversation with the game, indeed a more overt and reciprocal one than readers can have with written texts (which, as Plato long ago pointed out, cannot actually respond to us, see Gee 2011). The player and the game respond to each other in turn.

Although at this point the idea is speculative, it is possible that the notion of 'conversation' could be generalised to cover oral and written language, games (and perhaps other interactive media), and our interactions with the world. I believe that the way to do this would be through a notion well established in ecological psychology, the concept of affordances.

When we humans look at the world in a goal-driven way we actively seek *affordances* in the world. Affordances are what things are good for, based on what a user can do with them (Gibson 1979). For us humans, a hammer is good for pounding nails. That is one of its affordances. A hammer is also pretty good at being a paperweight or a murder weapon. These are others of its affordances. It is very bad at being a toy for infants and you simply cannot use it as food. These are not affordances of a hammer for humans.

Affordances are only affordances, though, given that a potential user of the object has the ability to use the object to carry out the action it affords. The user must have what we can call an *effective ability*, the ability to effect (carry out) the affordance. Humans usually have the effective ability to use hammers for pounding nails. Animals without an opposable thumb do not. They cannot properly hold the hammer. For us humans, hammers do not have an affordance as food. But if they have wooden handles, they do have such an affordance for termites. Termites have the effective ability to eat wood. We humans do not.

Human life and survival is all about finding affordances which one has the effective abilities to put to good use. Let's say you want to get across a creek. You look around. The log on the ground would afford you the opportunity to cross the creek if you have the ability to move it and good enough balance to walk across it. A line of rocks across the creek would afford you the opportunity to cross the creek, as well, provided you have the ability to walk on wet and perhaps slippery rocks. The creek affords you the opportunity to cross it by swimming across if you can swim across a fast-moving current. Your burly friend could get you across by carrying you if you can convince him to do so and you are able to put up with the humiliation of being carried across like a child.

We look at the world around us to find things with affordances that match our abilities so we can accomplish our goals. Let's call this process of seeking to align or pair affordances with effective abilities the process of 'aligning with the world'. People (and other animals) who are poor at aligning with the world risk danger, failure, and death.

There is a sense in which we humans have conversations with the world, conversations which are formalised in science (Gee 2013). When we form a goal and act on the world, we are looking for the affordances of things in the world, affordances that we have the effective abilities (within the constraints of a given identity) to use to accomplish our goals. Our actions are probes in the world or questions put to the world to see whether and how we can align our effective abilities with affordances of things in the world.

Our conversations with the world go something like this: We have a goal. We take an action in the world, an action that is a type of 'probe' or 'question'. The world responds in some way, answers back. Given that response we ask ourselves if the action led to a result that was good or bad for accomplishing our goal. We 'appreciate' the result of the action in terms of affordances for accomplishing our goal. We then act again and proceed in a probe–response–reflect–probe again cycle until we accomplish our goal, change it, or give up. Of course, things can get more complicated as we pursue more than one goal at a time.

This probe–response–reflect–probe again cycle is a type of conversation with the world. Like all conversations it requires us to listen to and respect our interlocutor (here, the world) if we want to have a good conversation. Science is a formalisation of this sort of conversation with the world we all have. Science has tools for new sorts of probes (questions) and new sorts of reflection on responses. But evidence in science is, at root, always a response from the world.

The probe–response–reflection–probe again cycle is at the heart of video game playing as well. Often via an avatar, gamers form a goal (based on the design of the game and their own desires), act to probe the game world, reflect on the result, see the result as good or bad, and act (probe) again in a chain of acts meant to accomplish their goal. Gamers seek to understand and use the 'rules of the game' to align themselves with the game (in terms of affordances and effective abilities) properly to succeed, just as scientists seek to understand and use the 'rules of the world'.

In a conversation between two people in language, we have goals we want to accomplish (e.g. bonding, informing, motivating, manipulating, or reassuring our listener or listeners). We probe our listener/s through moves in language (a form of action), reflect on their responses, and then act again based on these responses. In conversations with others, the other is the 'world' we are probing and we are in turn the other's world, since the other has goals as well when they respond to us and take their turn at talk. In conversations with others we seek affordances in their talk, attributes, abilities, desires, skills, character, and language resources for which we have the necessary effective abilities to use (yes, sometimes, manipulate) for our purposes (goals).

So we are arguing that when we humans talk, when we act in the world, whether as part of everyday life or science, and when we play a video game, we are having interactive, responsive, turn-based, conversations based around the search for affordances we can use. Just as Plato thought, reading is a sort of secondary or derivative conversation in which we as readers have to answer for the text (for the implied writer) with respect for that text as a different voice from our own (see Iser 1974 for the notion of implied writers and implied readers).

Note that in this theory, writing, game design, and the design of virtual worlds all involve designing conversational platforms or spaces. And, indeed, it is not for nothing that some scientists think they are coming to understand the 'mind of God' (Davies 1992) when they study the world, since they seek to understand the world's deep design, that is, the deep patterns that allow us to effectively act on and in the world.

The question then becomes: Can we show that conversations in language, interactions with the world in everyday life and in scientific investigations, and video game playing are, at a deep level, similar (though not of course identical)? Better yet, can we learn more about them all by seeing their similarities worked out in different ways in different contexts? If this pursuit turns out to be meaningful, then discourse analysis could be generalised quite far, indeed. We would need to develop more general theories of and tools for conversational interactions where it is not just people that answer back, but games, other media, and the world as well.

References

Bogost, I. (2007) *Persuasive Games: the expressive power of videogames*, Cambridge, MA: MIT Press.

Bogost, I. (2011) *How to do Things with Games*, Minneapolis, MN: University of Minnesota.

Davies, P. (1992) *The Mind of God: the scientific basis for a rational world*, New York: Simon & Schuster.

Gee, J. P. (2004) *Situated Language and Learning: a critique of traditional schooling*, London: Routledge.

Gee, J. P. (2007) *What Video Games Have to Teach Us about Learning and Literacy*, 2nd edn, New York: Palgrave/Macmillan.

Gee, J. P. (2009) 'Playing Metal Gear Solid 4 well: being a good snake', in D. Davidson (ed.) *Well Played 1.0: video games, value and meaning*, 263–274, Pittsburgh, PA: ECT Press.

Gee, J. P. (2011) *Social Linguistics and Literacies: ideology in discourses*, 4th edn, London: Taylor and Francis.

Gee, J. P. (2013) *The Anti-Education Era: creating smarter students through digital learning*, New York: Palgrave/Macmillan.

Gee, J. P. (2014a) *An Introduction to Discourse Analysis: theory and method*, 4th edn, London: Routledge.

Gee, J. P. (2014b) *Good Video Games and Good Learning: collected essays on video games, learning, and literacy*, 2nd edn, New York: Peter Lang.

Gee, J. P. (2014c) *Unified Discourse Analysis: language, reality, virtual worlds and video games*, London: Routledge.

Gibson, J. J. (1979) *The Ecological Approach to Visual Perception*, Boston, MA: Houghton Mifflin.

Holland, D., Skinner, D., Lachicotte, W. and Cain, C. (1998) *Identity and Agency in Cultural Worlds*, Cambridge, MA: Harvard University Press.

Iser, W. (1974) *The Implied Reader: patterns of communication in prose fiction from Bunyan to Beckett*, Baltimore, MD: Johns Hopkins Press.

Marr, D. (1991) *From the Retina to the Neocortex: selected papers by David Marr*, Boston, MA: Birkhauser.

Marr, D. (2010) *Vision: a computational investigation into the human representation and processing of visual information*, Cambridge, MA: MIT Press.

Paul, C. (2012) *Word Play and the Discourse of Video Games: analyzing words, design, and play*, New York: Routledge.

Petersen, J. (2012) *Playing at the World: a history of simulating wars, people, and fantastic adventures from chess to role-playing games*, San Diego, CA: Unreason Press.

Squire, K. (2011) *Video Games and Learning: teaching and participatory culture in the digital age*, New York: Teachers College Press.

Wolf, J. P. (2012) *Building Imaginary Worlds: the theory and history of subcreation*, New York: Routledge.

Chapter 3

Discourse, cybernetics, and the entextualisation of the self

Rodney H. Jones

The quantified self

More and more I find myself emotionally attached to my iPhone, not so much as a communication device, and not as a physical object that expresses my identity and social status (as described in Carrington's chapter in this volume), but, rather, as a 'servomechanism', a means for receiving constant feedback about my physical and mental well-being. One app on my phone holds the accumulated information of all the meals I've eaten for the past three years including calorie counts and calculations of my intake of key nutrients. Another records all of my runs and uploads them to my *Nike+* page, where my average distance and pace are compared to that of other men my age, and still another is wirelessly connected to an accelerometer that I wear around my wrist which records every step I take during the day and how much I toss and turn in bed at night. I have an app that gathers information from my Wi-Fi scale and can automatically tweet my weight, body fat percentage and body mass index to all of my followers on Twitter, one that reminds me to drink water and asks me to record how much, and one that asks me at random times during the day to take a picture of myself and record my mood using a colour coded scale that ranges from 'insanely great' to 'couldn't be worse'.

You may think me odd, but I'm not alone. Self-tracking apps like the ones I've described are becoming more and more ubiquitous. Some people use them to manage chronic diseases, others to motivate themselves to exercise or to lose weight, and others to conduct 'experiments' on themselves out of nerdy curiosity or a utopian belief that technology can help them to 'optimise' themselves. Many of these people identify with a loose organisation of self-trackers known as the Quantified Self Movement (Wolf 2010), whose members meet up regularly in cities all over the world to share their stories of self-discovery. Practices of digital self-tracking, however, are not confined to specialist communities of self-quantifiers and 'body-hackers' (Dembosky 2011), but are becoming more and more mainstream, evidenced by the proliferation of apps and devices for self-monitoring on the market, including the inclusion of a feature in Apple's new iOS 8, which gathers, integrates and analyses data gathered from multiple self-tracking apps in one application.

The idea of self-tracking is, of course, not really new. Humans have been creating textual representations of their bodies and their behaviours as a means of self-reflection and self-improvement for thousands of years. Such texts include journals, diaries, lists, and record books, charts and graphs and self-portraits in various media. One of history's most famous self-trackers was the American statesman Benjamin Franklin, whose *Autobiography* records how he ended every day by reviewing a list of thirteen virtues, placing a check mark next to a virtue whenever he violated it. But a lot has changed since Franklin's time. Now, new 'technologies of entextualisation' (Jones 2009) allow us to capture aspects of our bodies and our behaviour that were heretofore less visible to us, to compile, calculate and visualise that information in multiple ways, and to transmit it to large numbers of people over the internet. In the words of cardiologist and geneticist Eric Topol (2012: vi), for the first time in history, we can 'digitise humans', and the affordances and constraints offered by my 'digital self' are rather different from those of Franklin's 'analogue self'.

In this chapter I will consider practices of 'self-tracking' using digital media not just in terms of their consequences for people's relationships with their bodies, but also in terms of their consequences for people's relationships with texts and practices of reading and writing. The ways self-tracking apps gather data about their users and then reflect them back in the form of analyses, exhortations, reminders, and narratives, I will argue, is indicative of a more general characteristic of digital texts – their ability to 'read their readers' and 'write their writers' and to 'customise' their contents in real time based on actions that their readers and writers take. This reflective dimension of digital texts is, in many ways, a 'game changer', not just for ordinary people who use these texts, but also for discourse analysts who try to make sense of them. It has been the tendency for most approaches to discourse to treat texts as artefacts that are co-constructed through acts of authorship by writers and acts of interpretation by readers. How does our approach to discourse change when we start to see readers and writers as artefacts constructed by texts and the invisible algorithms that govern them? Under such conditions, more traditional questions regarding what a text 'means' or what people are 'doing with words' are less important than questions about how texts operate to 'process' their writers and readers and reflect back to them certain versions of themselves.

In considering these questions, I draw on an analysis of twenty-five of the most highly rated self-tracking apps available on Apple's App Store, each of which I used myself for a period of no less than a month, and in some cases, for several years. I have supplemented this analysis with other users' experiences taken from online reviews and blog posts, as well as from two focus group interviews with participants in the Quantified Self Movement conducted at their annual meetings in San Francisco and Amsterdam in 2013. The analysis relies on a number of approaches to discourse, including multimodal and mediated discourse analysis, as well as on insights from cybernetics and media theory.

Who's writing whom?

Most approaches to texts in the field of discourse analysis have focused either on how they are structured to encode meaning – as, for example, in Halliday and Hasan's (1976) attention to the cohesive relationships between clauses which create 'texture' – or on their communicative functions – as in Brown and Yule's (1983: 190) definition of a text as 'the verbal record of a communicative event'. In other words, discourse analysts have generally been more concerned with how authors construct texts (as opposed to how texts construct authors), and with how people use texts to communicate with others (as opposed to how they use them to communicate with themselves).

Meanwhile, work in cognitive psychology and media studies has suggested other ways of looking at texts and the media through which they are created, seeing them less as separate artefacts and more as extensions of their users (see for example Introna 2011; Latour 2007; McLuhan 1964). Among the most dramatic renditions of this idea is Andy Clark's (2003) argument that a fundamental characteristic of being human is our ability to enhance our cognitive and physical abilities by merging with tools, whether they be stone axes, written texts or iPhones. 'Human thought and reason,' he contends, 'is born out of looping interactions between material brains, material bodies, and complex cultural and technological environments' (11). The tools that have been most responsible for enhancing our cognitive abilities, Clark argues, are essentially forms of discourse, a list which

> begins with speech and counting, morphs first into written text and numerals, then into early printing . . . , on to the revolutions of moveable typefaces and the printing press, and most recently to the digital encodings that bring text, sound, and image into a uniform and widely transmissible format.
>
> (Clark 2003: 4)

What I will argue in this chapter is that digital media have made the 'looping interactions' between humans and our discursive tools dramatically more efficient. Whenever we search for something on Google, shop on Amazon. com, or enter data into a health or fitness app, what we write is algorithmically processed and reflected back to us as a version of our own interests, desires or actions. More and more, as we read and write texts, those texts are simultaneously reading and writing us back.

Of course, different kinds of 'technologies of entextualisation' and the texts they result in facilitate this phenomenon of reflexivity in different ways, which is one area where discourse analysts can make a contribution, addressing questions about the kinds of readers and writers that iPhone apps, social media sites and search engines create. Another way discourse analysis can contribute to our understanding of the reflexive quality of digital texts comes from its ability to link the discursive features of texts and the discursive behaviours of individuals to larger social formations, ideologies, and relationships of power (see chapters by Marsh, Snyder, and Sewlyn in this volume). Beyond the consequences of these different technologies of entextualisation for the ways we are able to 'author ourselves', what are their possible effects on the ways we are able to author our social relationships and our societies?

Texts as servomechanisms

Among the approaches to discourse analysis that have been most preoccupied with the role of discourse in mediating human actions and identities is mediated discourse analysis (Norris and Jones 2005; Scollon 2001), an approach which focuses less on texts as linguistic artefacts and more on the social actions that people use texts to perform. From the point of view of mediated discourse analysis, all actions are mediated through 'cultural tools', some of which are technological: computers, motion sensors and mobile phones, and some of which are semiotic: texts, images and other forms of discourse. These different kinds of tools impose different affordances and constraints on the kinds of actions people are able to perform (see Figure 3.1).

While at first glance this model does not seem very different from the communication-focused approach to texts discussed above, central to mediated discourse analysis's understanding of mediation is that cultural tools do not just mediate the interaction between the social actor and the outside world, but also crucially mediate the formation of the actor's 'inner world' or what Scollon and Scollon (2004) call 'the historical body'. Every time a tool is used to perform a new action, the affordances and constraints of

Social actor   Mediational means   Social world

Figure 3.1 Model of mediated action

that tool are slightly altered through the particular plans, intentions and experiences of the social actor. And every time a social actor uses a particular tool, the social actor also changes as the social practices associated with the tool are submerged into his or her 'historical body'. To use Clark's (2003: 7) terms, as we use tools, we 'dovetail our minds and skills to the shape of our current tools', and the tools 'dovetail back . . . actively, automatically and continually tailor[ing] themselves to us' (see Figure 3.2).

What is less thoroughly theorised in mediated discourse analysis, however, are the mechanisms, both cognitive and discursive, through which this 'dovetailing' between social actors and cultural tools occurs. Here, I argue, we can turn for insights to classical theories of cybernetics and information processing.

The term 'cybernetics' – from the ancient Greek word for 'steersman' – was adopted by Norbert Wiener to describe 'the science of control and communication in the animal and machine' (Wiener 1948). The central idea of cybernetics is that the workings of biological organisms, ecological systems, and many mechanical devices can be understood as a matter of how they use information to adapt to changing conditions in their environments, and central to this idea is the concept of 'feedback', the notion that information about the results of past behaviour can serve to guide future behaviour.

Although cybernetics has had a profound influence on many different disciplines in the sciences and social sciences, including engineering, computer science, biology, environmental science, psychiatry, management, and even some branches of linguistics, it has never really held much attraction for discourse analysts, chiefly because the 'mathematical theory

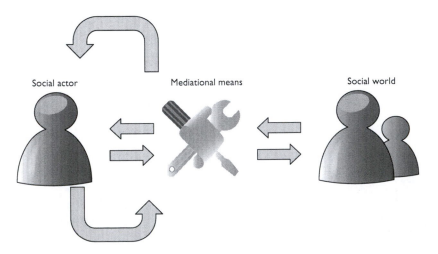

Social actor   Mediational means   Social world

Figure 3.2 Mediated action as a feedback mechanism

of communication' (Shannon 1948) it is based on treats 'information' as separate from both 'meaning' and 'context', two notions that are at the very heart of most theories of discourse. I would argue, however, that the cybernetic idea of interactive systems in which participants constantly adapt their behaviour based on feedback from their environments is also central to many models of discourse, including the 'probe–response–reflect–probe again' model that Gee (this volume) uses to describe our 'conversations with the world'.

How then, might we apply the cybernetic model of feedback to understanding how people use texts, and how texts 'dovetail' back on their users? A feedback loop typically includes data gathering, data processing, transmission of the data back to the organism, and action on the part of the organism (which produces more data). When all of these processes are operating in a system, that system constitutes what is known in cybernetics as a 'servomechanism', a 'feedback loop' consisting of a sensor (for data gathering), an amplifier or processor (for data processing), a transmitter (for data transmission), and an actor (see Figure 3.3).

In considering the role texts play as part of servomechanisms, as discourse analysts we are chiefly concerned with the affordances and constrains of different technologies for gathering data (the ways available for writers to 'write' texts), and for processing data (the ways available for these texts to 'write their writers' by changing what writers have entered into a different form and feeding it back to them).

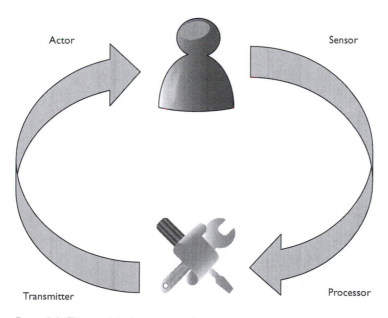

Figure 3.3 The model of a servomechanism

An example of such a servomechanism can be seen in the app *iDrated*, which I use to help me to maintain my goal of drinking more water. Whenever I drink water, I enter the amount by tapping the screen and choosing a size of bottle that best represents the amount of water I drank (see Figure 3.4). The program then processes that data in relation to my goal, immediately feeding back to me an image of a body representing how much water I have drunk and have left to drink (see Figure 3.5). If I like, I can also set an alarm so that the programme will remind me every time I need to take another drink.

Figure 3.4 Data entry screen on *iDrated*

Figure 3.5 Feedback screen on *iDrated*

This program helps to create an efficient servomechanism by the way it facilitates data gathering, helping me to easily record the amount of water I have drunk by presenting me with different sized bottles to choose from, and by processing the data in relation to my goals, helping me to see my progress. At the same time the semiotic systems that the app makes available also constrain the kinds of information that I can make relevant about my water drinking – I can only express the amount that I drank, not the kind (e.g. tap water, mineral water), nor the circumstances in which the drinking took place. Similarly, the figure of the human – in various stages of saturation – that is served back to me is utterly decontextualised, separated from factors like the time of day, the temperature and how thirsty I am when I view it, information which I must 'fill in' in order to make a decision about how to respond. In this, as in every servomechanism, then, agency (my control over drinking water) is distributed between the actor (me) and the tool, each both enabling and constraining the other (S. Scollon 2005).

Data gathering

As I argued above, different technologies of entextualisation make available different methods for gathering data from users, each with their own sets of affordances and constraints. The *iDrated* app makes it much easier for me to record how much water I drank than it would be if I had to write this information down in a notebook without the aid of pictures, and to remember to make an entry without the aid of an electronic reminder.

Different technologies of entextualisation, however, don't just change the relative convenience of inputting data. On a deeper level they change what it means to engage in the act of writing itself. Kittler (1999) notes how, in the twentieth century, the invention of the typewriter changed the way people wrote, making it more mechanical and less embodied. Digital technologies have further changed the experience of writing. As Derrida (2005: 23) observes:

> With pens and typewriters, you think you know how it works, how 'it responds'. Whereas with computers, even if people know how to use them up to a point, they rarely know, intuitively and without thinking . . . how the internal demon of the apparatus operates.

With the introduction of wireless sensors and algorithms that automatically convert online gestures (like clicking on a portion of a webpage) or physical actions (like going for a run) into acts of 'writing', writing has moved even further away from the deliberate act of inscription with which it is traditionally associated.

Taking these observations into account, the self-tracking apps I experimented with can be compared based on how 'automatic' they make the act of inputting data, and, conversely, how much agency the writer can exert over this input. At one extreme one can place apps such as *Fitbit*, which is paired with a wireless accelerometer that measures users' steps. In this case, the measurement and recording is done automatically: the user has no control whatsoever over the number of steps recorded. The only way to alter the number is to take more steps, which, in a way, is the whole point of this and many of the other apps I analysed: to put users in a situation in which 'writing' depends not just on inscribing information in a traditional sense, but in changing their behaviour in some more fundamental way.

At the other extreme, one can place apps with a relatively low level of automaticity and a high level of authorial control such as *DayOne*, a diary/ journal app which allows users to type entries, to which they may also add things like pictures, tags and location information. Of course, typing a journal entry on a smartphone keyboard is a substantially different experience from writing a diary with a pen, and this is likely to affect the length of the entries one writes and even the kinds of things one writes about. At the same time, this input system has certain affordances, including making it easier to compose a journal entry anytime and anywhere and making it easy to combine other modes with writing. There are, as well, certain automatic aspects to the input system of this app: users can set it, for example, to automatically record the time and location of an entry and the music the user is listening to when the entry is composed, and to automatically remind users to enter data. In fact, despite the considerable effort required to write journal entries, the main selling point of the app for many users still seems to be its 'ease of use'. In a review of this app on iTunes, one user wrote:

> I wanted an app that encouraged journaling, but some of the others actually made it a pain to create entries, so I never used them. With *DayOne*, I am eager to add entries, and it is quick & easy . . . I am very pleased with the auto-add of weather, GPS, and current music playing . . . I also love how easy the tags are to set . . . Even with multiple functions, it is very organised & can be personalised in just seconds.

One thing this review reveals is the complex relationship between automaticity and perceived control: functions that automatically collect data do not necessarily give users a feeling that they have less control over input if the app also allows them to 'personalise' the nature and level of the automaticity.

Nevertheless, some degree of surrender of authorial control – whether it is giving the app the ability to record your every step or simply to record your location when you use it – seems to be a characteristic of almost all of the apps I analysed. Proponents of these forms of 'frictionless' writing argue that they enable us to produce kinds of texts that were not possible with conventional methods of inscription. As Gary Wolf (2010), one of the founders of the Quantified Self movement puts it:

> When the familiar pen-and-paper methods of self-analysis are enhanced by sensors that monitor our behaviour automatically, the process of self-tracking becomes both more alluring and more meaningful. Automated sensors do more than give us facts; they also remind us that our ordinary behaviour contains obscure quantitative signals that can be used to inform our behaviour, once we learn to read them.

Critics, on the other hand, focus on the loss of human agency that accompanies automatic writing. As technologies increasingly intervene between the writer and the word, writes Introna (2011: 128), 'human agency becomes encoded as already being in the code of the machine'. Perhaps the most famous articulation of this concern comes from Kittler (1997: 145), who declares:

> We do not write anymore . . . writing passes instead through microscopically written inscriptions which, in contrast to all historical writing tools, are able to read and write by themselves . . . We simply do not know what our writing does.

Processing

The other important stage in the workings of a servomechanism from the point of view of discourse analysis is the way that it processes the data that is gathered from the user. As Cheney-Lippold (2011: 170) describes it, through processing,

> the implicit disorder of data collected about an individual is organised, defined, and made valuable by algorithmically assigning meaning to (it)–and in turn limiting the potential excess of meanings that raw data offer.

Processing, then, always involves a certain amount of focusing of meaning and reduction of complexity in which different aspects of the data are made 'criterial' (Jones 2013), and others are backgrounded. The apps that I analysed achieve this in three essential ways, which I refer to as resemiotisation, retemporalisation, and recontextualisation.

Resemiotisation

Resemiotisation (Iedema 2001) is the 'translation' of data from one semiotic mode to another. As meanings move across modes and media, they change, with different aspects being foregrounded or backgrounded. Different semiotic modes (such as language, numbers, pictures) and different textual materialities (printed texts, iPhone screens, audio recordings) come with different affordances and constraints regarding how the reduction and focusing of 'raw' data can be accomplished, and thus what is ultimately made 'criterial' to users. Numbers can express exact amounts, but those amounts may not be particularly meaningful. Verbal expressions (such as 'high' and 'low') add value to quantities, though they are unable to express the same degree of exactness. Charts and other graphical representations help people to 'see' quantities and to experience aspects of their degree and change spatially.

Obviously, the most important form of resemiotisation in the apps used by self-quantifiers is 'quantification'. The *Fitbit* app transforms the experience of physical movement into a series of numbers representing steps, kilometres, and calories burned. *MyFitnessPal* transforms the experience of eating and digesting a meal into a series of numbers representing calories, carbohydrates, fats, and protein, and tells users how many calories they can still eat to stay within their self-imposed limits. Quantification, however, is not always enough to allow people to understand this information in ways that encourage behaviour change. The real power of technologies of entextualisation associated with self-tracking is in their ability to *qualify* this information, to make it more experiential. After a day of eating, for example, *MyFitnessPal* presents me with a pie chart, which communicates graphically the ratio of carbohydrates, fats and proteins I have eaten (see Figure 3.6). One advantage of these graphic representations is that they help to communicate values and ranges in ways that non-specialists can better understand by resemiotising the typological, conceptual meaning of numbers back into

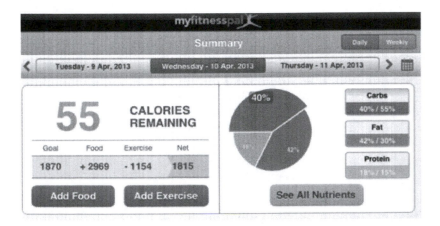

Figure 3.6 Screenshot of *MyFitnessPal*

the more topological, experiential meaning of shapes and colours (Lemke 1998).

The most important thing about resemiotisation, however, is not that it makes 'raw' data easier to understand and use, but that in doing so it assigns value to it, and, by extension, to the user from whom it was gathered. Seemingly innocuous values embodied in words like high, low, good, fair or poor, in colours from bright reds to cool blues, and in graphs with lines of different lengths and thicknesses, serve to support larger architectures of value or ideologies. The kinds of identities these texts reflect back to their users, as Cheney-Lippold (2011: 168) points out, 'focus not on essential notions of identity but instead on pliable behavioural models, undergirded by algorithms, that allow for the creation of a cybernetic relationship of identification.' In other words, the self gets defined solely within the parameters that the mediational means makes available, in much the way Serres (2007) points out basketball players are defined by the ball and the rules of the game. Proponents of self-tracking might say that this is exactly the point, to reflect back to the user an identity that is shaped and evaluated according to a particular set of values, such as 'good health'. Critics, on the other hand, would focus on how the modes and materialities of self-tracking apps limit the way we define self-knowledge (and ultimately, the way we define ourselves) based on the narrow semiotic categorisation practices these apps make available (see for example Cheney-Lippold 2011).

As these apps resemiotise data, then, they also resemiotise the users from whom this data has been collected. Some self-quantifiers, in fact, are very conscious of the kinds of identities such apps seek to impose on them, and the limitations of those identities. One participant in my focus group interviews said:

> There is something about every app that tries to paint you as a certain kind of person. So for example with Fitbit, the app already tells you that you're an active person because it gives you numbers about your physical activity, and the Lift app tells you that you are someone who is social, who wants to share goals with friends, because it gives you graphs comparing you with them. So you need to decide if you want to accept the identity that the app creates.

Retemporalisation

The second important aspect of data processing is what I call retemporalisation, the way technologies of entextualisation embed data into different 'chronotopes'. Bakhtin (1981) developed the notion of chronotopes in the context of literary studies: different authors, and different works, he observed, create different configurations of time and space within which actions are presented. Different chronotopes can either expand the scale of action or compress it. They can also function to create connections between different timescales, relating, for example, momentary actions to longer scale historical events. It is this aspect of chronotopes that Lemke (2000) focuses on when he speaks of activities taking place on multiple timescales with shorter timescale actions going to make up longer timescale ones, and longer timescale actions imposing constraints on what can occur on shorter timescales, a phenomenon Blommaert (2005) refers to as 'layered simultaneity'. The main difference, Lemke says, between naturally occurring eco-systems (such as the global climate) and human 'eco-social systems' is the ability of humans, through semiotic mediation (the creation of texts), to facilitate the communication of information across disparate timescales.

This ability is especially important in the context of health and risk. The way people understand and respond to health information depends crucially on the chronotopes within which it is communicated. The problem with most health behaviour is that the consequences of what we do now are usually not obvious to us. The negative feedback from eating an extra piece of cake, for example, is long term and gradual, while the positive feedback is immediate. Similarly, the positive feedback from exercising usually comes long after that first trip to the gym (Jones 2013). Retemporalisation situates information in either shorter or longer chronotopes, facilitating communication between different timescales. It might, for example, create feedback loops that operate on shorter timescales, providing people with more immediate information about their behaviour, as when my *Nike+* app provides me with a congratulatory message from a famous athlete right after I've finished a particularly gruelling run. Or it might involve plotting long-term trends, keeping track, for example, of a person's pattern of cake eating over time, recording on what days and at what times of day it occurs, and what usually 'triggers' it. The *Withings Health Mate* app connected to my Wi-Fi scale (a 'Withings Smart Body Analyzer'), for example, allows me not just to measure my body weight, fat percentage and body mass index, but also to monitor these values over time. This not only allows me to see when and how I am deviating from my goal, but also helps me to turn my weight gain or loss into a kind of 'narrative', linking the trend line to other episodes in my life such as holidays and love affairs gone wrong (see Figure 3.7).

In other words, retemporalisation creates the opportunity for us to engage with the 'layered simultaneity' (Blommaert 2005) of our behaviour. It also helps us to engage with our experience not just in a retrospective way, but also in an anticipatory way: seeing connections among moments in the past helps us to imagine the future (Jones 2009). Nicolas Felton, developer of an app called *Daytum*, argues that most people who collect data about their behaviour are not seeking 'answers' in a conceptual sense; rather, they are looking for ways to turn their lives 'into interesting narratives' (Hill 2011: 7).

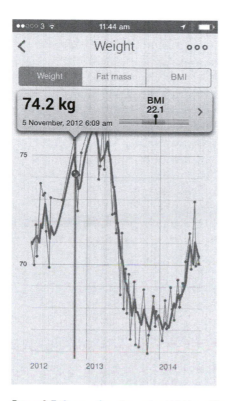

Figure 3.7 Screenshot from the *Withings Health Mate* app

One possible danger of such narratives, however, is the way they encourage what Blommaert (2005: 127) calls 'synchronisation', treating processes that are happening on different timescales as if they are unfolding 'in sync' with one another, thus obscuring the complex and contradictory relationships these processes might have with one another. This phenomenon is especially evident in apps that literally synchronise multiple data streams (like *TicTrac* and *Daytum*). Blommaert's concern with synchronisation is that it distorts our view of history, and that this distortion is often used as a tool by the powerful to make certain explanations of events or circumstances seem 'natural'. For self-trackers, synchronisation can lead them to jump to conclusions about the relationship between two or more processes (for example, my mood and my weight), while ignoring what might be more significant factors simply because they are less amenable to algorithmic retemporalisation. It can also encourage people to conflate correlation with causation, leading to forms of behaviour change that may have little or no impact on the issue they are trying to address.

Recontextualisation

The third aspect of data processing associated with the apps I analysed is recontextualisation. As mentioned in the introduction to this volume, digital technologies have destabilised traditional notions of context, making it more difficult for people to maintain strict boundaries between domains that before were seen as separate. Information flows freely across texts, across devices and across social situations. Since information acquires different meanings as it is imported into different contexts, the complex layering of contexts, and the ease with which information is decontextualised and recontextualised, compounds and complicates the meaning potential of texts

The apps I studied recontextualise data in three primary ways, by changing the physical context in which users interact with it, by changing its social context, and by changing the 'contextual frames' in which data are embedded. All of these forms of recontextualisation come with potential benefits and dangers for users.

Self-tracking apps change the physical context of data by making it available at times and places far removed from the contexts in which it was collected, and even from contexts in which one might be expected to use it for health purposes. Because these texts about ourselves are incorporated into mobile devices, they are, in fact, always available and, as a result, they have the potential to intrude into all sorts of situations. In some respects this is an affordance, allowing me, for example, to check my running tally of calories consumed at the very moment I am choosing dishes in a cafeteria line, or, in the case of apps like *My Medical* and *Glooko*, allowing medical practitioners stationed many miles away to get immediate information on the state of a patient. At the same time, data from self-tracking apps may intrude into contexts in which their presence might be deemed inappropriate or in which they might interrupt the flow of life in less positive ways, distracting users from an awareness of the here and now.

Another important way many of these apps recontextualise data is by altering the social context in which they appear, turning what was originally private behaviour into public information. Eighteen out of the twenty-five apps that I analysed allow users to share data with others, often via social networks such as Facebook and Twitter. The advantage of this for many self-trackers is that knowing that one's behaviour is observed can act as a strong motivator, and sometimes the people who are privy to this data respond with encouragement or advice. In other words, by making private data public such apps actually co-opt the people in the user's social network into the servomechanism, enlisting their help in providing further feedback. It also creates the conditions for these people to share their data back, and when they do, the context in which users are able to view their data changes dramatically. Suddenly they can compare their behaviour with that of their 'friends' and 'followers' and get an idea about what kind of behaviour is the 'norm' among different groups of people in their network.

Champions of self-tracking apps argue that their ability to recontextualise data across social networks is helping to create a new kind of health consciousness fuelled by communities of 'participatory biocitizens' (Swan 2012) who take greater responsibility for their own health and learn from one another. Critics, on the other hand, see the same phenomenon as evidence that digital technologies are helping to create 'societies of control' (Deleuze 1992) in which individuals are reduced to data points to be shared, compared, and evaluated.

Finally, recontextualisation often involves a kind of contextual 'reframing' of behaviour. One of the most common examples of such reframing that is built into many of the apps I analysed is the phenomenon of 'gamification' (Dembosky 2011): the reframing of health behaviour as a kind of competition or game. The app *GymPact*, for example, allows users to earn cash rewards for going to the gym, paid for by other members of the social network who fail to live up to their commitment to exercise. Similarly, the *Nike+* app allows users to 'race' with their friends, whether they are running at the same time or not. This gamification of health practices not only increases motivation, but can also contribute to self-reflection and learning. According to Gee (2003), the reason video games are so successful in engaging players in a process of rapid and effective learning include their interactivity, their ability to customise and personalise experience, and the way they provide 'just in time' feedback (48), all of which also seem to be characteristics of many of the most popular self-tracking apps.

Critics of gamification (Morozov 2014; Whitson 2013), on the other hand, warn that such attempts to make positive behaviours 'fun' might detract from people coming to appreciate the real personal or social benefits of such behaviours, and that they ultimately serve a neo-liberal political project that promotes individual responsibility and competition as the keys to progress and personal growth. Whitson (2013) raises another sort of political concern, warning that the basis of gamification is surveillance, and that any app which gathers and aggregates data from a large number of users, as do many of the apps I analysed, should be used with caution.

This concern points to a broader danger associated with the recontextualisation of data in the digital age, the fact that those data may eventually be recontextualised in places and for purposes that users are not aware of. The privacy policies of most of the apps I analysed state that users' data will not be sold to third parties, but a recent study by the Privacy Rights Clearinghouse (2013) found that the developers of a number of popular fitness apps either transmitted users data insecurely or passed it on to third parties without authorisation. Fears that such apps might eventually become tools for surveillance by advertisers or insurance companies were recently exacerbated when Facebook bought the popular activity tracking app *Moves* and immediately changed its privacy policy, informing users that their data may be used to 'understand and improve our Services' (Moves 2014), which presumably includes their services to advertisers.

Associated with these possible benefits and dangers is a larger, more fundamental issue: the fact that the logic governing the processing of users' data by such apps is rarely made explicit. It is based on algorithms that operate beneath the surface of the app's interface. As Whitson (2013: 175) argues:

> the danger of digitised processes (is) . . . we cannot open up the black box of the software that hides the rules from us. We cannot see why and how and when some of our actions are deemed successful and rewarded versus others that are not. We want to assume that these value judgements are achieved in a fair and impartial manner, but this is not always the case. There is no space in these systems for the mutual negotiation and agreement upon the rules.

In other words, users of self-tracking apps are rarely able to alter or even to question the ways their bodies are being resemiotised, retemporalised, and recontextualised. They have no choice but to simply trust the decisions of the algorithms. In fact, as Gillespie (2014: 179) points out, algorithms themselves have a way of acting as 'stabilisers of trust, practical and symbolic assurances that their evaluations are fair and accurate, and free from subjectivity, error, or attempted influence'.

This inherent opacity of algorithms is a challenge not just for users of digital texts, but also for discourse analysts seeking to analyse them. Evaluations performed by algorithms are intrinsically ideological, in that they 'always depend on inscribed assumptions about what matters, and how what matters can be identified' (Gillespie 2014: 177). While discourse analysts are well versed in uncovering the underlying ideological operations in more traditional texts, the kinds of tools they have developed are less suitable for uncovering the ideological assumptions embedded in code, which operates beneath the surface of texts. This is further complicated by the fact that algorithms themselves are, by their nature, constantly changing, adapting to the behaviour of users (Gillespie 2014).

Conclusion

In this chapter I have suggested a model for the analysis of digital texts based on principles from cybernetics and mediated discourse analysis. The texts I have analysed, self-tracking apps for health and fitness, may seem at first unique. The ways these texts gather data from their users, process it, and then reflect it back to them are, however, characteristic of many if not most of the texts we encounter online. Search engines like Google do not just provide a way for users to search the web, but also provide a way for Google and its advertisers to search users. The results such sites serve are not objective reflections of the information available, but rather selective reflections of users' past searching behaviour. Recommendation engines such as that used by Amazon.com form similar kinds of feedback loops, gathering information from searches and purchases by customers and feeding it back to them. Facebook rearranges stories on users' newsfeeds based on the kinds of stories and the kinds of people they have 'liked' in the past, and games such as those discussed by Gee, Hafner, and Marsh (this volume) engage players by transforming them into components in a 'cybernetic feedback system' (Whitson 2013: 166). One might argue, in fact, that the entire internet functions as a kind of servomechanism, growing, changing and forming new links among data that reflect the discursive activities of its users.

I am not arguing that this reflexive nature of digital texts is entirely new. As Clark (2003) reminds us, human beings have always been 'natural born cyborgs', entering into cybernetic relationships with the tools we develop to interact with our environments and monitor our behaviour. What I am arguing is that the cybernetic relationships that digital texts form with us are both more efficient and often less amenable to critical scrutiny. The purpose of most of the self-tracking apps I discussed in this chapter is to change users' behaviour by establishing efficient feedback loops between users and texts. Other digital texts also have the effect of changing users' behaviour, as web surfers, online shoppers, gamers and social media users continually modify their actions based on the feedback provided by the algorithms underlying these texts. 'As these algorithms nestle into people's daily lives and mundane information practices,' writes Gillespie (2014: 183), they change 'how they seek information, how they perceive and think about the contours of knowledge, and how they understand themselves'. The difference is that these projects of behaviour change are usually driven not by aspirations for self-improvement on the part of users but by the commercial and ideological agendas of internet companies and the advertisers who pay them.

References

Bakhtin, M. M. (1981) *The Dialogic Imagination: four essays*, trans. C. Emerson and M. Holquist, M. Holquist (ed.) Austin, TX: University of Texas Press.

Blommaert, J. (2005) *Discourse: a critical introduction*, Cambridge: Cambridge University Press.

Brown, G. and Yule, G. (1983) *Discourse Analysis*, Cambridge: Cambridge University Press.

Cheney-Lippold, J. (2011) 'A new algorithmic identity: soft biopolitics and the modulation of control', *Theory, Culture & Society*, 28: 164–181.

Clark, A. (2003) *Natural Born Cyborgs: minds, technologies, and the future of human intelligence*, Oxford: Oxford University Press.

Deleuze, G. (1992) 'Postscript on the societies of control', *October*, 59: 3–7.

Dembosky, A. (2011) 'Invasion of the body hackers', *FT Magazine*, 10 June. Online. Available HTTP: <http://www.ft.com/cms/s/2/3ccb11a0-923b-11e0-9e00-00144feab49a.html#axzz1pTueXXIL> (accessed 13 July 2013).

Derrida, J. (2005) *Paper Machine*, trans. R. Bowlby, Stanford, CA: Stanford University Press.

Gee, J. P. (2003) *What Video Games Have to Teach Us about Learning and Literacy*, Basingstoke, UK: Palgrave-MacMillan.

Gillespie, T. (2014) 'The relevance of algorithms', in T. Gillespie, P. J. Boczkowski and K. A. Foot (eds) *Media Technologies: essays on communication, materiality, and society*, 169–194, Cambridge, MA: MIT Press.

Halliday, M. A. K. and Hasan, R. (1976) *Cohesion in English*, London: Longman.

Hill, K. (2011) 'Adventures in self-surveillance: Fitbit, tracking my movement and sleep', *Forbes*, 25 February. Online. Available HTTP: <http://blogs.forbes.com/kashmirhill/2011/02/25/adventures-in-self-surveillance-fitbit-tracking-my-movement-and-sleep/> (accessed 6 June 2014).

Iedema, R. (2001) 'Resemiotization', *Semiotica*, 137(1-4): 23–39.

Introna, L. D. (2011) 'The enframing of code agency, originality and the plagiarist', *Theory, Culture and Society*, 28: 113–141.

Jones, R. H. (2009) 'Dancing, skating and sex: action and text in the digital age', *Journal of Applied Linguistics*, 6: 283–302.

Jones, R. H. (2013) *Health and Risk Communication: an applied linguistic perspective*, London: Routledge.

Kittler, F. A. E. (1997) *Literature, Media, Information Systems*, Amsterdam: Overseas Publishers Association.

Kittler, F. A. E. (1999) *Gramophone, Film, Typewriter*, trans. G. Winthrop-Young and M. Wutz, Stanford, CA: Stanford University Press.

Latour, B. (2007) *Reassembling the Social: an introduction to actor-network-theory*, Oxford: Oxford University Press.

Lemke, J. L. (1998) 'Metamedia literacy: transforming meanings and media', in D. Reinking, M. C. McKenna, L. D. Labbo and R. D. Kieffer (eds) *Handbook of Literacy and Technology: transformations in a post-typographic world*, 312–333, Mahwah, NJ: Lawrence Erlbaum.

Lemke, J. L. (2000) 'Across the scales of time: artifacts, activities, and meanings in ecosocial systems', *Mind, Culture, and Activity*, 7(4): 273–290.

McLuhan, M. (1964) *Understanding Media: the extensions of man*, New York: McGraw-Hill.

Morozov, E. (2014) *To Save Everything, Click Here: the folly of technological solutionism*, New York: PublicAffairs.

Moves (2014) 'Privacy policy'. Online. Available HTTP: <https://www.moves-app.com/privacy> (accessed 6 June 2014).

Norris, S. and Jones, R. H. (eds) (2005) *Discourse in Action: introducing mediated discourse analysis*, London: Routledge.

Privacy Rights Clearinghouse (2013) 'Mobile health and fitness apps: what are the privacy risks?' Online. Available HTTP: <https://www.privacyrights.org/mobile-Privacy Rights Clearinghousehealth-and-fitness-apps-what-are-privacy-risks> (accessed 14 June 2014).

Scollon, R. (2001) *Mediated Discourse: the nexus of practice*, London: Routledge.

Scollon, R. and Scollon, S. W. (2004) *Nexus Analysis: discourse and the emerging internet*, London: Routledge.

Scollon, S. W. (2005) 'Agency distributed through time, space and tools: Bentham, Babbage and the census', in S. Norris and R. H. Jones (eds) *Discourse in Action: introducing mediated discourse analysis*, 172–182, London: Routledge.

Serres, M. (2007) *The Parasite*, trans. L. R. Schehr, Minneapolis, MN: University of Minnesota Press.

Shannon, C. (1948) 'A mathematical theory of communication', *Bell System Technical Journal*, 27: 379–423.

Swan, M. (2012) 'Health 2050: the realization of personalized medicine through crowdsourcing, the quantified self, and the participatory biocitizen', *Journal of Personalized Medicine*, 2(3): 93–118.

Topol, E. (2012) *The Creative Destruction of Medicine: how the digital revolution will create better health care*, New York: Basic Books.

Whitson, J. R. (2013) 'Gaming the quantified self', *Surveillance and Society*, 11(1-2): 163–176.

Wiener, N. (1948) *Cybernetics: or the control and communication in the animal and the machine*, Boston, MA: MIT Press.

Wolf, G. (2010) 'The data driven life', *The New York Times*. Online. Available HTTP: <http://www.nytimes.com/2010/05/02/magazine/02self-measurement-t.html?pagewanted=all> (accessed 6 June 2014).

Chapter 4

Tagging on Flickr as a social practice

David Barton

Tagging is endemic on social media sites such as Twitter and for some time it has been an important feature of photo sites such as Instagram, Flickr and Delicious. A body of research on tagging has developed, and the existing literature examines how tags contribute to 'folksonomies', that is taxonomies created by combining the tags of many users. Typically these studies have examined large data sets of tags on particular sites and this work has been mainly from a web designer's and information scientist's approach, where tagging is used as a hyperlink bringing together all uses of a specific tag. In this chapter I am interested in complementing this approach with a user's view of tagging. This will be addressed by investigating in detail how people use tags on one particular site, Flickr, by drawing on a social practice view of language use online. This emphasises users' practices and how tags provide a writing space with particular affordances which users build upon. This study enables us to see people's purposes when tagging, how they design their sites in deliberate acts of curation, how tags are used more than just as parts of a folksonomy, and what is lost when discussing tags away from the pages where they are being used.

First, I will begin by explaining briefly a social practice view of language and how it is appropriate for studying tagging. This is followed by an overview of the methodology. The literature on tagging which relates to Flickr is then reviewed and this then leads on to the main part of this chapter, analyses of the tagging practices of two sets of users. The aim here is to understand people's practices, both in creating tags and in using them.

This chapter utilises a social practice approach to language online, developed from literacy studies (Barton and Lee 2013). This is an approach which can provide a way of examining texts and practices online. It starts out from what people do with language in their lives, locating this in broader social practices. What people are doing online can be described in terms of their language and literacy practices, in the sense of the commonly recognised patterns of activity where people bring their cultural knowledge to an activity. Practices are realised in specific events, such as uploading, tagging, searching and browsing. Emphasising the importance of language, a social practice approach sees online spaces as part of a textually mediated social world. Even an intensely visual site such as Flickr has a large amount of language on it and each photo can be surrounded by language serving many functions. For instance, when uploading a photo to Flickr the user is invited to add written titles, descriptions, tags, and more.

Methodology for investigating tagging as a social practice

The idea of online activity as consisting of a set of practices that are inferred from what goes on in events, which themselves are mediated by texts demands a research methodology that pays close attention to the detail of particular instances. This is an ecological approach which keeps to situated examples and is aware that what users do both affects and is affected by the perceived possibilities. There are not 'effects' of technology – rather there is the complex interplay of affordances in people's purposeful activities. This approach has the very strong idea of an active user, and not someone passively responding to the design of a site.

It is also important to stress that online life is essentially social and that the role of other people, online and offline, is crucial. Therefore a social practice approach is interested in the networks and other groupings people participate in, noting the fluidity and flows in such online participation. This is the approach which this paper is embedded in. The specific methodology involves revisiting existing data and locating tags in the context of their use. A related issue, the importance of how we talk about, visualise and represent tags, is a thread woven throughout the chapter, examining how different discourses and visualisations of tags represent or misrepresent tagging practices.

In this study evidence about tagging practices comes initially from examining the texts, that is the web pages containing the tags, and then from online interviews with some of the creators of the web pages. The web pages are treated as multimodal texts with distinct 'writing spaces' such as the spaces for titles, for tags and for comments. Each writing space has its own dynamics and has to be seen in relation to the other writing spaces on the page, to images and to overall layout. The tagging space is analysed in terms of content analysis and by drawing on linguistic analyses of discourse including examining cohesion and coherence, along with stance analysis.

After initial analysis of the web pages, some of the individual creators of the web pages were then contacted and asked to answer a generic online survey about their practices on Flickr. So for example, in a study about multilingualism they were asked general questions about which languages they used and what affected their language choice. This was followed up by individually tailored online interviews which asked questions about specific web pages, such as why they chose a particular language in relation to a specific image. The aim was to get the users to reflect on their practices by looking in detail at specific examples of their own pages. The analysis combined textual data with interview data.

This literacy studies methodology resonates well with approaches to discourse analysis which combine textual analysis with broader cultural knowledge, such as Wodak and colleagues' discourse-historical approach to critical discourse analysis (Reisigl and Wodak 2009) and mediated discourse analysis inspired by the work of Ron Scollon (Jones and Hafner 2012; Norris and Jones 2005). The methodology also links up with current work in Linguistic Ethnography (Tusting 2013). While not 'an ethnography' we would argue that this is an 'ethnographic approach' in that people's perspectives are highlighted, the analysis is situated in a broader cultural context and that it aims to be naturalistic with low levels of intervention. In this particular study there was also reanalysis of existing data meaning that we already knew a great deal about these users.

The study is multi-method and combines qualitative and quantitative approaches. The analysis of websites and the interviews led to a focus on individual cases, as will be seen in this paper. There is a repeated going back and forth between individual cases and a wider perspective as a way of seeing how individual interpretations hold up across broader data.

Tagging systems as folksonomies

Before examining the existing literature, and to introduce the topic of this chapter, Figure 4.1 provides an example of a set of tags related to one photo on a Flickr page. As can be surmised from the tags, the photo being described on this Flickr page consists of an Egyptian sculpture in a New York museum.

The photo page was created by a multilingual Spanish speaker from South America who was visiting New York. She was one of our informants on a study of how multilingual users of Flickr deploy their languages online

Figure 4.1 An example of tags (from http://www.flickr.com/photos/46836654@
N00/460544898/in/photolist-GGpXh-21NQnZ-5bb14d, last accessed
17 March 2014)

(Lee and Barton 2011). The page is also discussed in Barton and Lee (2013) and I will return to the example later in this chapter after reviewing some of the existing literature on tagging.

The idea of tags as being part of some form of folksonomy has been the prevalent view in research on tagging. A folksonomy is a taxonomy created by collating tags from a large number of people's tags and it was seen originally, when the term was invented, as an unintended consequence of individual people's actions (Vander Wal 2005). There was a cluster of studies around 2005–6, often collating tags from a large number of users into a folksonomy. These studies were often carried out from a librarian and information science perspective (such as Heckner et al. 2007; Winget 2006) or by the site designers themselves (as in Marlow et al. 2006 whose research was done in association with Yahoo).

In their useful early study of tagging, Marlow et al. (2006) point out that tagging systems work very differently on different sites and this must be borne in mind when discussing the particular case of Flickr. They compare Delicious (formerly del.icio.us) and Flickr, providing a set of seven aspects of design which affect the tagging. These are useful in demonstrating the variety of forms of tagging online and can be discussed here in relation to Flickr. Sites vary on what can be tagged and who can tag. By default any member of Flickr can add a tag to a photo. Sites vary in what support there is for tagging, whether there is a limited set of possible tags and how the tags are presented. Some tags may be provided by the site, such as date and make of camera. Tags then provide links to other photos with the same tag and they enable users to link with each other. In comparing Delicious and Flickr, Marlow et al. show how the two sites differ on all these dimensions. The idea that tagging differs from site to site can be seen by examining other sites such as YouTube, Twitter, Pinterest and Instagram. Looking at Flickr, not all the possibilities offered on the site are taken up by users. For example, although by default anyone can add tags, in practice most tags are created by the photographer and although they can add tags at any time they tend to create the tags when they initially upload the photo.

One study which has investigated people's motivations for tagging is a small qualitative study by Ames and Naaman (2007) which interviewed Flickr users. This work was also associated with Yahoo and the aim was to encourage users to tag more. They found that the motivations for tagging were many and varied and they identified a set of categories for motivations to tag. These included social reasons such as to make photos searchable to others, as well as personal reasons such as to help the user organise and find their own photos.

The designers provide the space which people act within. The list of differences between sites, discussed earlier, is a description of the possibilities they envisage for the site. People act within these possibilities, taking up some opportunities, ignoring others and creating new activities which the designers never dreamed of. It is this creative space between the designer and the user where the unexpected can happen which constitutes the affordances of tagging. Understanding the space between what the designers make available and what people then do within these spaces is the topic of this paper. In fact there is a remarkable range of possibilities on Flickr, many of which are hardly taken up, but at the same time there are strong constraints on what is possible.

To give an idea of what tags get used on Flickr, it may be useful to also show a visualisation of some of the most common tags on the site, as in Figure 4.2.

This is a tag cloud where size indicates number of instances of the tag. These are gathered together into an alphabetical list where the frequency is shown by the size of the word. This constitutes a folksonomy. It is an important visualisation of tags, and differs, for example, from a vertical justified alphabetical list of words all in the same font size. The form of these visualisations is created and made available by the designers of the site, not by the users. Visualisations of language are important and they can help and hinder us; here we see only the most common tags, and something else may be going on with the less common ones. Crucially it is in people's own words, and that is the important distinction from a scientist's or a linguist's taxonomy, or the anthropologist's folk taxonomy (which is in the anthropologist's words).

The list shows a certain range of topics as representing the discourse world of Flickr. There is international travel, holidays, family rituals and festivals. 'Wedding' is the most common tag (apart from the machine tags),

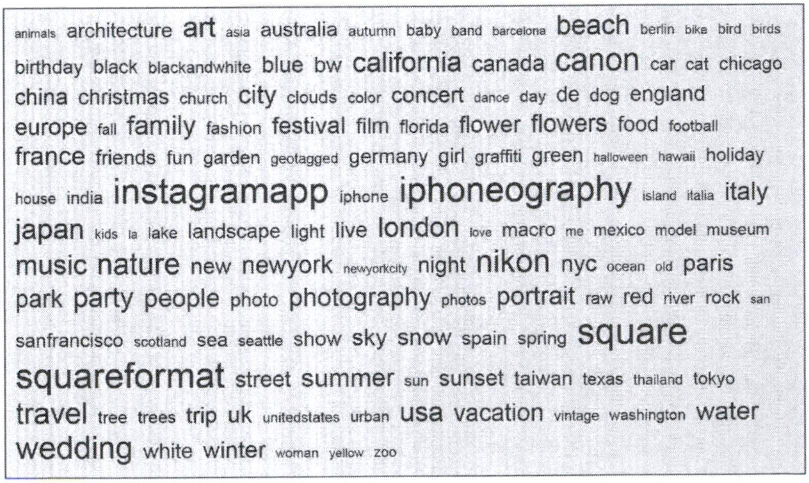

Figure 4.2 The most common tags on Flickr (http://www.flickr.com/photos/tags/, last accessed 12 February 2014)

with around 17 million instances. In terms of parts of speech, it is mostly nouns including places, along with adjectives of colour. Some are machine tags which are automatically added, such as the names of cameras Canon and Nikon. Other parts of speech are there, including the deictic pronoun 'me' which is used nearly 4 million times.

Looking more broadly at all the tags used on Flickr, rather than just the most common, there are all sorts of words including technical terms, dialect words, obscure words, abstractions, abbreviations, and many written languages are represented. All parts of speech are there. There is considerable deixis – 'here' has 80,000 instances and 'there' 46,000 instances. Even 'whence' has 213 instances and 'whenever' 492. There are several misspellings so, for example, 'writting' gets 8744 instances, some of which may be deliberate misspellings. Some aspects of the image are automatically added elsewhere on the page, such as when the photo was taken, and increasingly what make of camera, the camera settings and geotags of where it has been taken.

In the work of the mid-2000s comparing Flickr and Delicious, Guy and Tonkin (2006) review some of the literature on folksonomies, looking at what makes them work and listing some of the problems which other researchers identify. This is a useful review of the work at that particular time. They begin by pointing out that

> the number one gripe for those happier with more formal classification systems–is that the tagging terms used in those systems are imprecise. It is the users of a folksonomy system who add the tags, which means that the tags are often ambiguous, overly personalised and inexact.

They point out how many studies are critical of tags which are only used once as well as the use of 'nonsense' tags designed as unique markers that are shared between a group of friends or co-workers. The result is seen as an uncontrolled and chaotic set of tagging terms that do not support searching as effectively as more controlled vocabularies do. What they refer to as 'sloppy' tags included misspellings, compound words, single use tags and personal tags.

In their own study of tags on Flickr and Delicious, Guy and Tonkin found many such 'flaws'. 'By testing against multilingual dictionary software,' they write, 'we found that 40% of Flickr tags and 28% of Delicious tags were either misspelt, from a language not available via the software used, encoded in a manner that was not understood by the dictionary software, or compound words consisting of more than two words or a mixture of languages.' Overall, they state that 'Somewhere around a third of tags were indeed "malformed", in that they were beyond the grasp of a multilingual spell-checker for one reason or another.' Ironically, given the more recent ubiquity of hashtags on Twitter and many other sites, one of the complaints of that period was the use of symbols in tags and they observe that: 'Symbols such as # were used at the beginning of tags, probably for an incidental effect such as forcing the del.icio.us interface to list the tags at the top of an alphabetical listing.'

As a solution, Guy and Tonkin point out how researchers at that time were identifying the need to improve 'Tag Literacy' which would include 'Educating users to add "better" tags' and 'Improving the systems to allow "better" tags to be added', and they point to various lists of tag selection 'best practices' which could lead to general guidelines for users. These would include: 'using plurals rather than singulars; using lower case; grouping words using an underscore; following tag conventions started by others and adding synonyms'. In reviewing this area Guy and Tonkin are careful not to identify with this critique, which I would refer to as a 'deficit theory', very similar to other areas of public denigration of areas of literacy. This is seen in the terms used such as 'chaotic', 'nonsense', 'sloppy', 'flawed' and 'malformed'. (Elsewhere Marlow et al. 2006 mention another author referring to 'feral' tags.) Nevertheless, Guy and Tonkin are more even-handed. They see the problem for tagging systems as being the way they 'are trying to serve two masters at once; the personal collection, and the collective collection'. And that tags are not necessarily 'sloppy' or 'bad'. They point out that 'revisiting the data with another aim in mind might reveal usefulness in some categories of "sloppy" tag'. They raise questions about whether tags have a use beyond being search items. I would push this further and say that starting from people's tagging practices, a quite different view is apparent.

Tagging on Flickr

Turning to the present study and details of Flickr, it is a distinctly multi-modal site, where the central focus is on images but, nevertheless, a great deal of language is involved. On any online site there are distinct writing spaces, each with their own affordances. On a Flickr photo page these include space for a title, a description, tags and comments, and there is a link to the person's profile page. Photos are surrounded by writing. As part of the fluidity of the online world, this layout has been changed by the designers several times over the past few years, and the user has little control over the overall layout. As of May 2013, the title is in a larger bold font and superimposed over the bottom left hand side of the image. It is limited in length (apparently to 155 characters). Below this in a smaller font is the description space which can be empty or can contain several pages of text.

Tags appear as left to right text with a space between each tag (and, apparently, there can be up to seventy-five tags although in practice people rarely have more than twenty). Writing is also involved in describing the sets (themed groupings of one's own photos) and groups (themed groupings with other people's photos). Another important writing space, which will not be discussed in detail here, is the space for comments, which is available below the image.

The focus of this chapter is people's practices of tagging. What are users endeavouring to do? What are their purposes, and how do they use this writing space in relation to other writing spaces? The aim is to investigate how the act of tagging is situated in people's broader practices and what information is lost if tags are taken away from their context of use and used to create a folksonomy. This is a shift in perspective on what is going on.

The data to be analysed is taken from an earlier study of multilingualism and language choice on Flickr (Lee and Barton 2011) and from a study of deliberate learning on Flickr where people were participating in a '365 project' and taking a photo a day for a year (Barton 2012). Both of these studies are discussed in Barton and Lee (2013). So, I have returned to existing data, which was collected for different purposes, and have revisited it to investigate tagging practices. The methodology is to examine people's photo pages and, where available, to draw upon online interviews with the Flickr users.

Firstly, it is important to point out that people were emphatic that they use different sites for different purposes, so that they might use Flickr to display and to document, and for the photos to have a lasting presence there. This might contrast with a site like Facebook, where photos were more transient, were consumed quickly and quality was of less importance.

Examining the data from our multilingual study of thirty Flickr users, all of the Spanish users and around half of the Chinese speakers had tags in more than one language. In fact several had tags in more than two languages. For example, one Spanish speaker, Carolink, used Spanish, English and French. In our interviews with her she commented:

> I try to fit all the tags both in English (universalism) and in Spanish (my immediate Flickr public) and, since I know a little French, I put the French word when I remember it.

Another, Marta, tagged mainly in Spanish and Catalan, but also tagged in English and French, for example tagging a photo with 'playa', 'platje', 'beach' and 'plage'. The Chinese users sometimes tagged in both Chinese and English. With Chinese they also took advantage of the affordances of the scripts and sometimes tagged using both simplified and traditional characters and also romanised forms. For example, cjpanda tagged one photo in English as 'umbrella', in simplified Chinese characters as 伞 and in a romanised form of Chinese as 'shan'. In fact the tagging space was the part of the photo page which was most likely to exhibit multilingualism. So HKmPUA had a photo where the title and description were in English. However, the tags were in both traditional and simplified Chinese characters as well as being in English: 'Saikung, 西貢 [traditional Chinese], 西贡

[simplified Chinese], Hong Kong, 香港'. When interviewed about this, like several participants, HKmPUA stated that his aim was to get more hits:

> I want to get more views of my photos. I assume there might be lots of people in mainland China that might search for Queen's Pier photos, so I want my photos to come up in the search results when someone searches for Queen's Pier in simplified Chinese characters.

In such cases tags would be used as direct translations. These were usually straightforward terms which other people might also use. This can also be seen with the examples of 'beach' and 'umbrella', above, where people were aiming for general searchability.

At other times people put different information in different languages, so Saski reported that he often tagged in English but:

> When I post thinking about someone, a close friend or a known follower, I tend to post in Spanish . . . If I tag in Spanish, it has to be for a local (or personal, e.g. 'torollo') non translatable term.

These were often more idiosyncratic tags, such as 'disappear', 'heartbroken', 'desire', which were used by ädri. Some tags would require insider knowledge and would only be recognisable to other Flickr users, such as the tags '365' or '365Days', which Erick C used to indicated that the photo was part of his 365 photo project where he posted a photo a day for a year. So, in this data tags can be seen to been chosen for quite different purposes.

To illustrate how this works on particular photo pages let us now consider the tags on another photo, which was uploaded by a British academic and was not part of the multilingual study. The image consists of a man crouching on the ground and talking on his phone while at the same time writing on a piece of paper (and can be found at http://www.flickr.com/photos/drjoolz/25530138/in/photostream/, last accessed 22 August 2013). It is simply titled 'multimodal-guy'. There is no further description and, following a long tradition in photography, in many ways the photo 'speaks for itself'. I see it as a comment on the complexity of contemporary communication. Turning to the tags, there are four tags: 'UKLA', 'Conference', 'Bath', 'university' (see Figure 4.3).

Figure 4.3 Another example of tags

There are two important points to make about these tags. Firstly, unlike the tags in Figure 4.1, which repeated information that was already available elsewhere on the photo page, these tags provide new information. As another British academic, I can understand the tags as an explanation of the location of the photo. It was taken at the UK Literacy Association conference held at Bath University. I then notice the free conference bag in the photo and imagine a person having been phoned in an unfamiliar place and having to hurriedly write down a time or a place or a phone number. So, the tags are providing new information for making sense of the photo: for some readers at least, they are an essential part of the overall photo page. When talking to people as they examine a Flickr page we have observed that they often use the tags as part of their reading paths to make sense of the photo. This example confirms the point that people can be tagging in very different ways.

The second point to stress is that there is a 'grammar' to the tags: they make sense taken together and in this example the order of tags helps the meaning making. If the tags were considered in isolation then UKLA could mean many things. A brief search reveals that in the UK there is a 'Lubricants Association', a 'Laser Association', a 'Listing Authority' and a 'Locksmiths Association'. Looking more broadly, 'Ukla' is also the name of various towns around the world and of a business in Los Angeles. Similarly, taken alone, the word 'Bath' can be a town in the UK or, more frequently, it can be something full of water where one washes. The point is that taken together these tags have a meaning which they don't have when considered separately.

Visualisations and the creative use of tags

There are many uses of tags, and when re-examining the data collected as part of the earlier 365 study, where people take a photo a day for a year, there are good examples of how some photographers use the tagging space creatively. I will work through one example. On the first day of her 365 project one photographer used a photo of a garden gate (http://www.flickr. com/photos/60238368@N00/2065862805/in/photolist-49y63e-4a4Hsj-4agYuT, last accessed 15 August 2013). This is shown in Figure 4.4. (The original is in colour.)

It has the title ' . . . do I have to go? (1/365)' with the short description below: '26th November . . . dreaded trip to the dentist'. The idea of a gate seems a good image for starting out, both on the 365 project and on a trip to the dentist, and the first commenter on the image makes that point: 'Good luck (for 365 and dentist^^)'. The accompanying tags, shown in Figure 4.5, provide more detail of the day.

There is a strong narrative linking up the two activities of 365 and the visit to the dentist, and the tags can be read as a story. This idea of the 365

Figure 4.4 First day of 365 project

Tags

project365   365   gate   leaving   going out

dentist   torture   hate   fear   garden path

teeth   tooth   pain   dread   appointment

canon eos 400D   my day   snapshot   glance

day one   first   starting   digging my heals in

countryside   rural   bungay   suffolk   me

life   stress   everyday   myeverydaylife

Figure 4.5 First day tags

project being a tough challenge is common in the 365 data. Looking at this particular set of tags it follows some of the characteristics of the most common tags, listed earlier in Figure 4.2, in that there are several concrete nouns including places. However, there are also several abstract nouns and actions. There are several phrases, including 'project365', 'garden path' and 'myeverydaylife', a tag she uses often.

Figure 4.6 Last day of 365 project (http://www.flickr.com/photos/60238368@ N00/3059565140/in/photolist-5En587, last accessed 15 August 2013).

Moving to the last day of her 365 project, there is an image of someone standing in a field holding three balloons which spell out '365', as shown in Figure 4.6.

The title is ' . . . its time to let go (365/365)', and there is a long description explaining that her mother is holding the balloons and that because of the wind the photo was difficult to take. The tags are shown in Figure 4.7 and again there is a very strong narrative.

Interestingly, in the nineteen tags there are very few single words, but rather many phrases and whole sentences. These are comments, explanations and asides, all contributing to telling a story in a humorous way. In addition there are also exclamations such as 'eeeeeeeek!', which are also used by other photographers. Here she is not using tags as folksonomic hyperlinks to aid searching for similar photos; nor is she contributing to creating an overview of a vernacular structure of knowledge. Many tags are being used individually to express a contingent meaning and not to link outwards.

Looking at her 150 most common tags, shown in Figure 4.8, there are several elements of Flickr's overall most common tags, discussed earlier, including places and colours, and the word 'me'.

However, the list of the most common 150 words does not reflect the diversity of tags shown in Figure 4.7, the last 365 photo. The problem is that

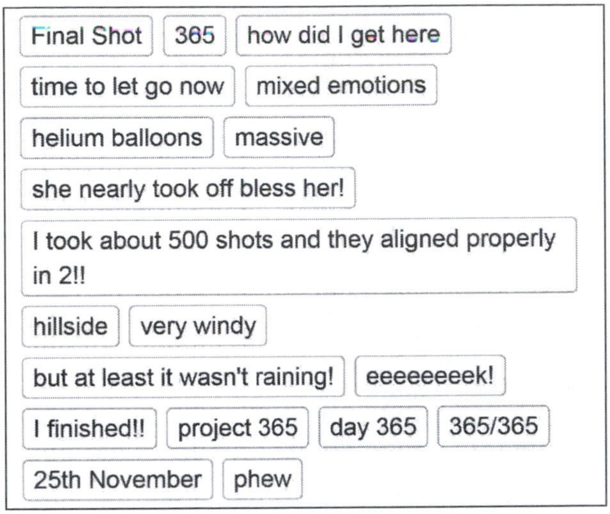

Figure 4.7 Last day tags

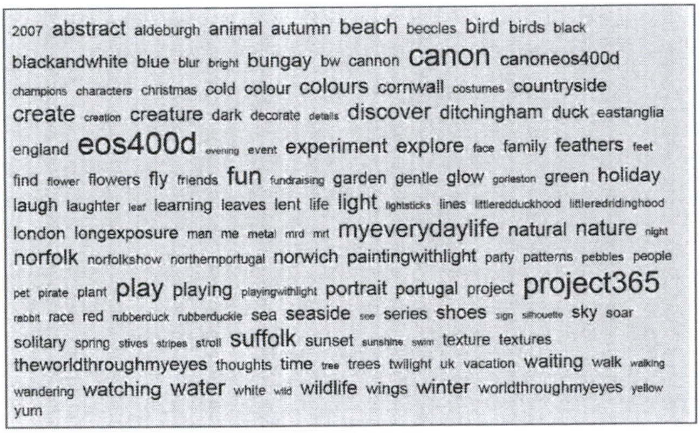

Figure 4.8 J's most common tags

the image of the 150 most common words is a particular visualisation of what is going on, and the less common phrases and sentences get left out. Looking at all of her tags, or just the first ones when displayed alphabetically, as in Figure 4.9, it is clear that overall her tags are not represented by the tag cloud of her 150 most common tags.

Firstly, there are several phrases, such as 'playingwithlight' and 'worldthroughmyeyes'. Some of these tags are particular to her, but several of the unconventional ones, such as 'adaywithoutrain', are also used

aaaaarrrgh abackupshotperhaps abandon
abighugtoallofyouwhoarealsofeelingitrightnow ability abitclichedbutmeh
abletodoansptoday aboutkneeheight above abreakfromthenorm abroad
absorbingitall absorbingreality abstrace abstract abstracted
abstractphotography abstracts abstractsp academia academic accessorize
acrobatic acrossthewater actually adaywithoutrain adeadbugortwo
adifferentlandmarkineachdirection adifferentperspective admin admitone adorn
adulloneatthat adventure ae afewminstorelaxatlast afewminutestowander
afewmoments afinecity africa africaalive
afriendgavemetheseflowersincomiserationofmytrashedkitchen afternoon afters
afunnyhappycolourforasaddepressedsite again againitwasallihadtimefortoday
aged ageing ageingprocess agile aging agingprocess agreatplacetowander
ahappyplace ahappywelcome ahhhhh ahhhijustnoticedthesetagsweretoonormal

Figure 4.9 All J's tags

by others. Maybe they are potential new lexical items, which others also invent or borrow. Certainly in many countries of the world the word 'adaywithoutrain' would prove useful. The problem with relying on her 150 most common tags is that it provides an overly conventional reading of her tags. The same difficulty can be seen with the representation of the overall most common tags on Flickr shown earlier in Figure 4.2. These visualisations give a very different picture of what is going on and we can see the importance of visualisations and how they shape the interpretation of data, drawing attention to some aspects but obscuring others.

Having provided some detailed illustrative examples it is worth looking across a set of Flickr users to see how widespread these broader tagging practices are. Are these examples unusual cases or are they to any extent representative of more general practices? I have examined this by returning to the group of Flickr users who were part of the original multilingualism study mentioned above. I have re-analysed the tags of twenty-two of the Spanish–English and Chinese–English Flickr users who participated in the study, looking mainly at their English language tags. It is worth pointing out that as well as being multilingual these people were all originally selected as being active users of Flickr, so it is not surprising that they all used tags. One person had only fifteen different tags, while most had many more, often several hundred. They all had tags which would be regarded as malformed by the critics of everyday tagging.

The most common form of deviant tagging, which they all had examples of was of multiword tags such as 'uglybird' and 'gloomysunday'. Both of these are plausible concepts which other users might find useful. Eighteen of the twenty-two users also had ones that could be regarded as more idiosyncratic. Often they were short phrases such as 'notmycat', 'farewellbritishcouncil' and 'doublehappiness'. Several even had longer phrases or sentences as in 'dontforgetthefrenchconnection', 'heshouldreceivethe-nobelprizeforliterature' and 'yesilikethatsongsomuch'. Half of the Flickr users had phrases which linked them to a particular Flickr group, indicating that they were participating in a group, as in the tag '365days'. Often these were groups which used the tags as awards, as in 'anawesomeshot' and 'Isawyoufirst'. Nearly a half of the users studied used tags with initials, mixtures of numbers and words, or they played with spelling or punctuation, as in 'pov', '5elements', and 'aaaa'. At least five people had a few multilingual tags like 'mujerwoman' and some tags were intertextual references to songs or other external material.

Looking at the tags in the context of the photos they related to, the function of the tag usually became clear, so that 'dontforgetthefrenchconnection' was an aside about the source of electric power in Spain with reference to a photo of electricity pylons. And 'farewellbritishcouncil' meant that someone was leaving a job. It is hard to provide figures about how many of the sets of tags had some internal ordering, as this is to some extent subjective. Nevertheless, many did and several had a strong sense of narrative and of a grammatical structure, as in:

'Spring — Lisbon — City — street — look — eye — woman — face — hair — outdoor — Feltlife — WowieKazoie — ILoveIt'

Although only a small sample of users has been investigated, this overview of the tagging carried out by a set of Flickr users suggests that the conclusions from the detailed examples, above, are in fact indicative of broader practices.

To return to what has been happening on Flickr and to what the designers of the site have been doing about tagging, there is more to be said about changes over time. Originally the tags appeared in a vertical list along with other 'metadata' on the left hand side of the image. Then as part of other changes it was moved to the right hand side. This may have affected the order in which users would tend to read the page, and the importance users would give to the tags (according to Kress and van Leeuwen 1996). Other changes over time affected what is mentioned in the tags. Now Flickr provides prompts of existing tags when a user starts typing. Also, before the availability of geotagging photos and the possibility of adding the photo to a map, users would sometimes add this location information manually in the tags. And, before this information was given automatically as machine tags, users would add camera details (e.g. Canon600D, 50mm) to signal their serious interest in photography.

A bigger change was when, in another redesign, the tags were put in a conventional left to right format as in the examples shown here. For the user a vertical list provides different affordances from a left to right layout. Alongside these changes, access to the tags became less straightforward as the tagging link was moved from being one of the buttons running along the top of the page to being buried in a list which had to be hovered over. In the most recent changes in May 2013, mentioned above, the tags are below the picture and on a normal computer screen the user has to scroll down the page to see them and cannot see both image and tags at the same time. And to add to this complexity, layout can be different on PCs, Macs, tablets and smartphones.

But does this 'downgrading' of tags matter? If the tags are merely meta-data then maybe this is not important. However, as shown in the examples above, for some users tags are an integral part of the photo page and essential to the user's meaning making. There is common folklore that users always complain about changes in platforms, but maybe in many cases there are tangible reasons for complaint. Users may be using sites in ways that the designers do not know about and are not interested in. Users have a stake in the site and see themselves as contributing to online curation. (See Snyder this volume; this topic is pursued further in Barton 2014.)

At the same time, users themselves are initiating changes and are finding new ways of expressing themselves. Hashtagging, for instance, has spread from Twitter to Facebook, Instagram and other sites. Initially the practices have been spread by users and then the designers have adopted and regularised the practices as an integral part of the platform. In relation to Flickr, students and other people around the world have taken to putting photos of their junk food meals onto the Flickr site, describing them in the titles in such terms as '#food #foodporn #yum #instafood #TagsForLikes #yummy #amazing #instagood . . . .' (as in this example http://www.flickr.com/photos/renattot/9518649062/). This idea of multiple hashtags would be frowned upon in Twitter etiquette but it seems to have a different function in Flickr.

In this way tags have moved out of a specific writing space and, by using the hashtag, words and phrases can be identified anywhere as tags. Maybe the time for a distinct tagging writing space is over?

Conclusions

This chapter has taken several routes into investigating people's tagging practices on Flickr. There has been an explicit methodology of going back and forth in a repeated cycle between detailed examples and general patterns. At the same time the analysis has zeroed in on people's individual Flickr pages to analyse individual tags, and then it has stepped back to analyse their overall tag lists. It has also drawn on interviews with some users to report on their stated purposes for specific tagging practices and it has briefly looked at changes over time in the design of Flickr pages which affect the possibilities for tagging.

There are many things going on in tagging spaces and it is not just about taxonomies, nor just about folksonomies. A complex picture of tagging practices emerges. First, tags are not isolated terms, but they relate to each other. They relate to each other internally within the tagging space and externally in relation to the whole photo page. Internally, there is a structure to a set of tags for an image and order and layout can be important. Taken together the set of tags can contribute to meaning making. There can be a strong narrative in the tags, reflecting almost a 'grammar' of tagging.

Looking beyond the tags to the rest of the page, tagging is a writing space situated within an assemblage of other writing spaces, images and layout. Whether they are creating the page or looking at the page, people are making meaning in relation to the whole page, including the tags. Tags are not just separate 'metadata' but they can be a central part of the meaning making, contributing to the overall coherence of the page. Tags are situated and often they do not make any sense outside of their context of use.

There are many individual differences between people in tag usage. Some people never use tags; others make tagging a central part of their pages. Multilingual Flickr users could be seen to use the resources of their languages strategically to make meaning when choosing what languages and scripts to put tags in. These many uses of tagging reflect how there are so many different possible relations between language and image.

People use tags for many expressive purposes. They can be used for existing information, for new information and to express affective stance towards images, including evaluations and feelings. They can be for making 'asides'. Tags can be individual words, phrases and even whole sentences. In what is in many ways a very serious site, there is at the same time a great sense of play on Flickr. In their tagging, people are inventing new concepts and exhibiting linguistic creativity. In a meme-like way these can get picked up by other users. There is great potential for new lexical items. This chapter has also examined some of the common visualisations of tags and has identified strengths and limitations of these visualisations. Finally, in the constant shape shifting of the internet, sites are constantly being redesigned, people are developing their practices and there may be significant changes in how and why people tag images.

References

Ames, M. and Naaman, M. (2007) 'Why we tag: motivations for annotation in mobile and online media', paper presented at CHI 2007 Conference in San Jose, California on 28 April – 3 May 2007.

Barton, D. (2012) 'Participation, deliberate learning and discourses of learning online', *Language & Education*, 26(2): 139–150.

Barton, D. (2014) 'How photographers use language and image to curate the internet', paper presented at Sociolinguistics Symposium in Finland, June 2014.

Barton, D. and Lee, C. (2013) *Language Online: investigating digital texts and practices*, London: Routledge.

Guy, M. and Tonkin, E. (2006) 'Folksonomics: tidying up tags?' *D-Lib Magazine*. Online. Available HTTP: <http://www.dlib.org/dlib/january06/guy/01guy. html> (accessed 17 March 2014).

Heckner, M., Muhlbacher, S. and Wolff, C. (2007) 'Tagging tagging: analysing user keywords in scientific bibliography management systems', paper presented at NKOS Workshop in Budapest, 21 September 2007.

Jones, R. H. and Hafner, C. A. (2012) *Understanding Digital Literacies*, London: Routledge.

Kress, G. and van Leeuwen, T. (1996) *Reading Images: the grammar of visual design*, London: Routledge.

Lee, C. and Barton, D. (2011) 'Constructing glocal identities through multilingual writing practices on Flickr.com', *International Multilingualism Research Journal*, 5(1): 39–59.

Marlow, C., Naaman, M., boyd, d. and Davis, M. (2006) 'HT06, tagging paper, taxonomy, Flickr, academic article, to read', paper presented at HT'06: Seventeenth ACM Conference on Hypertext and Hypermedia in Odense Denmark, 22–25 August 2006.

Norris, S. and Jones, R. H. (eds) (2005) *Discourse in Action: introducing mediated discourse analysis*, London: Routledge.

Reisigl, M. and Wodak, R. (2009) 'The discourse-historical approach in CDA', in R. Wodak and M. Meyer (eds) *Methods of Critical Discourse Analysis*, 87–121, London: Sage.

Tusting, K. (2013) 'Literacy studies as linguistic ethnography', *Working Papers in Urban Language & Literacies*, 105: 15.

Vander Wal, T. (2005) 'Folksonomy coinage and definition'. Online. Available HTTP: <http://vanderwal.net/folksonomy.html> (accessed 8 February 2014).

Winget, M. (2006) 'User-defined classification on the online photo sharing site Flickr . . . or, how I learned to stop worrying and love the million typing monkeys', proceedings of the 17th ASIS&T SIG/CR Classification Research Workshop, University of Texas at Austin.

Chapter 5

Intertextuality and interdiscursivity in online consumer reviews

Camilla Vásquez

Every spoken utterance, written text, or instance of computer-mediated communication (CMC) always bears traces of texts that came before it. Intertextuality refers to this historic relationship that exists among texts. In the process of constructing any text, speakers, writers, and users of digital media draw not only upon a whole range of intertextual links, but also on 'their intertextual knowledge of wider conventional genres as a whole' (Bax 2011: 29). Extending beyond simple reference to previous texts, intertextuality plays a large role in the meaning-making process. Intertextual awareness, therefore, is key as we construct new texts, and as we interpret given texts. Meaning does not reside in a single text, but rather each text derives its meaning as a result of its embedding in multiple layers of pre-existing texts, as well as in social and textual practices. Consequently, intertextuality is perhaps best conceptualised both as a text-creating practice as well as a discourse property of texts.

This notion of intertextuality – developed by theorists such as Bakhtin, Kristeva and Barthes, and originally applied to literary texts – encompasses a wide array of diverse textual practices: ranging from allusions made to other texts, to repetition, citation, quotation and paraphrase. Interdiscursivity, a closely related concept to intertextuality, refers to the appropriation of discourse conventions, resources and practices from one genre to another (Bhatia 2010). Thus, intertextuality can be conceptualised as drawing on the words of, or making reference to, some other text(s), whereas interdiscursivity refers to 'genre-mixing' or the 'hybridisation of one genre or text-type with another' (Bloor and Bloor 2007; as cited in Bax 2011: 28). Bhatia usefully characterises intertextuality as a 'text internal' phenomenon, and interdiscursivity as a 'text external' phenomenon (Bhatia 2010: 34). He also points out that while intertextuality tends to be fairly standardised and conventionalised, interdiscursive practices tend to be more complex and innovative, and result in generic hybridity.

The study of intertextuality has been traditionally associated with the analysis of literary texts; however, recent work on digital discourse and digital practices has shown that intertextuality can be found in virtually all types of online discourse. Focusing on genres ranging from email to wikis to Facebook status updates, scholars have documented both novel and well-established forms of intertextuality in digital texts. For example, Myers (2010) found that blogs and wikis are characterised by their links to other websites. Similarly, Lam (2013) identified hyperlinks as a key feature of online group buying offers. Besides hyperlinking, message intercalation, 'which involves editing a previous message in order to leave only that which is relevant to the response' (Benwell and Stokoe 2006: 260), is another intertextual practice that can be found in online discussion boards, instant messaging, as well as blog posts and comments. The 'retweet' (Herring 2013), in which one Twitter user forwards a message from another user, is perhaps the most recent iteration of this type of intertextual practice. Other forms of intertextual linking have been documented: for instance, when the same social network user posts as his/her Facebook status update a concise summary, or paraphrase, of a longer blog post that the same user wrote and posted earlier (Lee 2011; West 2013). Repetition is a common form of intertextuality found in all modes of communication, and one that is obviously not unique to digital discourse. However, in text messages (as Tagg 2012 explains) repetition serves the essential function of providing coherence between related acts of asynchronous communication. The 'second story'– that is when the telling of a narrative stimulates the telling of a second narrative that is topically related to the first – represents another form of intertextuality. Second stories were originally identified in spoken narratives, but have also been shown to occur in online genres, such as discussion forums (Page 2012) and email messages (Georgakopoulou 2007). While interdiscursivity has been less studied than intertextuality, recent research (Lam 2013) indicates that digital modes of interaction provide contexts where genre-mixing is quite common.

A focus on intertextuality and interdiscursivity in online discourse seems especially relevant because both phenomena highlight 'notions of relationality, interconnectedness, and interdependence' (Allen 2011: 5) that are central not only to digital communication, but also to modern cultural life. From a methodological perspective, examining intertextuality in online discourse enables discourse analysts to consider a much wider range of intertextual practices than were possible in analogue forms of communication. Internet discourse is often characterised as hybrid (Egbert and Biber 2013), and interdiscursive practices clearly contribute to that hybridity. In this chapter, I explore diverse forms of intertextuality and interdiscursivity found in one specific online genre: user-generated online consumer reviews. Online reviews can be described as an asynchronous, one-to-many, form of CMC, where users typically have no offline connections with one another. While the primary purpose of online reviews is for consumers to evaluate a product or service, reviews can be considered hybrid texts, in that they often also include description and narration (Vásquez 2014b).

In one of the earliest linguistic studies of online reviews, Pollach (2006) observed that intertextuality was quite unusual in online reviews. In fact, based on her analysis of a small corpus of reviews of electronics, she concluded that reviews

> remain in isolation. They are generally not linked textually or hypertextually to other relevant information. Also, authors do generally not seek to encourage readers to respond to what they have written.
>
> (8)

Similarly, in an analysis of recipe reviews, Mackiewicz (2008) characterised her review data as relatively non-intertextual, claiming that online reviews are a type of 'reactive' communication, which 'respond to the original discourse [. . .] and refer only to that discourse' (255). However, it is likely that as the number of online reviews has proliferated in recent years, discourse practices associated with reviewing have also changed and evolved. In my own more recent examination of online consumer review texts (Vásquez 2014b), I have found numerous examples of intertextuality. In the sections that follow, I take up this topic by illustrating and exploring diverse intertextual and interdiscursive practices that authors of consumer reviews engage in as they construct their online texts.

Data analysis

The data discussed below come from a small, specialised corpus of 1,000 reviews, which were sampled from five websites associated with reviews of various types of products: hotels (TripAdvisor), common consumer goods (Amazon), restaurants (Yelp), films (Netflix), and recipes (Epicurious). Because past discourse analytic research on online consumer reviews has tended to focus on reviews from only one or two types of sites (Mackiewicz 2008, 2010a, 2010b; Pollach 2006; Skalicky 2013; Tian 2013; Vásquez 2011, 2013, 2014a), the present study aims to widen the scope by examining reviews from a broader range of websites. The analysis began with an inductive process of identifying and coding of various types of intertextuality and interdiscursivity (with the assistance of an online coding program, dedoose. com). In the following section, I present overall trends found in the data, as well as a few closer textual interpretations of selected examples. By taking a contextual and functional approach (Bazerman 2004), I not only consider the types of texts and genres that reviewers draw upon as they engage in intertextual and interdiscursive practices, but I also consider how those particular texts and genres are used to position reviewers in making unique statements.

I begin by exploring common patterns of reference made to prior reviews, as well as to other types of texts (both online and offline), which occur in all the websites examined. I then illustrate how reviewers creatively appropriate conventions from other genres (literary, advertising, activist) in the constructions of their own reviews.

References to other reviewers and to other texts

The most common form of reference to other texts happens when authors of reviews refer to the texts written by other reviewers on that site. In the data set of 1,000 reviews, almost 15 per cent of reviews ($N = 148$) included reference to other reviews. These references include a variety of forms, including the obvious *review(s)/ reviewer(s)*, as well as others such as *many of you, some of you, the comments, people, others,* etc. Most often, these intertexual allusions to the comments of prior reviewers take the form of agreement with others' opinions. Referring to conventional interpretations of agreement as a sign of positive politeness (Brown and Levinson 1987), communication researcher Mackiewicz (2010a) has noted that agreement with other reviewers can be interpreted as a sign of solidarity. Agreement with other reviewers is a phenomenon that appears on reviews from all five sites, as illustrated in the following examples.

> 1.1
> Stayed in the [hotel name] and <u>agree with the other reviews</u> in how dirty and dingy this place is. [TripAdvisor]
>
> 1.2
> I <u>agree with the reviews</u> - 1/4 cup of rum is very strong [Epicurious]
>
> 1.3
> Unfortunately, I have to <u>agree with another review</u>. This tea tastes like an extract of pipe tobacco. [Amazon]

This consensus construction lends itself to a spirit of collaboration among participants. Furthermore, by referring to having read the reviews of others, these authors of reviews simultaneously position themselves as readers of reviews, and therefore as members of this particular review community. Reviews are embedded within other, larger, discourse systems – most obviously on the website where they appear. Reviewers make this embedding apparent when they explicitly refer to prior reviews or reviewers.

Of course, instances of disagreement can also be found on all of the sites, as reviewers occasionally disagree with the viewpoints and opinions of other reviewers.

> 2.1
> <u>Unlike some other Yelp reviewers</u>, the fish in our selections was very fresh [Yelp]

2.2
This recipe was great! Very easy to prepare, and I did not find the batter runny at all, <u>contrary to other reviews</u>. Will definitely keep this and make it again! [Epicurious]

2.3
I have to <u>disagree with the recent negative reviews</u> [Netflix]

Comparatively, the verb *agree* occurred twenty times in the data set whereas the verb *disagree* only occurred three times. Overall then, it is clear that more reviewers go 'on record' as agreeing (e.g. *I agree with . . .*) than as disagreeing. Furthermore, the preferred linguistic structure for disagreeing typically takes a less direct form (e.g. *Unlike others, contrary to*). While this difference in levels of directness between agreeing and disagreeing may reflect general politeness conventions in English (where disagreement is typically considered a 'dispreferred' response to an evaluation – e.g. Pomerantz 1984), less direct disagreement constructions are also especially useful in the specific context of online reviews. By using a construction such as *contrary to others* or *unlike other reviewers*, the reviewer implicitly acknowledges the uniqueness of consumer experiences, and the inherent subjectivity involved in their own evaluation. It is a means of expressing concession, and one which grants validity to the assessment of others, while nevertheless maintaining a difference of personal opinion. Even in the final instance in the disagreement examples (2.3), where the reviewer actually does use the word *disagree*, there is a subtle difference between this form and the majority of those expressing simple agreement. Whereas the general tendency for expressing agreement is simply *I agree*, the reviewer in example 2.3 inserts the semi-modal *have to* before the main verb (*I have to disagree.*) The semi-modal *have to* (whose meaning is similar to other modals and semi-modals of obligation and necessity, such as *must, ought to, need to*) connotes a sense of being compelled to take an action, perhaps one which is unavoidable. Interestingly, the semi-modal *have to* does also appear in one of the agreement examples, 1.3: *Unfortunately, I have to agree with another review. This tea tastes like an extract of pipe tobacco.* However, it is important to note that in this case, the reviewer is agreeing with a negative review, rather than with a positive review – which suggests that reviewers may be more reluctant to write a negative review (a view which is supported by Hu et al. 2009 and Kuehn 2011). Moreover, because the negative review with which he is agreeing appears in grammatically singular form (i.e. *another review*), it does not represent the majority or consensus opinion about this product. Therefore, a general sense of reluctance about expressing this negative assessment is accomplished here with the semi-modal *have to*, as well as with the adverb *unfortunately* which precedes it.

To sum up, when reference is made to other reviewers/reviews to express agreement, the agreement tends to be formulated in more direct, or explicit, terms. And disagreement, when it occurs, tends to be stated in more indirect, or implicit, terms. Situating one's own opinion within the context of existing opinions is a common strategy in online reviews, perhaps because reviewers are aware that 'how opinions are received depends on the relation of the content of a review to what other authors have written' (Otterbacher 2011: 428). Furthermore, as different groups of researchers have noted, comments expressing agreement or disagreement (which interact with overall review valence, and helpfulness ratings) do influence readers of reviews with respect to their attitude toward a product (Sparks et al. 2013; Walther et al. 2012).

Besides making reference to prior reviews and reviewers, reviewers also made intertextual references to other types of texts considered relevant to the product. These explicit references to other texts appeared in just over 10 per cent of reviews (*N*=114). Most common were references to online texts such as Wikipedia entries, YouTube videos, and other related websites. For example, on TripAdvisor reviews there were occasional references made to online booking services, such as hotels.com or kayak.com as well as to hotels' websites. Similarly, a few Yelp reviewers referred to a restaurant's website in their reviews. Interestingly, hyperlinks were not as common in the review data as they are in other forms of online discourse (Lam 2013; Myers 2010), appearing in less than 3 per cent of the reviews. It is possible that the site architecture of some review sites restricts reviewers from posting hyperlinks.

In addition to intertextual references to online sources, a nearly equal proportion of references were made to offline textual sources. These often cited a product's label or manual, referenced a sign found in a particular location, or referred to a popular media source. Very often, when references were made to other (either online or offline) textual sources, they provided readers with clarification, or additional information, about some aspect of the product.

The examples below are excerpted from two different Amazon reviews of tea. Both reviewers use the same intertextual strategy of embedding a direct quotation from another textual source into their review: in 3.1 it is from an online source (a Wikipedia entry), whereas in 3.2 it is from an offline source (the product's packaging).

3.1
I am also trying out hibiscus tea because I have read that there are clinical trials that show hibiscus lowers blood pressure. . . . From Wikipedia: 'A study published in the Journal of Human Hypertension has shown that drinking hibiscus tea can reduce high blood pressure in people with type 2 diabetes . . . ' [Amazon]

3.2
This Organic Green Tea Kombucha from [Brand name] is certainly unique. It tastes like a mixture of passion fruit, plum, ginger, and green tea. . . . [Brand name] writes this on the box about the tea's benefits: 'Green Tea Kombucha is based on an ancient remedy and offers a convenient form of Kombucha designed for daily use. Legend has it that some 2,000 years ago . . . ' [Amazon]

These types of references show intertextual links in action. As reviewers adopt and appropriate other sources in constructing their own texts, they not only embed the words of those sources through the use of quotations, but they also simultaneously draw upon the larger discourse systems in which those quoted texts operate. For example, both reviewers extol the health benefits of drinking certain types of tea. Both reviewers also use direct quotations to give their own texts a greater sense of authority. Yet there are also important differences between the two. Example 3.1, in which the reviewer quotes from the online source, Wikipedia, draws on the discourses of empirical investigation in western medicine, with its references to research findings published in a medical journal (i.e. a multi-layered form of intertextuality). In contrast, example 3.2, with its reference to the product label's description of the tea as an 'ancient remedy', draws upon discourses of traditional, holistic approaches to health and medicine. While these may not represent deliberate choices on the part of reviewers, the insertion of these particular texts into their reviews nevertheless implicates the reproduction of the larger discourse systems in which those quoted texts circulate. These examples highlight how intertextuality is central to the creation of a text's meaning as well as its possible interpretations.

Another subcategory of intertextual references consists of allusions to, or explicit mentions of, popular culture texts. The following example is similar to the previous examples of reviews of tea. In it, the author of a restaurant review makes an intertextual reference by drawing on discourses from popular television food and cooking programmes to frame her positive evaluation of a particular restaurant's ingredient-driven approach to food preparation.

4.1
When the food shows on Bravo or Food Network talk about Italian food, they always say something in the lines of "let the ingredients speak for themselves." Good Japanese food does exactly the same, but for some reason, it's described as minimal with some exposition about mastering technique. [Yelp]

Making reference to popular culture texts indexes a reviewer's consumption of, and taste in, specific forms of mass media. The inclusion of references to specific examples of television shows, films, or other forms of mass media within online reviews – especially when they are not only recognised but also shared by readers – can contribute to a sense of affinity or co-membership among individuals who interact with one another exclusively in online contexts. In addition, popular culture references in this genre may also serve a metaphorical function: comparing a unique, subjective experience to a larger cultural product, that is shared by many. For instance, in an earlier study, I found that a number TripAdvisor reviewers writing negative reviews often compared their specific hotel experience to something that might have happened in the popular British sitcom, *Fawlty Towers*. Because the setting of *Fawlty Towers* is a hotel where things continually go wrong, this reference itself automatically indexes a negative hotel experience, as can be seen in the following example from the opening line of a hotel review.

4.2
It's difficult to describe the sheer awfulness of this faulty towers-like [sic] establishment. [TripAdvisor]

Of course, the success of such a strategy in terms of interpretation and meaning making on the part of the reader depends on the extent to which readers are familiar with the particular form(s) of popular culture being invoked.

In addition to using popular culture references to compare individual, personal, and subjective experiences with recognisable images, settings, and personae from the mass media, reviewers can also use popular culture references to achieve other goals. For example, in the following excerpt, one Netflix reviewer makes a reference to a popular culture figure in order to directly address another reviewer who posted an earlier review of the same film on the same site. (It should be noted that Netflix reviews are all posted anonymously, because the site does not provide reviewers with the option of creating a profile or a user ID.)

4.3
If you watch this movie, be sure to watch it. Don't read, knit, or try to write a review to another movie, while you watch this movie (Gene Shalit, I'm looking at you), because this movie will require you use all of your cognitive thinking power to follow. [Netflix]

Here, the reference to North American television film critic, Gene Shalit, appears to be a tongue-in-cheek response to another Netflix reviewer who, in an earlier review, indicated that he/she had posted an evaluation of it on Facebook while simultaneously watching the film. The intertextual meaning in this text is therefore doubly embedded. In order to derive the meaning of this reference (which draws on the larger genre of film reviews in the mass media), readers will first need to be familiar with North American popular culture to know who Gene Shalit is. Second, the interpretation of who exactly the reviewer is addressing as 'Gene Shalit' is contingent on the reader's familiarity with the review history for this particular film on this particular website. In effect, there are two layers of intertextuality in this example: 1) a reference to a popular culture figure being used to make 2) a reference to a previous reviewer's comments. I will have more to say about the challenges associated with the identification of these types of intertextual references in the chapter's conclusion.

Interdiscursivity: intertextual relationships with other genres

Building on the previous discussion, I now turn to instances of interdiscursivity, in which reviewers appropriate recognisable discourse conventions associated with other genres in the construction of their reviews. I focus, in particular, on examples of interdiscursivity which involve the blending of artistic, advertising, or activist genres.

One example of creative self-expression can be seen below. This reviewer writes his film reviews in the form of a haiku, and numbers them.

> 5.1
> Haiku #713, BIUTIFUL: The nose of Bardem Its flatness brings him closer To the screen, and death [Netflix]

Example 5.1 provides a clear example of genre-mixing, as the author uses the haiku, a poetic form, as the structure for his film review. The Netflix haiku reviewer is noteworthy not only for taking a ludic approach to writing the review, but for transforming the prosaic genre of the consumer review into a literary genre. Although such examples are certainly not the norm in online reviews, there is evidence of haiku reviews of films, music, and books appearing on other internet sites as well. While the majority of consumer reviews do not appear in this poetic form, the author of Example 5.1 is clearly participating in a much larger internet phenomenon of haiku reviewing.

Not surprisingly, the predominant genres appropriated by online reviewers come from the fields of advertising, sales, and marketing. The following examples, all from recipe reviews, have a familiar, advertising-slogan-like quality. In other words, they come across to us as 'canned' messages, rather than providing any specific, or descriptive, information about the recipe being reviewed. Instead, these texts sound similar to something we might have heard on a commercial, or perhaps read in a print advertisement.

6.1

Love at first bite. [Epicurious]

6.2

It's the recipe that keeps on giving. [Epicurious]

6.3

. . . few things can top this! [Epicurious]

6.4

. . . do yourself a favour and make it tonight! [Epicurious]

6.5

You cannot go wrong – this is definitely a winner! [Epicurious]

Examples such as these reveal how the evaluative language that we use – as private individuals, consumers and 'prosumers' – is inevitably shaped by the discourses of media advertising that surround us. As endorsers of a product or service, individuals who write reviews appropriate elements of these advertising discourses and, in doing so, they 'sell' their readers on the benefits of products which they support and believe in. Some reviewers may adopt the conventions of those genres deliberately and self-consciously; however, others probably do so unwittingly.

The appropriation of advertising discourse also appears frequently in Yelp restaurant reviews. Very likely, Yelp reviewers' drawing on the genre of popular advertising (such as television commercials) is related to the site's emphasis on reviews that are 'funny' and 'cool'.

7.1

I'm sorry babe, but I'm leaving you for the man bringing me endless loaves of hot Cuban bread. [Yelp]

In example 7.1, the reviewer begins her text as a form of pseudo-address to her significant other, playfully informing him that she plans to abandon him for her waiter. It is not surprising that some reviews sound like commercial product advertisements, since that is essentially what they are – albeit created by private individuals rather than by marketing professionals. Consequently, it is not uncommon to observe reviewers drawing upon some of the discourse conventions of these closely related, pre-existing, commercial genres. The resulting texts can be thought of as hybrid discourses, in which reviewers appropriate discourses of advertising, as they blend cheery, jingle-like slogans such as 'Try it, you'll love it!' with narrative accounts of their own personal experiences.

I conclude this section with one of the most unusual examples of inter-discursivity. The author of this review of a high speed blender self-identifies as the wife of a man suffering from health problems caused by a diet soda addiction. Although the review begins as a personal narrative, the author also takes an 'activitist' stance, by inserting her message of ****ASPARTAME KILLS**** in two separate points in her review. This simple two-word message is reminiscent of what might be written on a protest sign, and it refers to an issue that actually has no direct relationship to the product being reviewed. The message is directly incorporated into the review text itself, and it is focalised using semiotic means (asterisks and capitalisation), rather than metalinguistically. The author of this review also blends genres in another way: by incorporating the texts of two complete recipes into her review of her high speed blender, as seen below.

8.1
I think the best thing about the 5200 is this: you CANNOT TASTE fresh spinach in ANYTHING. I got mine for Christmas. My husband will not TOUCH anything dark green. As a result of this and just as importantly is his serious illness from a DIET SODA HABIT (five to six cans per day) I had to figure out a way to sneak spinach into his ice cream smoothies. And aloe vera juice, unflavoured. And yogurt; he'd never touch them either. Here is a delicious recipe guaranteed to fool ANY picky eater:
1/2 to 1 cup fresh spinach, out of the bag, which I freeze;
1/2 cup unflavoured yogurt
1/4 fresh and/or frozen strawberries, partly thawed;
1/4 cup aloe vera juice, UNFLAVORED
strawberry ice cream, sugar free.
Put in [*brand name*], blend 5 seconds on one, then turn to ten for 5 seconds. It is delish.
ASPARTAME KILLS
For constipation—
1cup mint choc chip ice cream
1 little cup Milk of Magnesia
1/2 cup fresh spinach
1/4 CUP unflavoured aloe vera juice
Blend as above.
ASPARTAME KILLS [Amazon]

This is an especially interesting example because this particular reviewer makes the choice to insert a political agenda into her review, demonstrating what is possible (though not common) to accomplish in the space of the review text. Online review sites tend to position reviewers, first and foremost, as consumers; however, sites such as these could also, in theory, serve as spaces for alternative forms of social participation, such as activism. Of course in reality, they are rarely used for such purposes (Kuehn 2011). Nevertheless, this example shows how the intended function of the review space (to describe, evaluate, discuss the product being reviewed – in this case, a blender) is of little or no consequence to this particular reviewer, who appears to be more concerned with taking a stand against an artificial sweetener – and with providing readers with some recipes and 'nutritional' tips. In doing so, she constructs a highly interdiscursive review text, in which she appropriates features of a number of genres including the personal narrative, the recipe, and an activist mode of discourse.

Conclusions

Reviewers draw upon a range of existing texts, discourses, and generic conventions in constructing their review texts. In this chapter, I have shown what is commonly found in online reviews, by illustrating how some reviewers use intertextual references to others' reviews as a way to ground their own opinions, either to align with – or to oppose – the evaluations of other reviewers. I have also pointed out that other types of (online and offline) textual sources can be referenced or quoted in online reviews to lend authority to a reviewer's claims, or to further inform or educate readers. Among these, I have shown that references to popular culture and mass media texts can be a way for reviewers to perform their tastes and preferences and to possibly connect with readers who happen to share those tastes in culture and media. All of these forms of intertextuality appear frequently in online reviews. However, beyond showing what is common, I have also highlighted what is possible. What I mean by this is that although not all reviewers will insert a political agenda into their review, nor will they make use of an existing form of artistic expression to provide the structure for their reviews, a handful of reviewers *do* opt for these less-conventional modes of self-expression. Indeed, some reviewers demonstrate considerable creativity in the types of texts and discourses that they draw upon in the construction of their own texts.

Online reviews are a genre with no precise analogue precedent. Although professionally written consumer product reviews have been available in mass media venues for decades, this more recent ability for any consumer to publicly share his/her experiences and reactions to a product or service – and to reach a wide, global, interested audience in the process – represents a new vernacular literacy practice. As more and more users around the world create and share these types of online texts, the potential for numerous as well as more varied forms of intertextuality and interdiscursivity increases. At the same time, the exact audience of these review texts remains vast, indeterminate, and potentially global. This means that some intertextual references – particular those related to popular culture – can be risky, in the sense that they may not 'carry over' to readers from a cultural context which is different from that of the author and, as a result, some readers may be unable to interpret the meanings associated with those references.

On the other hand, despite the risk assumed by those reviewers who rely on intertextual references to create specific associations (i.e. some readers may not recognise and understand those references, and thus miss out on their intended meaning), intertextual references realise specific functions in these environments. For example, such references enable participants who do not know one another in an offline sense to identify with a review author on the basis of shared consumption and tastes in popular media. Intertextual references may also help to forge a sense of virtual co-membership among reviewers and reviewers who participate in shared discourse systems, as we saw with examples 3.1 and 3.2. In this sense, intertextual references both contribute to the discursive construction of reviewer identities and they also serve to create a connection between author and audience.

Just as these types of references sometimes pose challenges for readers, they may also pose similar challenges for discourse analysts, who may only be able to identify some intertextual references, and overlook others with which they are unfamiliar. Besides understanding the architecture and mechanics of the site on which a particular review is posted, and being well acquainted with the product being reviewed, it can also be beneficial for analysts to read the entire thread of reviews for that product to be able to follow references to other reviews. This suggests that for discourse analysts interested in studying intertextuality in online reviews, a 'sampling by theme' approach (Androutsopoulos 2013) – where analysts collect all of the topically related messages from a particular thread or forum – may be more productive than other approaches to data sampling. Moreover, for analysts studying intertextuality in other types of new media, a sustained period of participant observation of the site/community may also be useful – as well as perhaps interviews with contributors and readers. These secondary data sources may reveal additional insider understandings of intertextual references, practices and meanings (Barton and Lee 2013). However, as was illustrated by a few of the examples in this chapter, some review sites require reviewers to post anonymously, which restricts the type of additional insider information that can be accessed.

Consumer reviewing is a discursive practice, whose products are digital texts. In those texts, reviewers are able not only to communicate directly with other reviewers (as well as other imagined readers) – but they also construct their texts by making intertextual references to what others before them have written. In some cases, they make allusions to the reviews of others. In other cases, they use different textual sources, different communicative genres, or even larger discourse systems, as foundations for building their own review texts.

As resources for creating meaning, intertextuality and interdiscursivity rely on shared norms, references, and understandings. It has been argued that one of the motivations for individuals to post consumer reviews is because they serve as 'a way for people to construct social relations, assimilation, identity, or a sense of group coherence in response to the postmodern condition of alienation, isolation, and displacement' (Kuehn 2011: 50). Such an interpretation helps to explain how intertextuality and interdiscursivity play an important role in the construction of a real – or imagined – community of readers on online review websites.

References

Allen, G. (2011) *Intertextuality*, 2nd edn, London: Routledge.

Androutsopoulos, J. (2013) 'Online data collection', in C. Mallinson, B. Childs and G. V. Herk (eds) *Data Collection in Sociolinguistics: methods and applications*, 237–249, London: Continuum.

Barton, D. and Lee, C. (2013) *Language Online: investigating digital texts and practices*, London: Routledge.

Bax, S. (2011) *Discourse and Genre: analyzing language in context*, London: Palgrave Macmillan.

Bazerman, C. (2004) 'Intertextuality: how texts rely on other texts', in C. Bazerman and P. Prior (eds) *What Writing Does and How It Does It: an introduction to analyzing texts and textual practices,* 83–96, London: Routledge.

Benwell, B. and Stokoe, E. (2006) *Discourse and Identity*, Edinburgh: Edinburgh University Press.

Bhatia, V. (2010) 'Interdiscursivity in professional communication', *Discourse & Communication,* 4: 32–50.

Bloor, T. and Bloor, M. (2007) *The Practice of Critical Discourse Analysis: an introduction,* London: Hodder Arnold.

Brown, P. and Levinson, S. (1987) *Politeness: some universals in language*, Cambridge: Cambridge University Press.

Egbert, J. and Biber, D. (2013) 'Developing a user-based method of web register classification', in S. Evert, E. Stemle and P. Rayson (eds), 16–23, proceedings of the 8th Web as Corpus Workshop (WAC-8) @Corpus Linguistics 2013.

Georgakopoulou, A. (2007) *Small Stories, Interaction, and Identities*, Amsterdam: Benjamins.

Herring, S. (2013) 'Discourse in Web 2.0: familiar, reconfigured, emergent', in D. Tannen and A. M. Trester (eds) *Discourse 2.0: language and new media*, 1–26, Washington, DC: Georgetown University Press.

Hu, N., Zhang, J. and Pavlou, P. (2009) 'Overcoming the J-shaped distribution of product reviews', *Communications of the ACM – A View of Parallel Computing,* 52(10): 144–147.

Kuehn, K. (2011) 'Prosumer-citizenship and the local: a critical case study of consumer', Reviewing on Yelp, unpublished dissertation, Pennsylvania State University.

Lam. P. W. Y. (2013) 'Interdiscursivity, hypertextuality, multimodality: a corpus-based multimodal move analysis of Internet group buying deals', *Journal of Pragmatics*, 51: 13-39.

Lee, C. (2011) 'Microblogging and status updates on Facebook: texts and practices', in C. Thurlow and K. Mroczek (eds) *Digital Discourse: language in the new media*, 110–130, Oxford: Oxford University Press.

Mackiewicz, J. (2008) 'Reviewer motivations, bias, and credibility in online reviews', in S. Kelsey and K. St. Amant (eds) *Handbook of Research on Computer-Mediated Communication*, 252–266, Hershey, PA: The Idea Group Publishers.

Mackiewicz, J. (2010a) 'Assertions of expertise in online product reviews', *Journal of Business and Technical Communication*, 24(1): 3–28.

Mackiewicz, J. (2010b) 'The co-construction of credibility in online product reviews', *Technical Communication Quarterly*, 19(4): 403–426.

Myers, G. (2010) *The Discourse of Blogs and Wikis*, London: Continuum.

Otterbacher, J. (2011) 'Being heard in review communities: communication tactics and review prominence', *Journal of Computer-Mediated Communication*, 16: 424–444.

Page, R. (2012) *Stories and Social Media*, London: Routledge.

Pollach, I. (2006) 'Electronic word of mouth: a genre analysis of product reviews on consumer opinion web sites', proceedings of the 39th Hawaii International Conference on System Sciences, IEEE Computer Society.

Pomerantz, A. (2006 [1984]) 'Agreeing and disagreeing with assessments: some features of preferred/dispreferred turn shapes', in P. Drew and J. Heritage (eds) *Conversation Analysis*, vol. II, 26–43, Sequence Organization, London: Sage.

Skalicky, S. (2013) 'Was this analysis helpful? A genre analysis of the Amazon.com discourse community and its "most helpful" product reviews', *Discourse, Context & Media*, 2(2): 84–93.

Sparks, B., Perkins, H. and Buckley, R. (2013) 'Online travel reviews as persuasive communication: the effects of content type, source, and certification logos on consumer behavior', *Tourism Management*, 39: 1–9.

Tagg, C. (2012) *Discourse of Text Messaging: analysis of SMS communication*, London: Continuum.

Tian, Y. (2013) 'Engagement in online hotel reviews: a comparative study', *Discourse, Context & Media*, 2(3): 184–191.

Vásquez, C. (2011) 'Complaints online: the case of TripAdvisor', *Journal of Pragmatics*, 43: 1707–1717.

Vásquez, C. (2013) 'Narrativity and involvement in online consumer reviews: the case of TripAdvisor', *Narrative Inquiry*, 22(1): 105–121.

Vásquez, C. (2014a) 'Usually not one to complain but . . . : constructing identities in online reviews', in C. Tagg and P. Seargeant (eds) *The Language of Social Media: community and identity on the internet*, 65–90, London: Palgrave Macmillan.

Vásquez, C. (2014b) *The Discourse of Online Consumer Reviews*, London: Bloomsbury.

Walther, J. B., Liang, Y., Ganster, T., Wohn, Y. and Emington, J. (2012) 'The effect of online reviews and helpfulness ratings on consumer attitudes: application and test of congruity theory to multiple Web 2.0 sources', *Journal of Computer-Mediated Communication*, 18: 97–112.

West, L. (2013) 'Facebook sharing: a sociolinguistic analysis of computer-mediated storytelling', *Discourse, Context and Media*, 2: 1–13.

Chapter 6

YouTube as text

Spoken interaction analysis and digital discourse

Phil Benson

The rise of digital discourse raises questions about the adequacy of what we might call 'traditional' discourse analysis tools to the task of analysing computer-mediated communication (CMC). This chapter explores some of these questions in the context of a study of multimodal interaction on YouTube that draws upon tools for the analysis of spoken interaction. Historically, spoken interaction has been placed at the heart of discourse analysis by two major schools that have treated it as their primary object of interest: Conversation Analysis (CA) (Sacks et al. 1974) and the Birmingham school of discourse analysis (Sinclair and Coulthard 1975). While observing that technology-based interaction was a likely growth area for CA research, Seedhouse (2005) questioned how far CA principles could be applied to written asynchronous online interaction. The same argument could be made of any set of principles designed for the analysis of spoken interaction. Nevertheless, CMC researchers have largely relied on these principles, adapting them, in particular, to analysis of conversation-like interactions conducted through the medium of writing (Herring 2001; Herring et al. 2013).

CMC research initially focused on environments that allow written interaction to emulate spoken interaction, either synchronously (e.g. chat rooms) or asynchronously (e.g. threaded discussion forums). New multimodal text-types, such as blogs (Herring et al. 2005) and social media (boyd and Heer 2006), have also been seen as inherently conversational, although they have been positioned at some distance from the norm of face-to-face spoken interaction. Herring et al. (2005: 1) find that the blogosphere is only 'sporadically conversational', while boyd and Heer (2006) raise a number of questions about the differences between online and spoken interaction, among which the absence of clearly identified recipients and contexts for messages are especially important.

While the various forms of multimodal CMC clearly differ from spoken interaction, the degree to which they resemble it is an important issue. Because spoken interaction is often viewed as a fundamental mode of social interaction, any attempt to understand multimodal CMC in similar terms touches on the senses in which CMC texts are also products of social interaction. Through a case study of the multimodal discourse of YouTube, this chapter argues that, in spite of evident differences from spoken conversations, YouTube pages are products of social interactions that can be analysed using tools designed for analysis of the structures of spoken interaction. It asks what steps need to be taken in order to make these tools work in analysis of the multimodal discourse of YouTube, and what their limitations may be.

The context for this discussion is a case study of YouTube pages based on a series of videos, entitled 'Cantonese Word of the Week!', which have attracted a considerable number of views and comments since they were posted in 2011–12. These pages form part of the data set for a project designed to investigate evidence of informal language and intercultural learning in YouTube comments. This chapter focuses on the framework for analysis of YouTube discourse, involving application of the spoken discourse categories of 'exchange', 'turn', 'move' and 'act' (Coulthard 1985; Stenström and Stenström 1994), that was developed during the project. A key feature of this framework is the application of these categories not only to written comments, but to the broader multimodal processes that generate the text of the YouTube page as a whole.

YouTube as text

As the fastest growing web service of recent years, YouTube now ranks third behind Google and Facebook in measurements of web traffic. YouTube has also attracted academic interest in an emerging literature that tends to view it as a technological, media or cultural phenomenon (Burgess and Green 2009; Kavoori 2011; Lovink and Niederer 2008; Snickars and Vonderau 2009; Strangelove 2010). On the face of it, YouTube is a website where people watch videos, and not a 'text'. Nevertheless, YouTube pages are sometimes discussed in terms of text and discourse (Androutsopoulos 2013; Kavoori 2011) and several studies have pointed to the role of language in the management and retrieval of videos. Kessler and Schäfer (2009: 279) point out that, because YouTube cannot machine-read the semantic content of moving image files, information management relies on 'metadata that names, describes or categorises whatever there is to be seen', which comes in the form of 'user-generated input provided as text'.

This comment points to two different ways of viewing YouTube as text, which focus either on the use of writing or on the YouTube page as a whole. In their work on the image sharing site Flickr, Barton and Lee (2012: 285) observe that, '[a]lthough Flickr is a site primarily devoted to images, there is a great deal of user-generated writing on the site, especially writing around an uploaded image'. This user-generated writing includes titles and descriptions of images, tags and geotags, notes added to photos, and comments (see also Barton this volume). There is also a good deal of these kinds of writing on YouTube, and written comments on videos are prominent among them. Another way of viewing media sharing websites such as Flickr and YouTube as texts is to examine how pages are organised around samples of media, with writing and other semiotic modes playing complementary roles. The video is the focal point of a YouTube page. It is the main reason why people visit the page and, possibly, the only part of the page that most users pay close attention to. Yet it is also difficult to understand how YouTube works, both technologically and culturally, without attending to the ways in which various semiotic modes work together to make up the text of the YouTube page.

This second view of YouTube as text takes us into the terrain of multimodal discourse analysis (MMDA) (Baldry and Thibault 2006; Bateman 2008; Jones 2013; Kress 2010). Much of the research on CMC focuses on written interaction independently of its multimodal contexts. Herring et al.'s (2013) handbook on the pragmatics of CMC example, includes discussion of interaction in almost every chapter, but no chapter deals substantially with multimodal interaction. Baldry and Thibault (2006: 18), however, refer to 'the resource integration principle', which treats multimodal texts as '*composite* products of the combined effects of all the resources used to create and interpret them'. Applying this principle to YouTube, Androutsopoulos (2013: 50) comments that '[a]lthough each textual bit on a YouTube page can be viewed as a distinct textual unit, videos and comments co-occur in a patterned way and are interrelated in meaning making'. These comments suggest that, if tools for the analysis of spoken interaction are to be used in analysis of YouTube pages, written text should not be isolated from its multimodal context. Instead, interactional analysis should encompass the multimodality of the page as a whole.

Viewed in this light, three characteristics of YouTube as text stand out:

1   YouTube pages deploy *multiple semiotic modes*, including moving images, spoken word, music and sound, still images, written words, and a variety of clickable objects, icons and links. The number of identifiable communicative elements found on a YouTube page is typically more than 100, and this number increases as written comments are added. Each comment sits within a space that contains eleven different elements in addition to the comment itself, each of which leads to a different action when clicked.

2   YouTube pages are products of *multiple authorship*. A page is created when a user uploads a video and inputs written text to describe it, but much of the text of the page is machine-generated and includes boilerplate text from YouTube and text created by advertisers and other users. Users subsequently add to the text in various ways: by adding written comments, but also by actions that do not involve writing, such as 'liking' and 'disliking' the video or individual comments.

3   YouTube pages are *highly dynamic* in the sense that the text of the page constantly changes in response to user and machine-generated input. Simply by viewing a page, a user alters the number of views that is displayed below the video. The text of the page that surrounds a particular video also varies according to the location of the user, automatically or in response to user-defined settings.

These characteristics make YouTube particularly amenable to MMDA, but two further steps are needed to support the use of tools intended for analysis of spoken interaction in the context of MMDA. The first step involves treating YouTube as a form of social media, while the second involves treating YouTube pages as products of mediated social interaction. Zourou and Lamy (2013: 1) define social media as 'artefacts with a networking dimension, which are designed so as to make that dimension central to their use'. YouTube fits this definition well as a particular kind of social media, in which networking is mediated by uploading media (videos, images, written text) and commenting. This definition encompasses YouTube and other media sharing services, in which social interaction is mediated by the activities of uploading and viewing media.

The second step involves a particular understanding of the sense in which YouTube is 'interactive'. Rafaeli and Ariel (2007) make a useful distinction between two kinds of interactivity in digital media: one concerned with 'responsiveness' to user input, the other with interpersonal interaction. In the first sense, the interactivity (or responsiveness) of YouTube is a matter of how the interface responds to user input; in the second it is a matter of the quality of the social interaction that can be observed on YouTube pages. Adopting a discourse-based view, Rafaeli and Ariel define this second sense of interactivity as 'the extent to which messages in a sequence relate to each other and especially the extent to which later messages recount the relatedness of earlier messages' (73).

This definition of interactivity takes cohesion and coherence as the main indicator of the quality of digitally mediated social interaction. Herring's (2013) comparison of message sequences in a recreational Internet Relay Chat (IRC) chat room and YouTube comments also attends to linkages among messages. Herring found that comments on media sharing sites tend to be 'prompt-focused' and 'respond to an initial prompt, such as a news story, a photo, or a video, more often than to other users' responses' (13). Few comments are linked to a previous comment, which means that the 'stepwise' patterns of topic development observed on IRC chat are largely absent. This comparison is problematic, however, to the extent that it only considers linkages among written messages. Sindoni (2013: 205) goes a step further by positing a 'multimodal relevance maxim' for YouTube comments, which states that '[c]omments need to be consistent with the main communicative focus of multimodal interaction and the most salient semiotic resource: the foregrounded video'; but at the same time, she appears to remove the video from the field of interaction, by describing it as a 'master-text' and comments on it as 'meta-texts', or 'adjuncts' to the video (180). The framework that I will describe develops this view by treating the uploading of a video as an interactional turn, which begins a process of multimodal social interaction in which users 'respond' to the 'initiation' of the video using a variety of semiotic modes.

A framework for analysing YouTube interaction

The framework used in this study is based on the framework for analysing the structure of spoken interaction developed at Birmingham University in the 1970s (Sinclair and Coulthard 1975). Originally based on classroom interaction, this framework was later applied to analysis of everyday English conversation (Stenström and Stenström 1994; Tsui 1994). The framework identifies a hierarchy of nested units – 'transaction', 'exchange', 'move' and 'act' – through which participants organise spoken interaction. Transactions are composed of exchanges, which are typically composed of two or three moves (Initiation, Response, Follow-up). In Stenström and Stenström's (1994) account, on which this study is based, Sinclair and Coulthard's three moves are extended to eight: Summons, Focus, Initiate, Repair, Response, Re-open, Follow-up, Backchannel. In both accounts, an exchange minimally consists of two moves: an Initiation followed by a Response.

Stenström and Stenström (1994: 30) define a move as 'what a speaker does in a turn in order to start, carry on and finish an exchange'. An Initiation (I) begins an exchange and 'predicts' or 'constrains' the following move, which will normally be a Response (R) (Coulthard 1985). Stenström and Stenström insert the CA category of 'turn' (Sacks et al. 1974) between exchange and move. An IR exchange may take place over two turns, but the categories of move and turn are not coterminous. A turn that follows an Initiation often consists of two moves: a Response followed by an Initiation (R+I). Coulthard also gives an example of a single move that contains both a Response and an Initiation (R/I).

1	Teacher: can anyone tell me what this means	I
2	Pupil: does it mean danger men at work	R/I
3	Teacher: Yes . . .	R

Source: Adapted from Coulthard (1985: 135)

In this example, Turn 2 is both a Response to the Initiation in Turn 1 and an Initiation that elicits a Response in Turn 3. Importantly, R+I and R/I turns are a resource for speakers to produce sequences of topically linked exchanges and crucial to the stepwise topic development that Herring (2013) fails to find in YouTube comments. Exchanges typically flow into new exchanges through R+I and R/I moves, but terminate with turns that consist only of a Response move.

Act is the smallest interactional unit, signalling 'what the speaker intends, what s/he wants to communicate'. A move may consist of one, two or several acts. Coulthard (1985) emphasises that interactional acts differ from 'speech acts' (Searle 1969), because they are defined principally by their interactive function. The speech act 'statement', for example, might be classified interactionally as an 'inform' if it occurs in an I move, or as an 'answer' if it occurs in an R move responding to a 'question'. The speech act 'question' might also be classified interactionally as a 'challenge' or 'clarification check' if it occurs in an R move. Because moves are realised by acts, they predict both the move and the range of acts that must follow if the interaction is not to break down. An I move that contains a 'question', for example, predicts an R move containing an 'answer'. In the study discussed later in this chapter YouTube data were coded using a modified version of Stenström and Stenström's (1994) taxonomies of moves and acts, which are among several in the literature that differ considerably in their terminology and in the distinctions they make (cf. Tsui 1994). While the classification of moves and acts remains an inexact science, these taxonomies proved useful as heuristic devices for exploring interactional patterns within the multimodal discourse of YouTube.

In mapping YouTube discourse on to this framework, two assumptions were made. The first was that interactional moves need not be spoken or written. From the perspective of MMDA, a framework that could only be applied to spoken (or conversation-like written) interaction would be narrow, because interaction is invariably multimodal (Norris 2013). The second assumption was that an exchange may be multimodal in the particular sense that it begins with a turn that draws on one set of semiotic resources and is completed by a turn that draws on another. The premise of analysis was, therefore, that any action that modifies the content of a YouTube page potentially counts as an interactional turn that can be coded in terms of moves and acts. The relevant user actions are multiple and include, in addition to writing a comment or replying to a comment, uploading a video and 'liking' or 'disliking' a video or comment. The most important implication of this premise is the treatment of uploaded videos as complex I moves that predict R moves of various kinds. Rafaeli and Ariel's (2007) distinction between 'responsiveness' and 'interactivity' is again useful. By clicking on icons on the video player (play, pause, etc.) users produce a corresponding effect but they do not modify the text of the page. This is a matter of the responsiveness of the YouTube interface. By clicking on the 'like' icon below the video player, on the other hand, the user modifies the page by increasing the number of 'likes' displayed. This is a matter of interactivity, or social interaction. By clicking a 'like' icon a user makes an R move realised by an 'evaluate' act, producing a simple exchange that begins with the I move of the video and terminates with the R move of the 'like'. This approach to analysis also has an impact on our understanding of written comments, because it allows us to recast them as 'interactional turns' that can generally be classified as I, R, R+I, or R/I moves.

The study

The remainder of this chapter discusses how this framework was used in a study that aimed to uncover evidence of language and intercultural learning in comments on YouTube videos. The starting point of the study was an assumption that learning is a social process embedded in interaction (Seedhouse and Walsh 2010: 127), which, although previous research has focused largely on learning and spoken interaction, might also be evident in interactions among YouTube commenters. Videos involving the use of English and Chinese were identified and comments related to language and culture were identified for analysis. A first step in the study was the design of a framework to analyse the discourse of these comments, which gradually developed into a more comprehensive framework for analysing the processes of multimodal interaction that generate the text of the YouTube page as a whole.

The use of this framework is illustrated by data from the 'Cantonese Word of the Week!' series, in which Carlos Vidal (YouTube username, 'carlos-douh') explains the meaning of popular Cantonese colloquial expressions in an entertaining manner. The series elicited more than 6,054 comments, of which 1,296 were related to language or culture and analysed in detail. In the most popular video in the series ('I am a Hong Kong Girl with 公主病 [Gung Jyuh Behng]', which recorded more than 1.3 million views) Carlos introduces a Cantonese expression meaning 'princess sickness'. This video elicited 1,260 comments, of which 246 were language-culture related; this proportion (20 per cent) was similar to the proportion for the whole series (21 per cent). Comments on this video are used as examples in the following sections.

Turns

CA researchers treat conversation as an orderly self-managed system, analogous to the turn-taking systems that govern games (Sacks et al. 1974). Although interaction on YouTube is not a self-managed system of this kind, turn is relevant as a basic unit of interactional analysis. Turns are framed by the affordances of the YouTube interface, which governs how users' contributions will appear on the page. In this context, any user action that contributes semantic content to the page counts as a turn. This content may be produced offline, before the action is performed (e.g. writing a comment and then uploading it) or it may be embedded in the action (e.g. clicking a 'like' icon). In order for a turn to be interactive, this action, whatever its form, must somehow be linked to an action performed by another user. In other words, it must contribute to an interactional exchange.

By uploading a video, together with a title, description and tags, a user makes the all-important I move that begins the interaction that will generate the ongoing text of a YouTube page. This move is both multimodal and interactively complex. In conversation, an utterance becomes an I move when it is followed by an R move. A speaker may also make more than one potential I move in the same turn. The R move in the next turn, therefore, indicates how the next speaker orients towards the preceding turn as an I move (i.e. the part of the turn they are responding to and how they interpret it interactionally). This point is particularly important in understanding interaction on YouTube pages, because users typically respond to videos in a variety of ways, orienting both towards the act of uploading the video or towards some particular I move within the video or the written text that accompanies it. It is also worth noting that the uploader of the video also has the power to decide who will participate in this interaction, by allowing unrestricted comments, by limiting viewing and commenting to an identified group of users, or disallowing comments altogether.

Response moves

YouTube offers three semiotic modes for R moves: 1) video responses; 2) the 'like' and 'dislike' icons; and 3) written 'comments'. A video response responds to video through the medium of another video. 'Liking' or 'disliking' a video or comment is simply a matter of clicking an icon and represents a simple 'evaluate' act. Written comments represent a range of acts, among which 'evaluate' appears to be most frequent on most pages. An 'evaluate' in a written comment ('i like you XD', 'Funny!') is interactively equivalent to liking or disliking a video and differs only in its modality and specificity. Written comments also offer three distinctive interactional affordances: 1) they allow R moves to be directed at a particular aspect of the video; 2) they allow performance of a range of acts within R moves; and 3) they allow performance of I moves, which potentially lead to prolonged exchange sequences. Important as they are in the interactional world of YouTube pages, the 'like' and 'dislike' icons are interactively limited. They allow only one move (R) and act ('evaluate'), which terminates any IR exchange in which they play a part.

Analysis of written comments provides a good deal of evidence that they are not simply 'comments' on the video 'prompt' or 'metatext', but interactive turns that complete or prolong exchanges that begin with the uploading of a video. Comments that can be classified as simple R moves typically display different orientations towards the video as an I move. In the 'Gung Jyuh Behng' video, Carlos speaks directly to the camera and addresses

viewers as 'you'. The 1:27 minute video is divided into three segments:
1) Carlos begins by saying, in Cantonese with English subtitles, 'I am a
Hong Kong girl with Gung Jyuh Behng'; he then acts out several Cantonese
utterances as if they were spoken by such a girl (e.g. 'Hurry up and buy
me things! I want Louis Vuitton and Gucci!!'), repeating the phrase Gung
Jyuh Behng after each; 2) he explains the meaning of Gung Jyuh Behng in
English and finishes with his catchphrase for the series, 'Hear it! Speak it!
Memorise it!'; and (3) he ends the video by directing viewers to his other
videos, Facebook page and Twitter feed. Extract 1 shows five different orientations towards the video as an I move.

Extract 1

Comment	Orientation
1 Funny!	The whole video
2 i like you XD	Carlos
3 Omg! Your cantonese is amazing! And fantastically funny your rendition of Princess Syndrome!	Segment 1 (Carlos speaking Cantonese)
4 LOL I totally thought you mean princess cookie/pastry this whole time . . .	Specific item in Segment 1 (Carlos's pronunciation of 病)
5 Actually we call '公主病' Princess Syndrome instead of 'princess sickness'	Specific item in Segment 2 (Carlos's translation of 公主病)

Comments 1 and 2 are simple 'evaluate' moves, oriented to the video as
a whole and to Carlos's performance. The vast majority of non-language-
culture related comments for this video are of these kinds. Comments 2
and 3 are oriented towards the first segment of the video. Comment 2 is
an 'evaluate' of this of this segment, while Comment 3 points specifically
to Carlos's pronunciation of 病, which could be interpreted as 'cookie/
pastry', rather than 'sickness'. Most of the language-culture related comments for this video are of these kinds and orient towards Carlos's use of
Cantonese in Segment 1. Comment 2 is one of a small number oriented
towards the explanation in Segment 2, and none were found that oriented
to Segment 3.

Extract 1 shows how comments, typically, 'respond to', rather than 'comment on', videos or specific aspects of them. Three other kinds of evidence
for interactivity can also be seen in Comments 3–5. First, Comments 3 and 4
both use second person address, which is characteristic of comments on videos in which the uploader speaks directly to the viewer. All three comments
also begin with an 'uptake' act ('OMG', 'LOL', 'Actually') that explicitly
links the comment to the video. Lastly, comments are often marked for
affective and epistemic stance (Ochs 1996), which signals an orientation
towards commenting as an interactive event. In the comments above, it
is the 'uptake' acts that are affectively ('OMG', 'LOL') and epistemically
('Actually') marked (note also, 'I totally thought', in Comment 4). While

the stance markers used in YouTube comments tend to differ from those used in face-to-face interaction (notably the use of acronyms and punctuation marks as affective markers), their interactive functions appear to be very similar.

Complex moves in written comments

While the majority of comments on the 'Gung Jyuh Behng' video consist of a single R move, three other types are also found: turns that consist of both R and I moves (R+I or R/I) and turns that consist of a single I move. In the first case, the R move completes an exchange and a further I move is added. In the latter, the comment is usually linked to the video semantically, but not interactively. Comments 4 and 5 in Extract 1 are examples of R/I moves. Comment 4 clearly responds to Carlos's pronunciation of 病 ('evaluate') but also adds the commenter's opinion that it sounds like the word for 'cookie/pastry' ('opine'). Comment 5 differs in that an 'object' act both responds to Carlos's opinion on the translation and signals a new opinion. Extract 2 shows an example of an R+I move followed by an R move.

Extract 2

	Comment	Move
A:	OMG~ why can you pronounce cantonese so freaking well! and I have yr shelf behind u, IKEA product~ha	R+I
B (Carlos):	haha, yah i love that shelf!! :D	R

A's comment consists of an 'evaluate' of Carlos's Cantonese pronunciation, followed by an 'inform' referring to a shelf that appears behind Carlos in the video. The following R move, made by Carlos, closes the exchange. Extract 3 shows an example of an I move.

Extract 3

	Comment	Move
A:	Hey r u really non chinese? u speak mandarin really fluently~	I
B:	when did he speak mandarin??	R/I

A's comment is semantically related to the video, but it is clearly not a Response to it. Instead, A directs a 'question' to Carlos about his ethnicity (in fact, Carlos is not ethnically Chinese). B's response is a 'challenge' to this question, which implicitly refers to the fact that Carlos is speaking Cantonese, rather than Mandarin.

In all of these examples, new topics are raised in the I moves, which allow interaction to move forward. R/I and R+I moves are especially important in this respect because they can, in principle, be followed by further R/I and R+I moves ad infinitum. The longest sequence of this kind in the comments on the Gung Jyuh Behng video consists of ten comments. Incomplete exchanges, in which a potential I move is not followed by an R move, are also characteristic of the discourse of YouTube comments. Extract 3 exemplifies this as B's R+I does not elicit a Response. This tendency for potential exchanges to 'hang' for want of an R move is one important difference between YouTube interaction and spoken interaction, in which closure of exchanges is the norm.

Written comments – patterns of interaction

Based on the analysis presented so far, it is clear that the characteristic pattern of interaction in written comments is the IR exchange, in which the video functions as the I move. The vast majority of first comments in the 'Cantonese Word of the Week!' series consist of or begin with an R move directed at the video or some aspect of it, especially those that are not related to language or culture. Among the language-culture related comments extended comment sequences are more frequent. Of the 1,296 language-culture related comments in this series, 421 (32 per cent) were found in sequences of comments that begin with an R+I, R/I, or I move. There were 154 sequences of this kind with an average length of 2.7 comments. The fact that such sequences occur primarily among the language-culture related comments is also significant. Language and culture is, broadly, the substantive topic raised by the videos in the series. A language-culture related comment is a comment oriented towards the substantive topic of the Initiation that the video represents, and a sequence of comments represents a development of this topic. The number and length of exchange sequences are, in this sense, indicators of the semantic breadth and depth of interaction on the topic of a video.

The patterns that are found within sequences of written comments are varied and are somewhat similar to multi-party spoken interactions. Extract 4 illustrates some of the possibilities:

Extract 4

A:	Video: [Carlos saying 公主病]	I
B:	공주병 Wow it sounds really similar haha	R/I
C:	how does it pronounce?	R/I (reply to B)
B:	Gong ju byung. Something like that.	R (reply to C)
D:	That's cause Chinese is the oldest language compared to Japanese and Korean. The Japanese have 'kanji' and the Koreans have 'hanja', where they take some Chinese characters (called 'hánzi') and write them the same but pronounce them differently. They also have similar sounds for meanings, such as 공주병 and 公主病.	R+I (reply to B)
E:	i totally agree with you~~~many japanese and korean vocabularies sound like Chinese. I found lots of korean vocab have similar sounds to Hakka, one of the dialects of Chinese.	R+I (reply to D)

In Extract 4, there are five participants, including Carlos (A), whose pronunciation of 公主病 is the I move to which B responds. B's turn is coded as an R/I move, in which the I move is realised by the information that 公主病 sounds like a Korean phrase 공주병 with the same meaning. C then makes an R/I move asking B how the Korean phrase is pronounced and B responds by providing the pronunciation. The interaction continues with a comment from D in reply to B's first comment, offering an explanation of why the two phrases have similar pronunciations. Lastly, E responds to D with an R+I move, agreeing with D's explanation and adding the information that many Korean words sound like Hakka words. The sequence of comments 'hangs' at this point, as E's Initiation does not attract a response.

Extract 4 shows how a topic develops through commenters ending their turns with I moves. Occasionally, a topic develops in this way through a series of dyadic conversation-like comments posted by two commenters (typically when there is a point of dispute). However, multi-party interactions are more characteristic, in which topics develop in a 'chain' of comments, where, for example, A responds to B, C responds to B, D responds to C, and so on. In Extract 4, B makes the initial R/I move, C responds to B, and B responds to C and then plays no further part. D then responds to B's first turn and E responds to D. This pattern reflects the way in which asynchronous interactions develop, with participants not necessarily attending to the whole of a sequence of comments. In this context, it is worth noting that, in principle, interactive turns that contain I moves remain open for R moves indefinitely. This is especially true of videos; the Gung Jyuh Behng video has continued to elicit Responses over a period of three years. It is also true of written comments (note, for example, how B's first comment in Extract 4 elicited independent Responses from C and D), though less so because comments move out of view as they are replaced by newer comments.

Displaying interaction

The way in which comments that are available for response become less likely to elicit responses as they move out of view points to a tension between the textual product of the YouTube page and the interactional processes that produce it. While analysts of spoken interaction and conversation-like written interaction rely on records that reflect the sequence in which turns were taken, an interactional analysis of a YouTube page can recover this sequence only partially. 'Likes' and 'dislikes' can be understood as interactional moves, but they are recorded only as aggregate numbers; no trace is left of when or by whom these moves were made. The layout of written comments has some relationship to the chronological sequence in which they were posted, but the layouts of the comments section makes it difficult to read them in this sequence (see below). The fate of video responses is also interesting in this respect, because their name originally signalled an orientation on the part of YouTube towards interactive dialogue through the medium of video. In August 2013, however, YouTube announced the discontinuation of video responses, because they were 'little-used' (YouTube 2013). Users were encouraged, instead, to embed links to videos in written comments, or to indicate that their own videos are responding to others by using titles, tags and descriptions. Comments on the blog post that discuss this change suggest that many users saw this as a move away from an orientation towards 'conversation'.

The layout of written comments, in particular, reflects a tension between the sequential order in which they are posted and the ways in which the page designers assume that users prefer to read them. Comments are displayed using a modified version of a threaded discussion forum, in which it is possible to, for example, reply to a comment, or reply to a reply. Where comments are explicitly linked in this way, they are nested and displayed in sequential order. The comments section as a whole, however, is organised differently, so that comments can be viewed in one of two ways. By default, comments are displayed in descending order according to the number of 'likes' they receive (the 'top comments' option). The alternative is to display them in reverse sequential order, with the most recent comment appearing at the head of the list ('newest first'). In addition, only the most popular or most recent comments are displayed; users need to click 'all comments' to see the section as a whole. The effect is that it is both difficult and counter-intuitive to read comments in sequential order (and presumably only a discourse analyst would want to do so!). Nevertheless, comments can be read in this way and this is even encouraged by the layout of nested comments. The tension here is, presumably, between the imperative of providing a satisfactory multimodal reading experience, while at the same time representing YouTube as an interactional space.

Conclusion

The aim of this chapter has been to discuss the usability of tools designed for analysing spoken interaction in the analysis of YouTube pages. It has shown these tools have proved useful, not only in the analysis of written comments, but also in facilitating a broader understanding of the senses in which the multimodal text of a YouTube page is a product of interactional processes of various kinds. In this context, the basic ideas and categories associated with exchange structure are seen to have applications beyond spoken interaction. They remain usable and useful in the context of multimodal digital discourse because, in its essentials, communicative interaction has certain properties that are relatively independent of modality. They are also especially useful in analysis of texts such as YouTube pages, which do not at first sight appear to be records of interaction. Androutsopoulos

(2013: 50) describes YouTube as a 'participatory spectacle'; we are able to both view and participate in the construction of the text of YouTube pages as it evolves over time. What we observe in this 'spectacle' is interaction among YouTube users, albeit the structure of this interaction is somewhat concealed by the design of the page. Spoken interaction analysis tools, therefore, help us to see how the text of a YouTube page is, in fact, a product of interactional processes.

At the same time, there are clearly areas of YouTube to which exchange structure analysis is not immediately applicable. The analysis of videos as Initiation moves is probably the most problematic area in this respect. If interactional moves are made up of acts, then it is clear that the action of uploading a video involves a large number of acts. While it is relatively easy to identify the element in a video that commenters are responding to, it is often difficult to characterise this element as an act (see, for example, Extract 4, in which the comment responds to Carlos's pronunciation of a word). Although they do not appear in the data for this study, video responses and links among videos using tags and other cross-referencing devices add another layer of complexity. At one point YouTube appears to have imagined 'conversations' conducted through the medium of video; how would exchange structure analysis cope with conversations of this complexity? Another interesting area for further investigation is communicative actions that are clearly interactive but directed beyond the page, such as 'reporting' a video or comment as spam or abuse and 'sharing' a video through other social media services. The latter reminds us that the YouTube page on which a video is first uploaded is often not the only place on which it can be seen and discussed.

Acknowledgements

This chapter is based on a project funded by the Hong Kong Research Grants Council General Research Fund, entitled Informal Language Learning in Social Media Environments: A YouTube-based Study (Ref. No. 840211). I am grateful to Ada Fong for her work in collecting and analysing data for this project.

References

Androutsopoulos, J. (2013) 'Participatory culture and metalinguistic discourse: performing and negotiating German dialects on YouTube', in D. Tannen and A. M. Trester (eds) *Discourse 2.0: language and new media*, 47–71, Washington, DC: Georgetown University Press.

Baldry, A. and Thibault, P. J. (2006) *Multimodal Transcription and Text Analysis: a multimedia toolkit and coursebook*, London: Equinox.

Barton, D. and Lee, C. (2012) 'Redefining vernacular literacies in the age of Web 2.0', *Applied Linguistics*, 33(3): 282–298.

Bateman, J. A. (2008) *Multimodality and Genre: a foundation for the systematic analysis of multimodal documents*, New York: Palgrave Macmillan.

boyd, d. and Heer, J. (2006) 'Profiles as conversation: networked identity performance on Friendster', proceedings of the Hawai'i International Conference on System Sciences (HICSS-39), Kauai, HI: IEEE Computer Society.

Burgess, J. and Green, J. (2009) *YouTube: online video and participatory culture*, Cambridge: Polity Press.

Coulthard, M. (1985) *An Introduction to Discourse Analysis*, 2nd edn (1st edn 1977), London: Longman.

Herring, S. C. (2001) 'Computer-mediated discourse', in D. Schiffrin, D. Tannen and H. E. Hamilton (eds) *The Handbook of Discourse Analysis*, 612–634, Oxford: Blackwell Publishers.

Herring, S. C. (2013) 'Discourse in Web 2.0: familiar, reconfigured, and emergent', in D. Tannen and A. M. Trester (eds) *Discourse 2.0: language and new media*, 1–25, Washington, DC: Georgetown University Press.

Herring, S. C., Kouper, I., Paolillo, J. C., Scheidt, L. A., Tyworth, M., Welsch, P., Wright, E. and Yu, N. (2005) 'Conversations in the blogosphere: an analysis "from the bottom up"', proceedings of the 38th Hawaii International Conference on System Sciences, Kauai, HI: IEEE Computer Society.

Herring, S. C., Stein, D. and Virtanen, T. (eds) (2013) *Pragmatics of Computer-mediated Communication*, Handbooks of Pragmatics, vol. 9, Berlin: De Gruyter Mouton.

Jones, R. H. (2013) 'Multimodal discourse analysis', in C. A. Chapelle (ed.) *The Encyclopedia of Applied Linguistics*, Oxford: Blackwell.

Kavoori, A. (2011) *Reading YouTube: the critical viewers guide*, New York: Peter Lang.

Kessler, F. and Schäfer, M. T. (2009) 'Navigating YouTube: constituting a hybrid information management system', in P. Snickars and P. Vonderau (eds) *The YouTube Reader*, 275–291, Stockholm: National Library of Sweden.

Kress, G. (2010) *Multimodality: a social semiotic approach to contemporary communication*, New York: Routledge.

Lovink, G. and Niederer, S. (eds) (2008) *The Video Vortex Reader: responses to YouTube*, Amsterdam: Institute of Network Culture.

Norris, S. (2013) 'Multimodal interaction analysis', in C. A. Chapelle (ed.) *The Encyclopedia of Applied Linguistics*, Oxford: Blackwell.

Ochs, E. (1996) 'Linguistic resources for socializing humanity', in J. Gumperz and S. Levinson (eds) *Rethinking Linguistic Relativity*, 407–437, Cambridge: Cambridge University Press.

Rafaeli, S. and Ariel, Y. (2007) 'Assessing interactivity in computer-mediated research', in A. N. Johnson, K. Y. A. McKenna, T. Postmes and U. D. Rieps, *The Oxford Handbook of Internet Psychology*, 71–88, Oxford: Oxford University Press.

Sacks, H., Schegloff, E. A. and Jefferson, G. (1974) 'A simplest systematics for the organisation of turn-taking for conversation', *Language*, 50(4): 696–735.

Searle, J. (1969) *Speech Acts*, Cambridge: Cambridge University Press.

Seedhouse, P. (2005) 'Conversation analysis and language learning', *Language Teaching*, 38: 165–187.

Seedhouse, P. and Walsh, S. (2010) 'Learning a second language through classroom interaction', in P. Seedhouse, S. Walsh and C. Jenks (eds) *Conceptualising 'Learning' in Applied Linguistics*, 127–146, Basingstoke: Palgrave Macmillan.

Sinclair, J. M. and Coulthard, M. (1975) *Towards an Analysis of Discourse*, Oxford: Oxford University Press.

Sindoni, M. G. (2013) *Spoken and Written Discourse in Online Interactions: a multimodal approach*, London: Routledge.

Snickars, P. and Vonderau, P. (eds) (2009) *The YouTube Reader*, Stockholm: National Library of Sweden.

Stenström, A. and Stenström, B. (1994) *An Introduction to Spoken Interaction*, London: Longman.

Strangelove, M. (2010) *Watching YouTube: extraordinary videos by ordinary people*, Toronto: University of Toronto Press.

Tsui, A. (1994) *English Conversation*, Oxford: Oxford University Press.

YouTube (2013) 'So long, video responses . . . , Next Up: better ways to connect', post on the YouTube Partners and Creators blog. Online. Available HTTP: <http://youtubecreator.blogspot.ca/2013/08/so-long-video-responsesnext-up-better.html> (accessed 25 February 2014).

Zourou, K. and Lamy, M.-N. (2013) 'Introduction', in M.-N. Lamy and K. Zourou (eds) *Social Networking for Language Education*, 1–7, Basingstoke, UK: Palgrave Macmillan.

Chapter 7

Co-constructing identity in virtual worlds for children

Christoph A. Hafner

An important insight into the nature of discourse in digital contexts is that such discourse is frequently co-constructed. Reader and writer are often engaged in an overt, joint construction of text. Digital tools provide readers with possibilities to quickly and easily 'write back' to authors, a process that would have been cumbersome and time-consuming in the past. Furthermore, this kind of joint text construction has become a hallmark of digital texts: enabled, for example, through the comment functions available in blogs and social networking sites, the editing features of wikis and the annotation functions of certain social bookmarking sites. At one level then, these digital tools are all about enabling readers and writers to interact and negotiate meaning in digital texts, which both reader and writer contribute to. This chapter considers how such discursive interaction and joint construction can be analysed, in the context of the co-construction of identity in online virtual worlds for children. In order to do so, three key concepts are first described: 1) online identity; 2) affordances and constraints of digital tools; and 3) positioning theory as an analytical tool for interaction in digital discourse.

Identity in online virtual worlds for children

Online virtual worlds for children are graphically represented online spaces that children navigate through using an 'avatar' and where they can interact and play games with large numbers of others. They are also termed 'massively multiplayer online games' because they present game-like environments where millions of users interact. Examples include adventure games like Poptropica (Pearson Education) or social games like Club Penguin (Disney) and Moshi Monsters (Mind Candy). Such online virtual worlds for children are becoming an increasingly common part of children's play. Consequently, in the field of literacy studies, there has been increasing interest in studying them. Some have considered children's practices in such worlds when part of educational contexts (Fields and Kafai 2009; Merchant 2009; Wohlwend et al. 2011); others have examined children's independent, out-of-class literacy practices, including the nature of play and engagement with texts in these spaces (Black 2010; Marsh 2010, 2011).

One particularly interesting point of focus for such studies is children's virtual representation of self. As with other online spaces, virtual worlds provide an opportunity for users to create a 'second self' (Turkle 1985), with the potential to establish a 'fresh' identity (or set of identities) online. The conception of identity that is invoked here is informed by a sociocultural perspective, which sees identity not as a fixed, static entity but rather as something that is fluid and evolving. It involves a dynamic, ongoing performance as a 'certain "kind of person", in a given context' (Gee 2000: 99). In this sense, identity work is never complete; instead identities are constructed and reconstructed in the face of changing social circumstances. In addition, such a performance of identity involves the representation of self through a variety of semiotic resources, which can include the way one dresses, the way one uses gesture and body language, the way one talks and the way one writes. Therefore, discourse can be seen as an important tool through which identity in this sociocultural sense is indexed.

One question is how the available tools can be utilised in order to create such a 'second self' in the digital context. According to Thomas (2007: 8–9), internet users draw upon a 'semiotics of identity' when they participate in online spaces, using a range of available semiotic resources in order to perform identity. These resources include the way in which they: 1) represent the body (e.g. age, gender, ethnicity); 2) represent emotions; 3) demonstrate affiliations and relationships with others; 4) create a sense of belonging to particular cultural groups; 5) adopt storylines and discourses (e.g. socially, or in imaginative role playing or online gaming). Similarly, drawing on the work of Erving Goffman (1959), Jones and Hafner (2012) suggest that internet users manage the impressions that they make on others by making use of the 'equipment' available in particular settings, especially equipment for displaying information about the self and equipment for concealing such information. In addition, impression management strategies can be realised through particular linguistic and multimodal semiotic resources.

In their study of the shifting identities of Zoe/bluwave, a tween user of the virtual world Whyville, Fields and Kafai (2012: 236) note that designing an avatar and creating an acceptable look 'can be more challenging than one might think'. According to them, users have to consider what kind of avatar they want:

- one that looks like them;
- one that has something they don't (e.g. big lips, an adventurous haircut);
- one that displays an affinity for something;

- one that wears popular items;
- one that is simply aesthetically appealing.

They also highlight some of the social and ethical challenges of play in online virtual worlds, asking:

> In a site with over a million participants, how does one begin making friends? How much of one's real-life self ought one to share? When is it okay to pretend to be another gender or another age or simply lie?
>
> (228)

Following Zoe/bluwave over a six-month observation period, Fields and Kafai show how she adopted multiple identities and how these developed. Some identities were harder to construct than others. In particular, Zoe's attempts to represent herself as an African American with dark brown skin colour were often frustrated as it was difficult to trade items for her avatar that came in that skin colour. In addition, the authors note that there were some identities that 'seeped across' from the 'real world' social context to the virtual world (like her strong identification as an African American), and others that did not.

In summary, the kind of online virtual worlds for children in focus in this chapter require users to make a range of choices that impact on the construction of identity. The aim of this chapter is to consider how one particular virtual world facilitates the performance of certain identities by its users. In doing so, it is helpful to consider such worlds in terms of a set of digital tools for the representation of self, all of which have their own particular affordances and constraints.

The affordances and constraints of digital tools

One way to analyse the discourse of a digital environment like a virtual world would be to treat it as a text or set of texts. However, such an approach risks overlooking the essentially fluid and dynamic nature of the virtual world, which is to a large extent constituted of the actions of its users. As suggested above, a more satisfactory approach would be to conceptualise the virtual world as a set of cultural tools, which have been put in place by designers and provide users with various affordances and constraints for discursive action. The notion of 'cultural tool' originates in the work of Vygotsky (1978), who sees all human action as mediated through physical or cultural tools. A physical tool like a hammer mediates action on the physical world, while a cultural tool like language or discourse mediates interaction both with others and with ourselves. The concept has been further developed by Ron Scollon and his colleagues (Norris and Jones 2005; Scollon 2001), as an important element in mediated discourse analysis, an approach which focuses on the way that social actors use cultural tools (including discourse) in order to achieve mediated action.

In the virtual world, the cultural tools available to users would include any digital tools that facilitate representation for action and interaction. The most obvious ones include the player's avatar and means of communication such as a profile or messaging system. Importantly, all such digital tools have both affordances and constraints. The concept of affordances, introduced by Gibson (1979) in his work on visual perception, essentially refers to opportunities for meaningful action that can be taken up by an individual in a given environment. Gibson emphasises that different individuals may perceive different affordances in a given tool and also that they may differ in the extent to which they choose to take up the affordances that they perceive. Therefore, affordances are not only characteristics of tools, they are characteristics of tools as they are used by individuals in meaningful activity (see also Wertsch 1998). With respect to digital tools, we can define affordance as 'A feature of a cultural tool which makes it easier for us to accomplish certain kinds of actions' (Jones and Hafner 2012: 192). Constraints are the flipside of affordances. Just as a digital tool may enable certain kinds of actions, its design may also constrain others.

For present purposes, I want to draw attention to the way that meaning in the online virtual worlds in focus is co-constructed. In some respects, the context is analogous to that described by Gee (2003: 82) in his analysis of video games. There, he refers to the particular kind of stories that video games tell as 'embodied stories' because the narrative arises out of, and so is embodied in, the choices and actions that the player takes. Therefore, in constructing the game plot, video game designers must plan for the various choices that the player may make. The storyline in a game is thus co-constructed, arising from the choices of both game designer and player. In line with this, the affordances of the tools in the game world tend to make some choices more likely/possible while their constraints make others less likely/possible. In this way, designers can influence a player's choices, a feature that can extend to choices about identity. Similarly, the affordances and constraints of tools in virtual worlds for children can have an impact on users' choices, including choices about the discursive representation of self.

Positioning theory

In order to investigate the way that identity is co-constructed in virtual worlds, an analytical tool that accounts for interaction in the construction of identity is called for. Positioning theory, as developed by Rom Harré and his colleagues (Davies and Harré 1990; Harré and van Langenhove 1999), is one such tool. This social psychological theory was developed in response to a perceived shortcoming of existing work on the discursive construction of self, with its reliance on the relatively static notion of 'role'. In contrast, the concept of 'positioning' is seen as more dynamic, constantly shifting as the discourse unfolds. As Davies and Harré (1990: 48) note:

> Positioning, as we will use it, is the discursive process whereby selves are located in conversations as observably and subjectively coherent participants in jointly produced story lines. There can be interactive positioning in which what one person says positions another. And there can be reflexive positioning in which one positions oneself.

The basic idea is that, in any conversation, speakers make available a range of subject positions for themselves and their conversation partners and these positions are understood according to cultural 'storylines'. Because of the co-operative nature of conversation, participants must take up the positions that are offered if they wish to continue to jointly develop the storyline. Nevertheless, it is possible to negotiate positions by invoking competing storylines. As an example of this, a person who is seeking a divorce might complain to their lawyer bitterly about their spouse's actions, positioning themselves as victim and the lawyer as sympathetic listener. Resisting this positioning, the lawyer might treat such complaints as 'irrelevant' and respond only by providing legal tactical advice, firmly positioning themselves as legal counsel. In doing so, the lawyer changes the storyline underpinning the interaction as well as the subject positions that are available to the participants.

As should be apparent, positioning theory was developed primarily with conversation in mind, though it can indeed also be applied to writing (see, e.g., van Langenhove and Harré 1999). Here, I argue that the virtual world can be seen as an interaction, even a kind of conversation, between designer and user (see also Gee, this volume). The designer's choices, including aspects of the virtual environment, its cultural tools and the particular constellation of affordances and constraints selected, interact with the actions of the virtual world user. In this chapter, I consider mainly the way that the choices made by the designer construct different subject positions for the user as well as the way that these positions may be taken up by users as they co-construct their online selves. This is done with reference to one particular online virtual world for children, Moshi Monsters.

Moshi Monsters

Moshi Monsters is an online virtual world for children created by Mind Candy, a UK registered entertainment company founded in 2004. According to the Moshi Monsters website, it is intended for 'kids of all ages'. The site operates a freemium model, whereby users can register an account for free and can later upgrade to premium membership (with a monthly fee) in order to gain access to additional features, like areas of the virtual world that are closed to ordinary members. At the time of writing, there were over

95 million registered users. The premise of the site is that users adopt and look after a pet monster. The first thing that users do is select the monster that they want to adopt, by choosing from six different types and selecting a customisable colour combination. They also provide a username and some basic information about themselves, like gender and age. Once registered, users can: visit their monster in its home; care for, feed and play with their monster; take their monster to 'Monstro city'; play mini-games, either on their own or with other users; go shopping and buy items for their monster or for their monster's home; interact with other users, by leaving notes on the pinboard in that user's room or by sending them gifts. In order to buy anything in Moshi Monsters, users have to first earn 'rox', the virtual currency of the virtual world, which they do mainly by playing mini-games.

The Moshi Monsters interface is shown in Figure 7.1. Here, the monster is shown in its own room, standing in front of the door. Icons to the left and right of the screen serve to provide information about the user and monster (on the left), and provide tools that help the user to interact with the virtual world (on the right). At the top of the screen are tabs where the player can set their own mood and check updates from their friends. Users can also rate each others' rooms, at the bottom of the screen. The zoo and garden icons take the monster to other areas of its home and the daily challenge opens a puzzle game with other users. As mentioned, the pinboard is where other users leave notes and the gift room is where gifts (postcards, animations) are received. Finally, clicking on the friends tree opens a list of friends that the user has approved, similar to the friends list in a social networking site. Friend requests also appear here. To begin with, a monster's room looks very bare but over time, users gradually decorate the room with items bought in virtual stores for virtual money. As should be apparent, the virtual world provides plentiful opportunities for identity play and for constructing a discursive representation of self online.

The study

The main aim of the study was to analyse the affordances for the representation of self made available in Moshi Monsters. As noted earlier, this involves an analysis of the affordances and constraints of the digital tools in Moshi Monsters and the way that these are perceived and acted upon by members of the virtual world. The analysis was informed by my two children, Lily and Jack (pseudonyms chosen by the children who, at the time of the study, were aged ten and eight respectively). The children had considerable experience with the Moshi Monsters virtual world, having at one time been regular participants. Before the study, the children had participated in Moshi Monsters over a number of years, first as regular members and then as premium members of the site. I observed this participation informally during that time. At the time of the study, both children's accounts had been inactive for about six months and their premium membership

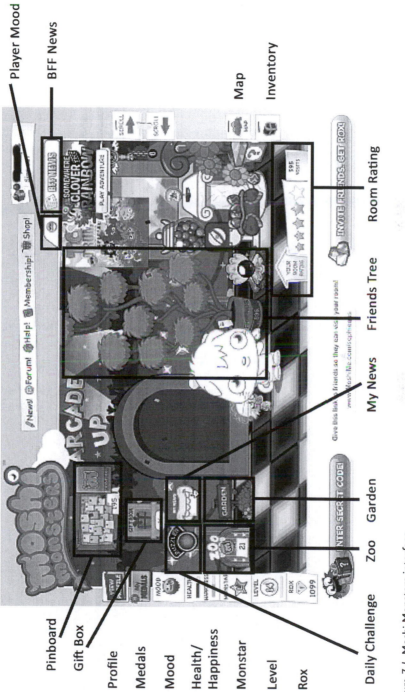

Player Mood

BFF News

Map

Inventory

Room Rating

Friends Tree

My News

Garden

Zoo

Daily Challenge

Pinboard

Gift Box

Profile

Medals

Mood

Health/Happiness

Monstar

Level

Rox

Figure 7.1 Moshi Monsters interface

had been cancelled. Before inviting the children to take part in more formal observations, as described below, informed consent was obtained from their mother, and the procedures involved were also approved by the research ethics committee at my university. The children agreed to the observations and seemed intrigued and excited by my interest in their virtual world activities. In observations, the children were not obliged to answer my questions if they did not want to, and the approach to questioning adopted sought to empower them as experts on play in Moshi Monsters.

Data were collected over a six-week period and consisted of four observations and accounts per child. These observations/accounts were divided into three main kinds:

1   Guided tour (session 1): The children were asked to provide a guided tour of Moshi Monsters, showing me their monster's home and the virtual world locations they most liked to visit.
2   Individual 'gameplay' (sessions 2 and 3): The children individually recorded a thirty to sixty minute session of their activity. The children then took part in a stimulated recall session, in which the session was replayed and they were prompted to provide an account of their activities (especially through the use of the question 'what is going on here?').
3   Final reflection (session 4): With Moshi Monsters open in front of them for reference, the children were interviewed about key issues relating to identity in the virtual world, including: 1) their monster's personality and to what extent it reflects their own personality; 2) aspects of the monster's identity that they might have chosen themselves: for example type, colour, name, gender, age, likes/dislikes, feelings; 3) particular texts/tools (e.g. profile) and what those tools allow them to disclose to others; 4) other spaces, e.g. mobile app, forum, fan videos.

In order to allow for a comparison, in sessions 1 and 2 the children used regular accounts and in sessions 3 and 4 they switched to premium member accounts. All sessions were recorded using screen recording software to capture activity on the screen as well as recording the users themselves. Gameplay was transcribed paying attention to time, activity and salient texts. Speech, including the children's accounts of their activities, was also transcribed. Field notes were recorded after every session. The resulting data set was coded using qualitative data analysis software (MaxQDA, Belous 2012), in order to identify patterns, especially those relating to co-constructed representations of self in the online virtual world.

Observations

The transcribed sessions show that Lily engaged in a wider range of activities than Jack: she logged nineteen different kinds of activities, ten of which were judged to implicate identity, while Jack logged eleven, only three identity-related. Examples of activities that implicate identity include some which involve the creation of representations of self: shopping for items to decorate room/monster, decorating room/monster, planting seeds in garden (creating a visual display of plants), collecting 'Moshlings' (monster pets which are displayed in the user's 'Zoo'). Interactions with other users also potentially implicate identity: playing multiplayer puzzles, reading/approving messages on pinboard, viewing gifts, viewing profile, adding friends. Other activities do not clearly involve such interactions or representations: for example playing single-player puzzles, mini-games, missions and earning rox, among others. The analysis shows that play in the virtual world is co-constructed, as the designer positions the player through the texts and tools that are made available and the player interacts with these texts, tools and positions. Three main positions are made available:

1   Player as monster.
2   Player as monster owner: carer.
3   Player as monster owner: game player.

Player as monster

The basic premise of Moshi Monsters, that players adopt a monster, positions the player and the monster as separate entities. However, in some activities players are invited to take up the monster's position by role playing their monster. These activities include: playing mini-games, mini-missions or so-called super moshi missions (more complex adventure games where the player goes on a quest, for members only). The designer achieves this positioning through multimodal discursive resources. For example, in one mini-game, 'The Ice Screams Game', the monster serves ice cream in an ice cream parlour in order to earn rox. This involves responding to the cues of customers (other monsters) by providing them with the correct combination of ice cream flavours. Visually, this is represented using a first person perspective, that is, the player sees what the monster sees – a counter with cones and ice cream bins, which is approached by other monsters wanting ice cream. Linguistic resources used in messages in this game also appeal directly to the player as monster, through use of imperatives and the second person pronoun:

'Bella! You did it!'
'Amazing! Today you were a gold employee!'

In missions, the player as monster can go on a quest to solve a problem in the virtual world. Visually, these missions are portrayed from a third person perspective, in other words, the player sees their monster on the screen and

uses their monster as a kind of avatar to interact with non-player characters and the virtual world. At the same time, the linguistic resources again
appeal directly to the player as monster:

'Super Moshi I need <u>your</u> help!'
'Now I need <u>ye</u> help putting that colour back in me rainbow'

The children's accounts show that they largely take up this positioning. When
asked 'what is going on here?' they frequently respond through use of 'I', for
example 'I'm just collecting some Cosmic Rox' (Jack, session 3). At times,
though, the ambiguous nature of the subject position offered comes through
in the way that the children describe their activity, as in this example from Jack:

> J: [reading] 'Fizzy is going to shoot some fizzy into a pile of Cosmic
>   Rox beneath our escape pod.' And then boom! The escape pod
>   will explode. Nah, just kidding. It'll just explode the bottom so
>   the escape pod will go up. [watching video and reading] 'One tiny
>   drop.' OK. <u>They</u> are actually going back up in really fast . . . [read-
>   ing] 'To be continued.'
> C: Who is 'they'?
> J: Like <u>me and whatever his name is</u>, Casper?
> C: The other moshling?
> J: Ya, the other moshling.
>
>   (Jack, session 3)

In this example, Jack describes the monster and his accomplice using the
pronoun 'they' but switches back to 'me and whatever his name is' on
questioning.

Player as monster owner: carer

The player is positioned as monster carer primarily when they are in their
home interacting with their monster/feeding their monster or out shopping
for their monster. This positioning is again achieved through multimodal
discursive resources, with the monster making sounds and utterances that
express appreciation, requests and even complaints. Players can interpret
their monster's utterances in conjunction with the monster health and
happiness bars that appear on the left of the interface (see Figure 7.1).
Examples of different speech acts observed include:

Appreciating:
[Shopping expressions/noises, cooing, gurgling]
[In shop] 'Mmmm . . . yum, that'll taste good in my belly.'

Requesting:

[In room] 'How about some grub?'

[In room] 'Aw I want everyone to see that I've got this . . . Maybe I can wear it as a hat?'

Complaining:

[In room] 'Better talk to the hand cause I'm not moving.'

Through these kinds of speech acts the player is positioned as the monster's carer, that is the person that the monster looks up to and depends upon for play, for food, for shopping trips, for renovations and for emotional support. Here, the designer creates a separate identity for the monster, which the player can interact with. In the process, players get to know the monster's likes and dislikes, as below, where Lily demonstrated her monster's reaction to tickling:

L: Yea you can tickle them. It's just . . . [monster starts crying] [both laugh]

L: See I've tickled it too much.

C: It doesn't like being tickled too much.

(Lily, session 4)

The children fulfilled their role of monster carer differently, indicating that the positioning can be taken up in different ways. Lily responded directly to requests, providing her monster with food to make it happy. Jack mostly found this to be unnecessary, explaining that 'when you go to lots of games, you don't normally need to feed your [monster] 'cause his happiness goes high. And when you do quests, his health goes quite high. So you don't really need to buy any food' (session 4). Thus, although Jack didn't feed his monster, he still took up the position of monster carer.

Player as monster owner: game player

The player is positioned as 'game player' mostly when using tools for inter-action and communication. In this case, the designer has provided various 'social networking features' or tools that afford interaction with other play-ers which may be taken up (or not). Here, the player is positioned independently of the monster that they have adopted, as a human user of the virtual world who can interact with other human users. Some discursive positioning occurs through texts in the virtual world. As players navigate the virtual world using their monster as avatar, they encounter other players' monsters. In Moshi Monsters, unlike some other virtual worlds for children, in most locations it is not possible for players to interact directly with one another (for example, through chat). Instead, they must use the pinboard in the monster's room to leave messages. In spite of this constraint on interaction, other monsters nevertheless appear to directly address the player in public areas of the world. Speech bubbles (presumably automatically generated) appear above other monsters and solicit interaction:

> 'You should visit my owner's room'
> 'You should leave a message on my owner's pinboard'

In addition, the designers encourage identity play through community competitions, such as the room of the week competition, organised through the Moshi Monsters website. The designers also provide the following tools/affordances for representation of self and interaction with other users: 1) Mood icon, profile; 2) Friends tree, BFF news, pinboard; 3) Room and room ratings, garden, zoo. Among these, there are two different kinds of tools – those that allow the player to explicitly make identity claims, for example adjusting the mood icon to show emotional state, and those that allow the player to implicitly make identity claims, for example in the choice of wallpaper for their room.

Both children had taken up the available tools and affordances for the representation of self, either through multimodal displays (e.g. their monster, their room) or through interaction with other members using the room ratings, friends tree, gift room and pinboard. The children were particularly enthusiastic about presenting themselves favourably through the design of their rooms. In this extract, Lily describes how she hopes to be perceived by visitors to the room:

> C: What if they look at your house? What can they tell about you?
> L: Um.
> C: If somebody was at your house . . .
> L: They think <u>I'm very fashionable</u> or something cause I always put two things that fit well together like um this like paparazzi thing and disco floor, it looks good together, and up here I have two floors cause <u>I was a member</u>.
>
> (Lily, session 4)

Here, the choice of the word 'fashionable' to describe own personality is very apt because decorating the room is very much like dressing up, experimenting with different 'looks' and the kind of effects that such 'looks' might achieve. Interestingly, another identity category that is invoked in this account is the category of 'member' – a category that is also invoked in the profile and which seems to provide children with social capital, given all of the benefits that members enjoy (Marsh 2011). In addition, the children could also evaluate other users through the visual design of their rooms, as when Jack concluded (rightly or wrongly) that one user was Chinese based on a preference to include lanterns and a sign with Chinese script in the monster's room.

In observations, the profile and pinboard were rarely used, perhaps because the children were 'returning' to Moshi Monsters after a long period of absence and were 'out of touch' with their virtual friends. Nevertheless, there is evidence that they perceived affordances for the representation of self in these tools. Indeed, most of the categories in the profile are explicit identity categories relating to mood, preferences, gender, age, location, favourite colour, favourite music, favourite food and some in-world specific categories like number of visits to room. The pinboard, where notes can be left for other users, allows for both explicitly claimed identities (e.g. 'I love soccer') and implicitly claimed identities (e.g. demonstrating group membership by using register features like slang and emoticons appropriate to online youth culture).

Discussion and conclusions

The focus of this study has been on the tools and affordances of the virtual world of Moshi Monsters and how these are perceived and acted upon by two child users. This focus could be seen as limiting – the study has not delved further into the social practices of the virtual world, which undoubtedly play an important role in aspects of identity construction. However, the perspective adopted, which sought to apply tools of discourse analysis in order to understand the co-construction of identity in an online virtual world, has yielded some interesting insights. In particular, adopting this perspective allows us to see clearly how identity, and other forms of user action in virtual worlds, is a jointly negotiated, interactive process between designer and user. In this, the focus on notions of 'cultural tool', 'affordances' and 'constraints', as well as the positioning framework derived from interactional sociolinguistics has been very useful.

Thus, in this study, the virtual world is conceptualised as a site of interaction, where meanings are jointly negotiated, according to the tools, affordances and positions made available. The technique of stimulated recall, where participants view their online activity and then provide a guided account of it, is essential to arriving at an ecologically valid interpretation. With respect to this protocol, the participants in this study sometimes became so engrossed in their gameplay videos that they stopped talking and providing an account. As a result, I often paused the video and prompted the children for comments. However, such prompting needs to be done in a careful and sensitive way, especially if the focus of the study is on identity. One fairly obvious tip is to ask open questions so that the participant can select the focus of their account for themselves. Even open questions can embed particular assumptions about the activity though. For example, I carefully avoided questions like 'what are you doing now?' which makes an assumption about agency and would have led the children to respond with 'I'. Instead, I preferred the more neutral question (from the point of view of agency), 'what is going on here?' This strategy has allowed me to infer, through their own use of language, the extent to which the children took up the positionings offered.

The analysis shows how the design of multimodal discursive resources that draw on language, visuals, sound, combines with the design of tools/ affordances in order to strategically position children in Moshi Monsters. In terms of positioning analysis, as different storylines are introduced by designers, different discursive resources are mobilised. These storylines have to do with assumptions embedded in different kinds of activities: in a mission, the player is constructed as hero solving problems in the Moshi Monsters world; in pinboard exchanges, as ('real-life') child user experimenting with social interaction. Positioning theory predicts that such positions would be difficult to resist: they must be accepted if the child is to successfully co-construct the story that the virtual world is telling. Indeed, the positions made available in Moshi Monsters were largely taken up by the children in this study. It is worth pointing out that a more detailed study of social practices would likely uncover more dramatic resistance to positions as well as alternative, unsanctioned positions. This was the case in Fields and Kafai's (2012) study of Whyville, where cheating and scamming practices, and associated identities, were observed in the focal participant. Similarly, Fink (2011) describes the practice of 'griefing' in Second Life, showing how this subversive practice challenges and disrupts assumptions about activity (i.e. storylines) in the virtual world.

Nevertheless, such alternative positions are most likely constructed only by more expert users. Most users likely conform to the positions that are made available to them through the available affordances. As such, some of the positions made available in Moshi Monsters are in need of critical evaluation. In particular, there is a strong discourse of consumerism, represented in some texts in the virtual world. For example, this discourse is evident when players are positioned as monster carers who can make their monsters happy by going shopping and purchasing virtual items to 'improve' their monster's life. Such a discourse seems to be common in other online virtual worlds as well. Ultimately, the players themselves are positioned as consumers/customers of the virtual world, and non-members are frequently served ads that illustrate the benefits of membership and solicit sales (in one thirty-seven minute session observed for this study, six ads were served, roughly one every six minutes). The study suggests that an important 'digital literacy practice' for young children who are participating in online virtual worlds is the ability to critically interpret texts that they come into contact with. They are frequently positioned in quite subtle ways and so it would seem to be worthwhile to develop age appropriate ways to explore questions like: 1) How are text consumers positioned? 2) By whom and for what purpose? 3) When/how can such positionings be resisted?

References

Belous, I. (2012) MaxQDA 11 [Computer software], Marburg: Verbi Software. Online. Available HTTP: <http://www.maxqda.com/> (accessed 30 June 2014).

Black, R. W. (2010) 'The language of Webkinz: early childhood literacy in an online virtual world', *Digital Culture and Education*, 2(1): 7–24.

Davies, B. and Harré, R. (1990) 'Positioning: the discursive production of selves', *Journal for the Theory of Social Behaviour*, 20(1): 43–63.

Fields, D. A. and Kafai, Y. B. (2009) 'A connective ethnography of peer knowledge sharing and diffusion in a tween virtual world', *International Journal of Computer-Supported Collaborative Learning*, 4(1): 47–68.

Fields, D. A. and Kafai, Y. B. (2012) 'Navigating life as an avatar: the shifting identities-in-practice of a girl player in a tween virtual world', in C. C. Ching and B. Foley (eds) *Constructing the Self in a Digital World*, 222–250, Cambridge: Cambridge University Press.

Fink, E. (2011) 'The virtual construction of legality: "Griefing" & normative order in second life', *Journal of Law, Information, and Science*, 21(1): 89.

Gee, J. P. (2000) 'Identity as an analytic lens for research in education', *Review of Research in Education*, 25(1): 99–125.

Gee, J. P. (2003) *What Video Games Have to Teach us about Learning and Literacy*, New York: Palgrave Macmillan.

Gibson, J. J. (1979) *The Ecological Approach to Visual Perception*, Boston, MA: Houghton Mifflin.

Goffman, E. (1959) *The Presentation of Self in Everyday Life*, Garden City, NY: Doubleday.

Harré, R. and van Langenhove, L. (eds) (1999) *Positioning Theory: moral contexts of intentional action*, Oxford: Blackwell.

Jones, R. H. and Hafner, C. A. (2012) *Understanding Digital Literacies: a practical introduction*, London: Routledge.

Marsh, J. (2010) 'Young children's play in online virtual worlds', *Journal of Early Childhood Research*, 8(1): 23–39.

Marsh, J. (2011) 'Young children's literacy practices in a virtual world: establishing an online interaction order', *Reading Research Quarterly*, 46(2): 101–118.

Merchant, G. (2009) 'Literacy in virtual worlds', *Journal of Research in Reading*, 32(1): 38–56.

Norris, S. and Jones, R. H. (eds) (2005) *Discourse in Action: introducing mediated discourse analysis*, Abingdon: Routledge.

Scollon, R. (2001) *Mediated Discourse: the nexus of practice*, London: Routledge.

Thomas, A. (2007) *Youth Online: identity and literacy in the digital age*, New York: Peter Lang.

Turkle, S. (1985) *The Second Self: computers and the human spirit*, New York: Simon & Schuster.

van Langenhove, L. and Harré, R. (1999) 'Positioning and the writing of science', in R. Harre and L. van Langenhove (eds) *Positioning Theory: moral contexts of intentional action*, 102–115, Oxford: Blackwell.

Vygotsky, L. S. (1978) *Mind in Society: the development of higher psychological processes*, Cambridge, MA: Harvard University Press.

Wertsch, J. V. (1998) *Mind as Action*, New York: Oxford University Press.

Wohlwend, K. E., Vander Zanden, S., Husbye, N. E. and Kuby, C. R. (2011) 'Navigating discourses in place in the world of Webkinz', *Journal of Early Childhood Literacy*, 11(2): 141–163.

Chapter 8

Recreational language learning and digital practices

Positioning and repositioning

Alice Chik

Recently, *The Guardian* asked: 'Can I successfully learn a language online?' (Codrea-Rado 2014) and invited three writers to use online language learning tools to learn a language over a six-week period. The three writers used three popular platforms (Duolingo, Rosetta Stone and Skype) to learn Spanish, French and Russian.

At the time of writing this chapter, these learners had just started their journeys, and the readers had yet to know of the learning outcomes: could they or could they not learn a foreign language using just online language learning tools? The fact that *The Guardian* devoted the space to discuss and 'road test' online language learning tools shows the emerging popularity of such tools. One reason these tools have captured the public's imagination is because many of them combine foreign language learning with social networking features, giving them the status of 'language learning social network sites' (LLSNSs). Ironically, the media documentation of the use of such online language learning tools also reflects the concerns of a current body of research on online language learning which involves examining the features of these websites, how users use them, and the processes of language learning they engage users in.

Language learning social network sites

Language learning websites with social networking features are still relatively new, so currently there are more reviews by bloggers and tech magazines than analyses by academic researchers; however, there is a growing body of published research on the usability of these websites (Zourou 2012). In this chapter, I use LLSNSs as an umbrella term for online learning tools which include features that allow users to:

1 construct a public or semi-public profile within a bounded system;
2 articulate a list of other users with whom they share a connection; and
3 view and traverse their list of connections and those made by others within the system (boyd and Ellison 2007: 5).

Several LLSNSs that have attracted a large population of users include Live-mocha, Busuu, Duolingo, Babbel and LingQ; and these different LLSNSs have slightly different configurations of features. The utility of the social networking features and degree of interactivity they promote depend on learners' willingness to communicate (Clark and Gruba 2010; Lloyd 2012) and on the type of learning content available on the websites (Brick 2012; James 2011; Liu et al. 2013; Orsini-Jones et al. 2013; Stevenson and Liu 2010).

Usability has been the main focus of most research on LLSNSs. Clark and Gruba (2010) use an auto-ethnographic approach to Clark's learning of Korean on Livemocha over a four-week period. They found that certain social networking features like connecting with native speakers for chatting, were highly motivating, but the audio-lingual method and decontextualised grammar-translation drills were frustrating and demotivating. Zourou and Lamy (2013) argue that the ways learners and teachers engage with the social networking features of social media, for both LLSNSs and SNSs, determine the quality of learning. Linking such learning to computer-assisted language learning (CALL), they argue that in order for learning to happen, there should be genuine social interaction beyond institutional led interaction. Liu et al. (2013) used a survey to get learners' use and perception of three learning sites, Livemocha, Busuu and English Café over a six-week period. Liu and her colleagues found that though affordances for language learning were present, the challenges of limited content and social networking functions did not yet favour full classroom integration.

Another approach to examining LLSNSs is to focus on evaluating the learning material on such sites. Harrison and Thomas (2009: 120) suggest that while many of these LLSNSs claim to use social networking functions to mediate foreign language learning, these sites resemble 'ready-made "Virtual Learning Environments"' that use a courseware approach to deliver learning. This claim aligns with Tomlinson's (2012: 143) suggestion that commercially produced materials focus mainly on 'informing their users about language features and on guiding them to practise these features'. Tomlinson (2012) also recommends that electronic materials should provide additional benefits such as collaborative and supportive learning opportunities, organisational convenience, localised adaptation, and integrated environments for out-of-class learning. For the evaluation of traditional print materials, the first step is often the examination of the author's claims (Pinter 2006; Tomlinson 2012). For LLSNSs, the claims can come from different sources: textual information on the website (e.g. 'About Us', 'FAQ', blog, press release), visual information on the website (e.g. icons, images, colour schemes), the interactive process of 'learning', textual and visual information from other social media platforms, media reports and interviews. Following Littlejohn's (2011) suggestions for English Language Teaching (ELT) materials analysis, it is important to examine not only the content, but also how learning and learners are represented in these descriptions to understand the evolving public discourse. This is where a discourse analytical approach may provide a more holistic approach to understanding the learning, learners and materials on LLSNSs. Current research on LLSNSs tends to focus on the *process* and *materials* of learning and treat LLSNSs as an emerging dimension of CALL. The present study aims to widen the scope by taking a discourse analytical perspective to examine the positioning of language learners in LLSNSs.

Positioning theory and digital practices

One way we can learn more about the public discourse of learning and the actions of learners on LLSNSs is by using positioning theory. Positioning theory was first developed to examine selfhood in psychology (Davies and Harré 1990). Harré and van Langenhove (1991) suggest that we can use the notion of 'positions' instead of 'roles' to understand discourse; while roles tend to be seen as more rigid, positions are constantly being negotiated in interaction. Harré and van Langenhove (1991: 395) argue that

> positioning can ... be understood as the discursive construction of personal stories that make a person's actions intelligible and relatively determinate as social acts and within which the members of the conversation have specific locations.

Positioning theory states that in conversation, people position themselves, position others, or are positioned to take up, develop, unfold or maintain a storyline (Davies and Harré 1990). A storyline can be understood as a narrative that unfolds, develops, is supported or questioned during the conversation. Davies and Harré (1990: 49) argue that 'story lines are organised through conversation and around various poles, such as events, characters and moral dilemmas'. In other words, every act of self or other positioning during a conversation will determine the development of a storyline. As a storyline is rooted in conversation, it is then, by extension, embedded in cultural and social conventions. In addition to notion of the storyline, Harré and van Langenhove (1991) introduced various modes of positioning:

- First and second order positioning – first order positioning refers to how persons position themselves and others by using existing social categories and storylines; a second order positioning happens when the parties involved in the conversation question the first order positioning, and is thus open for negotiation.

- Performative and accountive positioning – in first order positioning, the speaker makes a deliberate positioning statement to perform the act of positioning himself and others, and can be understood as a performative positioning act; and in response to a performative first order positioning act is the accountive second order positioning. It is accountive because a response to first order positioning involves talk about talk.
- Moral and personal positioning – moral orders can be understood as social norms within certain institutional structures in contrast to individual and personal attributes and characteristics.
- Self and other positioning – when a person initiates self positioning, he/she simultaneously positions the other.
- Tacit and intentional positioning – most first order positioning will be considered as tacit except in cases of lying or teasing, but second and third order positioning are all intentional in nature.

In recent years, positioning theory has been advanced for use at institutional (e.g. universities) and national levels to understand global issues and conflicts (e.g. global warming). This expansion in scale allows analysts to reconsider the ways issues and actions are understood and undertaken by different parties due to differences in positioning, the understanding of the storyline, and the demand of rights and duties. In discussing technology assessment, van Langenhove and Bertolink (1999) extend the perimeter of conversation beyond exchanges to include written artefacts. The same approach can be applied to the understanding of the discourses of learning on online platforms. LLSNS developers make various claims to position themselves and their websites as learning partners, which are the initiating statements that constitute first order positioning. Developers may also 'other-position' the learners through these claims (Davies and Harré 1990). Learners enter a 'conversation' with the websites through the documentation of the websites when they read the website description, which are the responses to the initiating statements that constitute second order positioning (van Langenhove and Bertolink 1999; Table 8.1). The intentional positioning in conversation can be either performative or accountive to achieve four distinct forms in different situations: 1) deliberate self-positioning; 2) forced self-positioning; 3) deliberate positioning of others; and 4) forced positioning of others (Harré and van Langenhove, 1991). On LLSNSs, while researchers have examined the creation and use of user profiles (Harrison 2013; Stevenson and Liu 2010), there are other discursive practices used on these websites to position learners for the maintenance of the storyline of certain forms of foreign language learning. On LLSNSs, we need to pay attention then not only to the written texts, but also to the use of other semiotic resources such as colours, visual and spatial manipulation.

Table 8.1 Types of intentional positioning

	Performative	Accountive
Self-positioning	Deliberate self-positioning	Forced other positioning
Other positioning	Deliberate positioning of others	Forced positioning of others

Source: Harré and van Langenhove (1991: 400).

Methodology

Like other researchers on LLSNSs, I was first attracted to and curious about the process of language learning on these sites. I then took an auto-ethnographic approach (Ellis et al. 2011) to test drive the websites, Duolingo (Italian) and Busuu (Spanish), over a four-week period from March to April 2013. Though both websites are available as apps, and I have also downloaded both apps, I found the apps not as user-friendly when I had to listen to or read lessons on noisy streets or public transport. As with other LLSNSs, both Duolingo and Busuu update on dedicated Facebook pages and blogs, so I 'liked' the Facebook pages and subscribed to the blogs. Both websites provided regular Facebook updates on various topics, from company news (e.g. new website development and user number) to language learning content (e.g. 'How do you say this in your language?'). Over the four-week learning period I became interested in the discourses of learning and learners on these websites. The use of an auto-ethnographic approach allows the learner–researcher to critically view learning as a situated process and learners as sociocultural beings (Block 2007; McNamara 2013). In my data collection, I took screenshots of my lessons and discussion forums, and downloaded relevant webpages on language learning and company information. I also took notes and interpreted the data reflectively to tease out relevant data on the learning process and positioning of learners.

Duolingo.com was launched in November 2011, and now claims 25 million users with 12.5 million active users (Lardinois 2014). Duolingo operates as a free ('forever') language education platform (von Ahn 2013). With no advertising banners on the website and no charge for the learning content, the revenue comes from translation services. The website requires a login signup via an email, Facebook or Google account. It offers six languages for learning (English, Spanish, French, German, Portuguese and Italian) with other language courses at various incubation stages.

Busuu.com was launched in May 2008, and now claims more than 35 million users (Busuu 2013). Busuu operates on a 'freemium' model, which means the basic study materials are available for free but grammar units and multimedia functions like voice recording and podcasts are only available to paid premium members. Currently it offers twelve languages (English, Spanish, French, German, Italian, Portuguese, Russian, Polish, Turkish, Arabic, Japanese and Chinese). It also partners with three external corporations (Collins, PONS, Macmillan Dictionary) for the supply of materials. The website requires a login signup via an email, Facebook or Google account.

In the following sections, I will examine the foreign language learning frame and positioning of language learners on Duolingo and Busuu websites. It should be noted that the findings were based on the analysis of the data gathered in March and April of 2013. Since then, both Duolingo and Busuu have updated and made slight changes to their interfaces. However, the basic principles have not changed.

The foreign language learning frame

According to Harré (2010), 'prepositioning' sets up the 'frame' for a storyline. On the websites I analysed, this 'frame' constitutes the way foreign language learning itself is represented. In order to become successful with learning, or at least not resistant, learners enter the conversation with the website to subscribe or agree to certain approaches to foreign language learning. Both Duolingo and Busuu are explicit in representing their conceptualisation of foreign language learning. I will start with the description of both home pages as statements of learning and then discuss the ways I experienced the learning spaces on both websites.

Home pages

When visiting Duolingo.com for the first time, visitors are first welcomed by the cartoonish website mascot, Duo the green owl, standing on a sea of clouds with his wings opened against a background of green mountains and forest under a light blue sky. Then visitors are greeted with the slogan 'Free language education for the world' on the top of the webpage, followed by prompts to sign up with either a Facebook or an email account. Next, visitors are reminded that Duolingo offers six language courses, as represented by respective national flags. (Curiously, English is represented by the American flag, and Portuguese by the Brazilian flag.) At the bottom half of the home page, visitors encounter four icons:

1   A 'free' batch: 'It's free, for real' and then in smaller print 'No fee, no ads, no gimmicks. A college-quality education without the pricetag.' Visitors are then encouraged to click on a hyperlink to a YouTube video explaining the business model of Duolingo and how it can provide language courses for free, forever.
2   An atomic symbol: 'Scientifically proven' and then in smaller print, 'An independent study found that Duolingo trumps university-level language learning.' Visitors are guided to read a research report by Roumen Vesselinov, PhD and John Grego PhD (Vesselinov and Grego

2012). On the cover of the report, the academic posts and affiliations of both authors are provided.

3   Three hearts (like those used in digital games): 'Learning, gamified' and 'Lose hearts with incorrect answer, practice against the clock, level up. Duolingo is addictive.'

4   A mobile phone: 'Also on the go' and in finer print, 'Make your breaks and commutes more productive with the Duolingo iPhone app.' At the time (April 2013), the Android app was not yet available.

As potential users read these statements, they are also entering a conversation with Duolingo in which Duolingo performs the first order positioning with their conceptualisations of learning: 'free', 'scientifically proven', 'gamified' and 'on the go'. While Duolingo positions itself, users are positioned to accept these conceptualisations that learning on Duolingo is free, scientific, game-like, and mobile. The conversation on language learning continues with the presumed reading of the research report or further reading into the 'About Us' section, which includes the basic philosophy of using translation as both the learning and business model, 'Community Guidelines' and 'Please don't use Duolingo to . . . ' sections. In the 'Community Guidelines' section, Duolingo reiterates that language learning should be free and collaborative ('Help and support across all skill levels') and language diversity should be respected ('Embrace and share regional language differences'). At this point, Duolingo has intentionally positioned themselves as superior providers of language learning ('trumps university-level language learning') and idealistic ('free for the world'). These statements are performative acts, constructing a storyline about language learning that users will either accept or question as they start using the platform.

Visitors to Busuu.com are greeted with a very different and a more colourful home page. On the top banner is the sunny Busuu garden with different kinds of cartoonish trees, and the slogan 'Your language learning community – join now for free!' Then the website is quartered with four icons:

1   A laptop with a collection of national flags: '**Learning language online** with interactive language courses and lessons'.

2   A collage of mobile devices: '**Download our mobile apps** to learn languages on the go'.

3   A collage of learner profile pictures around a globe: '**Connect with our worldwide community** to practice your language skills'.

4   The logos of Collins and PONS: '**Get access to Grammar Guides** provided by leading publishers'.

Visitors then see a banner with the words, 'In partnership with', followed by the names of a number of publishers and media companies, and 'as seen on' followed by the names of a number of traditional and digital media companies. Underneath the list of partners and media companies, two learner testimonials are given. The testimonials are randomly generated from a pool of about twelve. Each testimonial contains a profile picture, a testimonial statement of the benefits of being a Busuu member, a user name, age, country, language spoken and learning. Many of these testimonials are contributed by premium members. Scrolling down further, visitors are given brief information on the sixteen available languages; for instance, next to the Spanish flag button,

> Spanish is the second most studied language in the world. With Busuu. com you can learn from wherever you want and track your progress. Give it a try with our interactive exercises. Find out more about our online Spanish courses or try out our Spanish exercises!'

On this home page, Busuu initiates first order positioning by first claiming that learning is community-based and implying that materials are provided by established and reputable publishers.

The conversation about language learning continues in the 'About busuu.com' with first the bolded sentence '**busuu.com is an innovative online community for learning languages.**' Visitors are then reassured that 'We have personally suffered from the traditional way to learn a new language which we always found expensive, difficult and boring. Therefore, we decided to create a new concept of language learning by offering you the following advantages', which include 'learn from native speakers', 'learn with our materials', and 'learn for free'. Visitors are also able to access 'The busuu.com Language Barometer 2012' (Busuu 2012), a survey conducted by IE Business School on trends in language learning. Busuu deliberately self-positions as a sympathetic learning partner to a community of needy global learners; potential users are also positioned to accept that native speakers are superior language teachers.

The language learning processes

Once a visitor becomes a member and logs in to the website, the learner is now presented with a learning path. On the dashboard page (see Figure 8.1), Duolingo learners see a flow chart, the 'Skill Tree', with categories of vocabulary and phrases like 'Basics 1', 'Food', 'Plurals' . . . etc. Learners have to complete and unlock lessons as they progress. On the top right hand corner, learners are also informed of the number of words and consecutive days they have learned, experience points (xp) earned, and the 'lingots' earned. Lingot is the digital currency on Duolingo and can be used to purchase virtual items such as bonus lessons. Learners earn experience points to advance to the next level, which can be

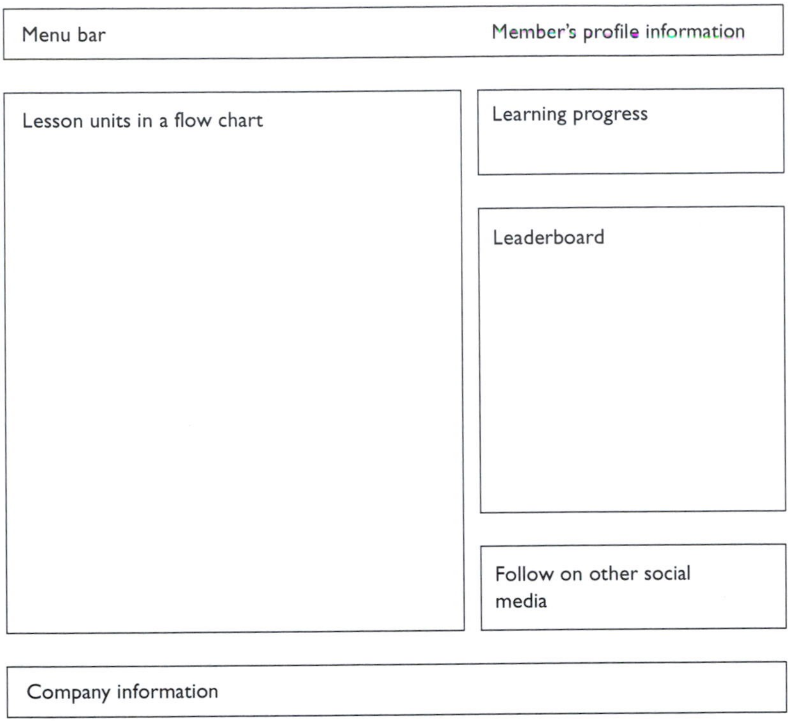

Menu bar	Member's profile information

Lesson units in a flow chart	Learning progress
	Leaderboard
	Follow on other social media

| Company information |

Figure 8.1 A graphic representation of Duolingo dashboard

published on Facebook. Learners can also opt out of lessons by taking tests to advance to the next level. The column on the right hand side includes a leaderboard with friends' records and activities on Duolingo during the week.

Duolingo uses translation as the main pedagogical approach, so most exercises are audio-lingual and translation drills. Each lesson includes twenty questions and learners are given three hearts, or three opportunities to make mistakes; when the hearts are used up, the broken hearts on the ground notify the learners that they have to retry the lesson. The questions are usually accompanied by an audio clip, and are of different types, such as Italian to English or English to Italian translation, multiple choice (with or without pictorial cues), listening (dictation from Italian) and, recently added, the voice recording function. When learners hover over the Italian words or phrases with their mouse, translation and grammar points are provided. Underneath each question, members can discuss the grammar points or raise questions in the comment box. Learners can also follow the discussion to receive updates. Learners might have to translate a vocabulary word (e.g. *L'uomo*) or a sentence (e.g. *La salsiccia è nel ristorante*). All materials are free; learners are only barred from certain materials simply because they have not yet completed the required lessons. There are no advertisements or promotional banners on the website.

When learners join a Duolingo lesson, they are positioned to accept the prescribed linear learning process and content. For each lesson, there is no skipping of questions (without losing a heart) and interaction with other learners is minimal. The only space to interact with other learners is through the discussion board underneath the answer. However, the discussion board is not available until the learners have submitted the answers. Once in the discussion, learners are free to post a comment or a question about the answers (usually grammatical, but as shown in the following section, comments can be playful). This is also the space where one learner can follow another learner, like a comment/response, and give lingots. However, the design of the discussion dictates that users have to click 'Follow Discussion' to be able to come back to the same discussion board. If users do not remember to click 'Follow Discussion', users have to redo the exercise (and hope that the same question will pop up) in order to participate in any ongoing conversation. It is possible to say that though there are different social networking features on the discussion board, learners are forced to take certain actions (click the 'Follow Discussion') to maintain their positions as participants.

Busuu members encounter a more commercial dashboard page (see Figure 8.2). The dashboard is designed as a two-column interface, with the profile information bar on the top of the page. On Busuu, members can be both teachers of languages they speak and learners of languages they would like to learn. Membership is divided into free and paid premium. The premium sign, a golden crown (as denoted by $ in Figure 8.2), is prominently placed on top of the dashboard page. Underneath the profile bar, learners can view their Busuu language garden on the left hand side, a visualisation of their language learning and collaborative efforts. The lushness of the cartoonish trees reflects the effort of the members. The language garden is followed by language learning units, and a large advertising banner. Another section of learning units is presented underneath the banner, followed by a big section on members' efforts in correcting others' work and the corrections they received. Members earn a Busuu berry for every correction they make; the berries can then be used to purchase virtual items for garden decoration (I purchased a cartoon hedgehog for my garden). Busuu berries can also be purchased with actual currencies. In the virtual shop, most items are available to premium members only. On the right hand column, members first encounter the Busuu promotional prompt to upgrade to premium membership, followed by a to-do list, Busuu berries status, and goal setting. Another advertising box heads the Community section, followed by a promotional prompt to join Busuu partner PONS community

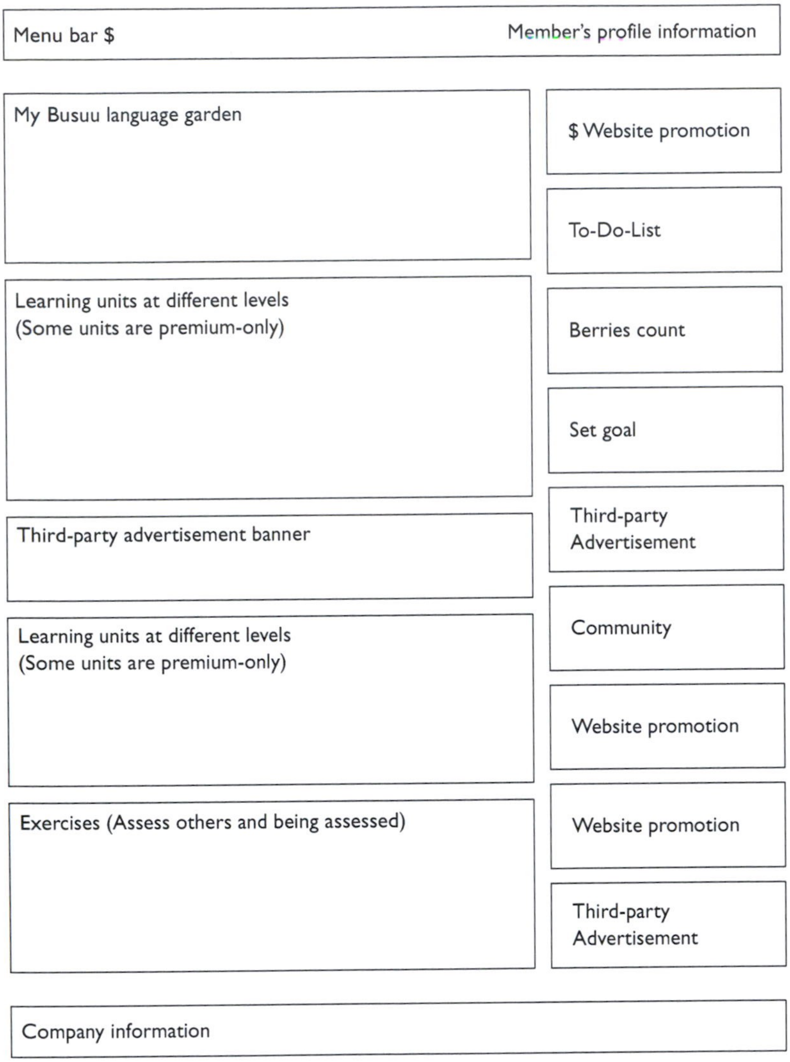

Menu bar $	Member's profile information

My Busuu language garden	$ Website promotion
	To-Do-List
Learning units at different levels (Some units are premium-only)	Berries count
	Set goal
	Third-party Advertisement
Third-party advertisement banner	Community
Learning units at different levels (Some units are premium-only)	Website promotion
Exercises (Assess others and being assessed)	Website promotion
	Third-party Advertisement

Company information

Figure 8.2 A graphic representation of Busuu dashboard

(premium only) and take recommended units, and ending with another advertising box. The company information is provided at the end of the page. Throughout the page, little golden crowns spice the page as reminders to join premium membership or to deter free members from clicking on premium content.

On the Busuu dashboard, users are positioned as either free or premium members, and members are constantly reminded of their positions.

The use of an icon (golden crown) is a visual positioning device to either attract free members to become premium members or deter free members from enjoying certain spaces and learning content. It is clear that unless users pay for premium membership, hence deliberately self-positioning as premium members, users are constantly reminded of the identity differentiation. Premium members enjoy ad-free dashboards, but free members have to accept three prominent advertising banners on their dashboards. The advertising banners serve as visual discursive devices to deliberately position free members as potential consumers of third-party products and services.

Busuu learners are free to complete any unit at any level to personalise their learning. When choosing a unit, learners see a third-party advertising banner sandwiched between instructions. Learners can choose to start with vocabulary, dialogue, writing, busuutalk, voice recording (premium only), review, printable learning materials or a podcast (the last two are for premium members only). The vocabulary learning is bilingual (with Spanish audio clips) and illustrated with photographs, and premium members can listen to the vocabulary item used in context. For instance, '*la cabeza*' is read aloud to all members, but the audio clip of '*Llevo un sombrero en la cabeza*' is only available to premium members. Free members have only very limited access to textual and audio learning materials in different sections. When members submit their writing exercises, they have to wait for other members to provide feedback. The busuutalk provides an instant voice chat function and members can connect with other members; however, I was never able to connect with any Spanish-speaking member during my four-week trial. All Spanish-speaking members were always 'busy', and I was urged by an automated message to keep trying. When learners join a Busuu lesson, they are positioned as part of the company's business operations first before members of a learning community as advertised on the Busuu homepage. The architecture of the website is designed to position Busuu users as consumers: either of Busuu or third-party products or services.

Positioning of language learners

Similar to other SNSs, language learners using Duolingo and Busuu can use the user profiles for identity construction by choosing from a number of options. On Duolingo, users can upload a profile picture, indicate a current location and write a micro autobiography (140 characters) (see Figure 8.3). However, all these steps are optional. On the profile page, users have a wall displaying recent activities where others can leave comments. Users can view their friends' activities and progress, and leave comments on their walls. In creating an account, a user is forced to choose a linguistic identity from established categories:

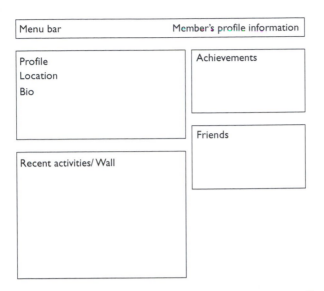

Figure 8.3 A graphic representation of a Duolingo user profile page

- I want to learn Spanish/German/French/Portuguese/Italian (I know English).
- Quiero aprender inglés (yo sé español).
- Quero aprender Inglês (eu sei Português).
- Voglio imparare inglese (io parlo italiano).
- Je veux apprendre l'anglais (je parle français).

My user profile should have been a space to construct my autobiography, but these pre-set bilingual categories do not provide any space for negotiation or questioning. Here, Duolingo's conceptualisation of bilingualism is a performative act to other position all users as only speakers of one of the five languages represented.

On Duolingo, it is almost a given that the users/learners have to come to terms with using the grammar-translation method. The question sentences are generated from online sources and, inevitably, there are a number of nonsense sentences. In cases like this, Duo users sometimes have fun making fictional scenarios out of these nonsense sentences. In a food lesson, for example, I was asked to translate *La salsiccia è nel ristorante* ('The sausage is in the restaurant'). In the Discussion section, different Duo users posted their responses:

QXQ: I wonder if the sausage is having a nice time in the restaurant, what's he eating?
portrayt: He's waiting for the mashed potato to turn up.
Elena18:   to turnip, you mean?:)

The playful attitude to nonsense can be seen across sections. When I came across *Il loro elefante beve il latte* ('Their elephant drinks milk') in a Possessive lesson, here are the comments I found:

Curlygirly: Possibly la elefante beve al stesso ristorante che dove il leone con la bistecca e Signo Salsciccia
[Possibly the elephant drinks at the same restaurant where the lion with the steak and Mr. Sausage]

Muttley71:   Forse l'elefante bevel nello stesso tesso ristorante dove c' è il leone con la bistecca e [didn't get that] :-)
(Perhaps the elephant drinks at the same restaurant where there is the lion with a steak and [didn't get that] :-))

Curlygirly: Ha ha – it is from anther question – the mysterious sentence that says 'The sausage is in the restaurant' . . . I imagined it to be a reference to a person waiting in a restaurant :)

In this thread Curlygirly responds to the question *il loro elefante beve il latte* by imagining another scenario in the same restaurant where one can find an elephant drinking milk, a sausage eating, and a lion having a steak. And Curlgirly does not use *la salsiccia* (the sausage), but the more respected form *Signo Salsciccia*, (presumably a spelling mistake of *Signor Salsciccia*, Mr Sausage). In response to her question, Muttley71 makes an attempt to understand the imagined scenario by rephrasing while correcting Curlygirly's original response. The corrections include contracting the article *la elefante* to *l'elefante* and correcting the adverb *che dove* (there where) to *dove c'è* (where there is). There are other similar playful responses to nonsense sentences. It could be argued that the question discussion section is the only space for Duo users to resist the prescribed pedagogy and is also the only space to truly communicate with other users.

On Busuu (see Figure 8.4), members have a greater number of choices when constructing user profiles: City and Country, Gender, Birthday, Occupation, Relationship status, About me and profile photograph. Free members are only allowed to upload one photo as a profile photo, but premium members can upload more photos to set up a gallery. Again, members are constantly reminded to upgrade to become premium members. On the member's profile page, three third-party advertising banners and five website promotional banners are integrated. Members can also use Busuu berries to purchase items to decorate their Busuu language garden as an alternate way to display identity.

On both websites, learners are other positioned both textually and visually. On Duolingo, the desire to learn a new language becomes a fixed bilingual identity. From a quick search, it was found that the social network features were not used much by Duo users. However, the discussion boards provided unexpected spaces for users to playfully resist the

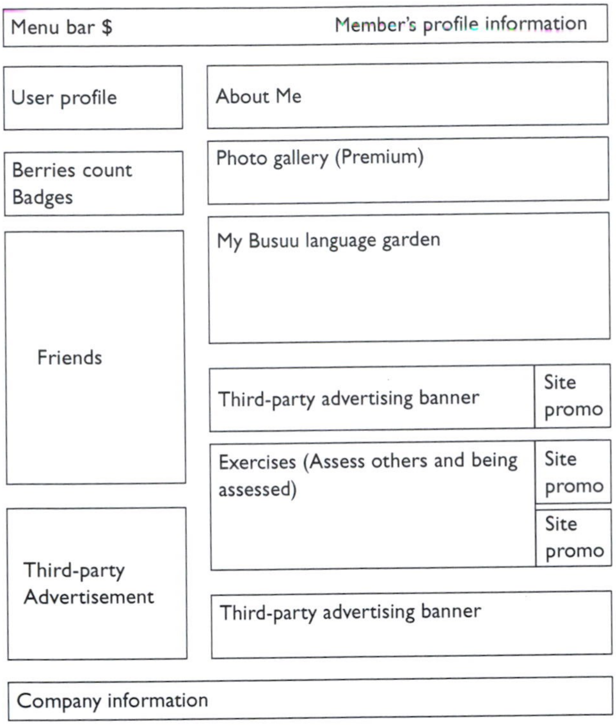

Menu bar $	Member's profile information

User profile	About Me

Berries count Badges	Photo gallery (Premium)

My Busuu language garden

Friends	

	Third-party advertising banner	Site promo
	Exercises (Assess others and being assessed)	Site promo
		Site promo

Third-party Advertisement	Third-party advertising banner

Company information

Figure 8.4 A graphic representation of a Busuu user profile page

learning materials and also connect with other playful users. On Busuu, users are first visually positioned as consumers of website premium membership and unsolicited billboards for third-party advertising. In this conversation with Busuu, there is no second order positioning for users to resist the first order positioning because there is no way out of being a target of a third-party advertising billboard other than paying for the premium membership.

Conclusion

The current scholarship on LLSNSs focuses on website usability, especially on the potential and processes of learning, and the impact of social network features on language learning. The scholarship has yet to agree on the long term benefits of using LLSNSs for language learning, but many scholars have expressed concern about classroom integration based on the quality of learning materials and potential 'dangers' of the social network features (Liu et al. 2013; Orsini-Jones et al. 2013). The alleged potential dangers include researchers' concern that some LLSNS users may use social networking features for 'flirting' or non-language learning purposes. Researchers have also pointed out the shortcomings of repetitive grammar drilling (Clark and Gruba 2010). While all of these studies have made valid contributions to our understanding of this new form of language learning, the present study has attempted to examine the discursive practices on these LLSNSs. I tried to highlight the positioning of learners through websites' claims about their pedagogical approaches, the learning activities provided, and the opportunities given to users to create profiles. Before users self-register, they are other positioned by websites to accept certain conceptualisations of foreign language learning. The discursive devices used to achieve these various positionings include both textual and other semiotic resources, like an atom model for 'scientifically proven'.

I have also argued that, though it is important to pay attention to the textual analysis, it is equally important to pay attention to other semiotic resources on the website interfaces. On a website, users are not only sensitive to the language used, they are also aware of other modes. It is not possible to ignore the golden crowns on the Busuu website, because they are everywhere. Their omnipresence is a discursive device to other position users. The space for deliberate self-positioning through profile creation on Duolingo is limited, but Duo users subvert the discussion spaces, which is intended for serious grammatical discussion, for playful and creative resistance to the rigid audio-lingual translation pedagogy.

The attention to semiotic and spatial resources should extend beyond the examination of profile pages and discussion boards. The adult participants in some studies (Orsini-Jones et al. 2013; Stevenson and Liu 2010) note that some LLSNSs employ cartoonish background colours and figures, and they wonder whether these LLSNSs were designed for adult or teenage users. The Duolingo mascot is a cartoonish green owl, who has undergone different modifications over the last year, and has become even rounder and more *kawaii*. The Busuu language garden can host a number of *Farmville*-style animals and statues. Perhaps one future direction for understanding LLSNSs is to examine the discursive practices of infantilising learners as a display of power relations. After all, am I really happy with having a shy hedgehog in my Busuu language garden?

References

Block, D. (2007) 'The rise of identity in SLA research, post Firth and Wagner (1997)', *The Modern Language Journal*, 91: 863–876.

boyd, d. and Ellison, N. B. (2007) 'Social networks: definition, history, and scholarship', *Journal of Computer-Mediated Communication*, 13(1): 210–230.

Brick, B. (2012) 'The role of social networking sites for language learning in UK higher education: the views of learners and practitioners', *International Journal of Computer-Assisted Language Learning and Teaching*, 2(3): 35–53.

Busuu (2012) 'The busuu.com Language Barometer 2012', *Busuu Blog*, 28 March. Online. Available HTTP: <http://blog.busuu.com/the-busuu-com-language-barometer-2012-results/> (accessed 12 January 2014).

Busuu (2013) 'busuu's mobile app reaches 20 million downloads', *Busuu Press Release*, 18 September. Online. Available HTTP: <http://www.busuu.com/files/press/releases/enc_20_mil_press_release_2013.pdf> (accessed 12 January 2014).

Clark, C. and Gruba, P. (2010) 'The use of social networking sites for foreign language learning: an autoethnographic study of *Livemocha*', proceedings of ASCILITE – Australian Society for Computers in Learning in Tertiary Education Annual Conference 2010, 164–173, Asclilte. Online. Available HTTP: <http://www.ascilite.org.au/conferences/sydney10/procs/Cclark-full.pdf> (accessed 15 May 2013).

Codrea-Rado, A. (2014) 'Can I successfully learn a language online', *The Guardian*, 21 February. Online. Available HTTP: <http://www.theguardian.com/education/2014/feb/21/can-i-learn-a-language-online> (accessed 23 February 2014).

Davies, B. and Harré, R. (1990) 'Positioning: the discursive production of selves', *Journal for the Theory of Social Behaviour*, 20(1): 43–63.

Ellis, C., Adams, T. E. and Bochner, A. P. (2011) 'Autoethnography: an overview', *Historical Social Research*, 36(4): 273–290.

Harré, R. (2010) 'Positioning as a metagrammar for discursive story lines', in D. Schiffrin, A. de Fina and A. Nylund (eds) *Telling Stories: language, narrative, and social life*, 51–55, Washington, DC: Georgetown University Press.

Harré, R. and van Langenhove, L. (1991) 'Varieties of positioning', *Journal for the Theory of Social Behaviour*, 21(4): 393–407.

Harrison, R. (2013) 'Profiles in social networking sites for language learning – *Livemocha* revisited', in M.-N. Lamy and K. Zourou (eds) *Social Networking for Language Education*, 100–116, Basingstoke, UK: Palgrave Macmillan.

Harrison, R. and Thomas, M. (2009) 'Identity in online communities: social networking sites and language learning', *International Journal of Emerging Technologies & Society*, 7(2): 109–124.

James, N. P. (2011) 'Busuu.com vs. Lang-8: evaluating the acquisition of the writing skills', *International Journal of Education and Development Using Information and Communication Technology*, 7(2): 78–87.

Lardinois, F. (2014) 'Duolingo raises $20M Series C led by Kleiner Perkins to dominate online language learning', *Techcrunch*, 8 February. Online. Available HTTP: <http://techcrunch.com/2014/02/18/Duolingo-raises-20m-series-c-round-led-by-kleiner-perkins-wants-to-dominate-online-language-learning/> (accessed 20 February 2014).

Littlejohn, A. (2011) 'The analysis of language teaching materials: inside the trojan horse', in B. Tomlinson (ed.) *Materials Development in Language Teaching*, 2nd edn, 190–216, Cambridge: Cambridge University Press.

Liu, M., Evans, M. K., Horwitz, E., Lee, S., McCrory, M., Park, J.-B. and Parrish, C. (2013) 'A study of the use of social network sites for language learning by university ESL students', in M.-N. Lamy and K. Zourou (eds) *Social Networking for Language Education*, 137–157, Basingstoke, UK: Palgrave Macmillan.

Lloyd, E. (2012) 'Language learners' "willingness to communicate" through *Livemocha.com*', in F. Demaizière and K. Zourou (eds) 'Social media and language learning: (R)evolution?', *Apprentissage des Langues et Systèmes d'Information et de Communication*, 15(1). Online. Available HTTP: <http://alsic.revues.org/2437> (accessed 25 March 2014).

McNamara, T. (2013) 'Crossing boundaries: journeys into language', *Language and Intercultural Communication*, 13(3): 343–356.

Orsini-Jones, M., Brick, B. and Pibworth, L. (2013) 'Practising language interaction via social networking sites: the expert student's perspective on personalized language learning', in B. Zou, M. Xing, Y. Wang, M. Sun and C. H. Xiang (eds) *Computer-assisted Foreign Language Teaching and Learning: technological advances*, 40–53, Philadelphia, PA: IGI Global.

Pinter, A. (2006) *Teaching Young Language Learners*, Oxford: Oxford University Press.

Stevenson, M. P. and Liu, M. (2010) 'Learning a language with Web 2.0: exploring the use of social networking features of foreign language learning websites', *CALICO Journal*, 27(2): 233–259.

Tomlinson, B. (2012) 'Materials development for language learning and teaching', *Language Teaching*, 45(2): 143–179.

van Langenhove, L. and Bertolink, R. (1999) 'Positioning and assessment of technology', in R. Harré and L. van Langenhove (eds) *Positioning Theory: moral contexts of intentional action*, 116–126, Oxford: Blackwell.

Vesselinov, R. and Grego, J. (2012) 'Duolingo effectiveness study: final report', *Duolingo*. Online. Available HTTP: <http://static.duolingo.com/s3/DuolingoReport_Final.pdf> (accessed 15 April 2013).

von Ahn, L. (2013) 'Duolingo now translating BuzzFeed and CNN', *Duolingo Blog*, 14 October. Online. Available HTTP: <http://blog.duolingo.com/post/64024962586/duolingo-now-translating-buzzfeed-and-cnn> (accessed 21 March 2014).

Zourou, K. (2012) 'On the attractiveness of social media for language learning: a look at the state of the art', in F. Demaizière and K. Zourou (eds) 'Social media and language learning: (R)evolution?', *Apprentissage des Langues et Systèmes d'Information et de Communication*, 15(1). Online. Available HTTP: <http://alsic.revues.org/2436> (accessed 30 June 2014).

Zourou, K. and Lamy, M.-N. (2013) 'Introduction', in M.-N. Lamy and K. Zourou (eds) *Social Networking for Language Education*, 1–7, Basingstoke, UK: Palgrave Macmillan.

Chapter 9

Investigating digital sex talk practices

A reflection on corpus-assisted discourse analysis

Brian W. King

> [C]omputer-assisted text analysis [is] an activity best employed not in the service of a heightened critical objectivity, but as one that embraces the possibilities of that deepened subjectivity upon which critical insight depends.
>
> (Ramsay 2003)

Corpus-assisted discourse analysis (CADA) is an approach that is used either on its own or in support of other forms of discourse analysis (Baker 2010). It takes lexical markers (i.e. words and phrases) as its focus, deploying computer software to count and compare these markers in order to learn more about the discourses of which they are a part. To the uninitiated, CADA and research on digital practices would appear to be a perfect match because data is generally pre-digitised, with no transcription required (two processes which vex corpus compilers of printed text and spoken discourse). But as I have explored elsewhere (see King 2009), CADA itself has both affordances and constraints in relation to data, people and practices in digital research, and this reality produces formidable challenges for corpus compilation and analysis. Here these points will be reviewed and updated, but with a shift in focus towards the practice orientation of this volume (see also Jones 2013; Norris and Jones 2005; Scollon 2001), which will permit a more direct focus on things that participants and researcher are using language to *do*. That is, rather than framing chat room discourse strictly as text, I will frame it as one component of a set of digital practices.

Towards such a framing, I will structure this chapter as a retrospective of an investigation into chat room discourse. In place of a tidy narrative, I aim to open a portal into the 'messiness' of a multi-stage process of getting started with corpus compilation and using CADA to identify 'sex talk' as a potential practice of interest in these chat rooms. In other words, when talk about sex emerges in chat rooms, what is being *done with* such talk? By placing the social actor at the centre, and making practices the unit of analysis (Scollon 2001), new insights into 'sex talk' online can be gained. In line with the spirit of this volume, I will highlight the ways in which digital practices have shaped my use of CADA methodology and how CADA has provided distinctive tools for the investigation of digital practices. The insights gained from this process have prompted me to reflect on the quotation which heads this chapter in which Ramsay (2003) questions the purposes for which analysts of texts might want to deploy computer assistance. For although CADA (as a computer-assisted methodology) can indeed at times provide a useful level of critical objectivity during discourse analysis, what emerges in this study is the perhaps higher level importance of another affordance that CADA provides; what Ramsay refers to as '*deepened subjectivity*'.

Practices

In this chapter I align to a view (compatible with this volume) in which 'practice' is viewed in countable form, as 'practices'. In other words digital chat is framed as a series or 'nexus' of specific practices which come together to create a recognisable sequence of events (Gee 1999; Gee et al. 1996; cited in Scollon 2001). Practices in this sense are actions that have become internalised as dispositions (Norris 2011: 36); that is, they have become part of a set of routine actions which have come to be taken for granted by certain people in certain situations (at least most of the time). But rather than being abstract and difficult to label or pin down (as practice in the abstract can be), they are material actions and can therefore be 'clearly defined' (Norris and Jones 2005: 98) making them more readily analysable. This view of practices applies to research practices as much as chatting practices. In this study the data is drawn from a corpus of online chatting transcripts.

Digital data

The corpus that forms the basis of this study was compiled by me (see King 2009 for details), and I refer to it as the Queer Chatroom Corpus. I became interested in investigating 'sex talk' in this body of data upon noticing that there are abundant lexical markers in it that point to sex in some way. I came to this realisation upon creating word lists from it, an exercise in which software (in this case Wordsmith Tools) is used to create a list of all the words in the corpus in order of frequency counts. While examining this list, numerous sex-related words caught my attention, and these included items that refer to sexual acts as well as sexualised body parts (i.e. foci of sexual attraction) and appearance. These particular lexical items serve as 'traces' of the discourses used during talk about sex (Baker 2010: 123) and therefore it follows that they also serve as traces of situated digital practices which people perform using those discourses (see Jones, Chik and

Hafner, this volume). Thus I resolved to count and analyse the use of these markers in order to determine what the participants were doing with them. What types of sexual practices were these participants at least sometimes demonstrating?

The vast majority of the markers occurred as *hapax legomena*, or words found only once in a given corpus. Being so rare in the data, these words are often ignored during corpus analysis because it is impossible to produce any statistically significant results on them individually. However, they may prove useful when categorised carefully, grouping them based on the ways they are used in discourse (Baker 2004: 352–353). This is one reason that I resolved to bundle them together and focus on analysing each resulting word category. Another reason was that in the process of forming these word categories I first became aware of some rather basic ways in which digital practices affect the methods of CADA, and word categorisation provided solutions to these problems.

Word categorisation in corpus study is often done using tagging software which automatically goes through the corpus and 'tags' the lexical items based on semantic categories (Baker 2006). Unfolding in real time, however, text-only chat conversations give rise to certain digital practices which pose challenges for the software. Certain typographical practices, for example word truncation (abbreviations) and 'cyber-orthography' (Al-Sa' Di and Hamdan 2005), greatly limit the effectiveness of this type of software, and so I was forced to carry out a manual analysis and group the words into categories by hand (for details see King 2009). Tables 9.1 and 9.2 (below) outline the types included in the word categories *Sexual Parts* and *Sexual Acts*.

Table 9.1 Sexual Parts

arse	bod	butt	erection	hole	meaty	nuts	shoulders
arsehole	body	chest	fur	hot	muscle	penis	stud
ass	bone	cock	genitals	hung	muscular	pole	sweat
asshole	boner	crack	goodlookin	hunk	naked	privates	thick
balls	bubble	dick	hairy	inches	nipple	pubes	tight
big	bum	erect	handsome	meat	nude	rump	tongue

Table 9.2 Sexual Acts

bang	cum	fuck	kinky	pig	root	spank	threeway
beat	cybering	grope	kiss	poke	scat	strip	top
blow	desperate	hard	laid	pork	screw	stroke	versatile
blowjob	dildo	horny	lick	pound	sexy	suck	virgin
bottom	drool	hump	masturbate	quickie	shag	swallow	wank
camming	fetish	jack	oral	ram	smooch	tease	whip
cruise	fisting	jerk	orgy	rim	snuggle	threesome	

The words sit out of context in the word list, so in order to more accurately determine which tokens (i.e. instances of each type) should be included in the counts, I searched for the words and read portions of the original conversations surrounding these words to clarify their meanings in use. During this process, numerous tokens were identified as false positives (i.e. mistaken matches), and I removed them from frequency counts. As Baker (2014: 51) points out, reading the original corpus text is a reliable but burdensome method of identifying sometimes elusive interactional phenomena. This corpus reading process also prompted me to notice false negatives (i.e. missed sexual connotations) that had at first escaped my attention when I examined the word list (e.g. 'fun' as a euphemism for sex, or adjectives that sexualise body parts as in 'hot arms'). Doubtless some subtle sexual connotations will still have been missed, but by adapting CADA methodology and using a combination of reading and automatic corpus searches, I can confidently assert that I have come much closer to 'full recall' of types and tokens for the word categories than would have been possible with one approach used in isolation (see also Baker 2014: 71).

Thus I hope it is clear by now that certain digital typographical practices force the CADA analyst to spend considerable time adapting chat transcripts for inclusion in a corpus. Without this level of care and attention, there would be too many missed instances of the word categories which could potentially lead to a partial picture of the data. Before continuing with analysis, I would first like to address the ways in which practices of digital research require adaptations in terms of digital research *ethics*.

Digital people

Corpus linguistic research certainly has its own established ethical codes (see Baker 2010; Kennedy 1998), but there tend to be different sets of criteria applied to already published written documents versus transcribed samples of spoken discourse. Print that has already been published requires publisher permissions due to copyright, and with recordings of spoken conversation, written informed consent is the established practice. But online discourse that is copied and saved from a publicly available chat room is a form of ephemeral interactive writing that falls somewhere in a cline between published writing and recorded spoken conversation. This ambiguity has led to considerable disagreement amongst digital research practitioners in general about the levels of ethical caution required when studying it. To apply offline ethical practices to corpus-assisted research of digital practices is not a straightforward enterprise, for the internet is not a direct spatial reflection of the offline world (Bassett and O'Riordan 2002). For example, chat room communication is neither inherently public nor private; rather it depends on how each participant sees the context of communication (Lawson 2004; Nissenbaum 2009). For this reason, seeking informed consent is a way to discover how participants feel about that context. Additionally, as Zimmer (2010) has stressed, those who participate in computer-mediated communication likely do not imagine that their words will be taken to another public domain for display there, domains such as corpora and academic reports (or book chapters). Therefore to do so without permission can be considered an affront to their dignity and a violation of privacy. For these reasons I resolved to approach all of the 1,332 participants in the corpus and get their permission for their words to be included (for a full breakdown of participant characteristics, please refer to King 2009).

Even if one resolves to pursue such a course of action, however, obtaining informed consent online can be intensely difficult because of participant anonymity. Fortunately, the nature of the portal site where the data for the present study were gathered allows for communication with anonymous participants via email, and in this way it was possible to contact the participants and secure informed consent, albeit a rather altered form of it. In short, participants were emailed and told that their conversations in the main ('public') chat room had already been saved to my hard drive, and the participants were then directed to another website (accessible strictly by invitation and only to those who might potentially have viewed those conversations in the first place) where they could peruse these saved transcripts and request deletions or the complete withdrawal of all their contributions (see King 2009). They were told that a null response would indicate consent, and this was done as a way of permitting them to remain anonymous if that is what they desired. This arrangement acknowledged that even though that chatting was done in 'public', it was only intended for a *certain* public – the men who seek out those chat spaces, register a nickname, and spend time chatting there.

One final point applies to cyber-research more generally, but deserves mention here. It has been argued by some that in spite of any perceived differences between offline and online inquiry, researchers need to maintain the standards of their field (e.g. D'Arcy and Young 2012). This is a pertinent observation when one considers the researcher's ethical obligations not just to participants, but to other researchers. To treat digital data as inherently public and freely available, and to gather data with impunity, is to risk 'poisoning the well' for future researchers. As Chen et al. (2004) have emphasised, to behave like online research 'paparazzi' with our metaphorical cameras in everyone's digital faces is ultimately likely to be counter-productive on top of being disruptive to digital communities and relationships. Therefore I would like to argue that proceeding with CADA in the face of the difficulties previously mentioned does indeed necessitate some creativity and adaptation. By adapting CADA to the digital practices of chat room discourse (as distinct from either print data or transcripts of spoken discourse), corpus compilation and subsequent analysis becomes plausible.

Digital practices

After adjusting for digital data and the challenges of informed consent, the corpus could in fact be compiled and prepared and analysis could fully proceed. In any investigation of discourse one must start somewhere, and in this case I resolved to begin by counting the incidences of each word category to gain a more detailed picture of who uses it and how often. The location of the participants (USA or Australia) and age (over forty or under forty) served as variables in this study rather than numerous other quite valid alternatives. Historical accounts place a shift in dominant attitudes towards gay identities around the late 1980s and early 1990s, a time when those born in the late 1960s were reaching adulthood (see Reynolds 2002). Many older ways of doing gay identity came under criticism at that time, suggesting that those born in the mid-1960s (i.e. age forty in 2005, the year of corpus construction) might have 'come out' in a different social climate than those born before, potentially resulting in differences in language use. The age split at forty was settled on because it also allows for a more even total word count of data across the participant categories. In terms of location, the USA and Australia were chosen so as to include one country from North America and one from elsewhere, and there were abundant data available for these two countries. Once the variables had been chosen, it was time to find out which type of participant was using each word category and how often. I would like to re-emphasise that my goal with such counting was not simply to pursue objectivity or to impose any kind of essentialist reading of these people or the language they were using. Although a certain level of objectivity is added by this 'who and how often' information, the value added is slight, and my main interest was to enable a deeper subjective and interpretive view of the data.

Discerning practices

To facilitate analysis, all tokens (i.e. incidences of a word, or 'type') in each category were tagged with the category name (e.g. Sexual Parts) so that the Wordsmith Tools software could identify which tokens should be counted as part of each category. The software was then used to make raw frequency counts, and the counts were then run through Rayson's (2008) online Log-Likelihood Calculator (cf. King 2009). That is, word counts of each word category were recorded for four different participant groupings (US+40, US-40, AU+40, AU-40) and for each grouping I recorded the total number of all words that those participants had contributed to the corpus. These numbers were entered into the calculator in order to determine whether some explanation other than chance would explain the results. Log-likelihood is a calculation put forward by Dunning (1993) as an alternative to the chi-square test when using smaller data sets, and it has been used by

Baker (2005) and Meyer (2002) amongst others. Rayson (2008) provides a detailed explanation of how the log-likelihood test is conducted mathematically, but I decided to trust the calculator's results (cf. King 2009). In order to reliably uncover patterns of similarity and difference in the frequency of the two word categories, four 'null hypotheses' needed to be either rejected or accepted (see Table 9.3). In other words, the participant groupings needed to be compared, one to each of the others, so as to determine whether any differences in frequency were statistically significant. Table 9.3 contains the results for the category Sexual Parts.

Table 9.3 reveals, following statistical analysis, that null hypotheses 1 and 3 must be rejected because there is a higher frequency of Sexual Part terms in the US+40 sub-group and this variation cannot be attributed to chance. It is clear that Americans in the corpus who are over forty used this word category more often than all of the other sub-groups did, with analysis demonstrating that any differences in frequency between the other sub-groups are chance results. For this study, the probability (p) that a difference is merely a chance result must be less than 1 per cent (i.e. $p < 0.01$) to be judged adequately significant. One per cent is a commonly cited cut-off point in corpus linguistic study, while $p < 0.001$ is widely considered to constitute high significance (Oakes 1998). Table 9.4 summarises the results of the same procedure for Sexual Acts as a category.

Table 9.3 Null hypotheses for Sexual Parts (locality and age)

Null hypothesis		Result
1	Differences in the *frequency of Sexual Parts* between *AU over 40 and US over 40* are a result of chance.	Rejected (strong)
2	Differences in the *frequency of Sexual Parts* between *AU under 40 and US under 40* are a result of chance.	Accepted
3	Differences in the *frequency of Sexual Parts* between *US over 40 and US under 40* are a result of chance.	Rejected (strong)
4	Differences in the *frequency of Sexual Parts* between *AU over 40 and AU under 40* are a result of chance.	Accepted

Table 9.4 Null hypotheses for Sexual Acts (locality and age)

Null hypothesis		Result
1	Differences in the *frequency of Sexual Acts* between *AU over 40 and US over 40* are a result of chance.	Accepted
2	Differences in the *frequency of Sexual Acts* between *AU under 40 and US under 40* are a result of chance.	Rejected (strong)
3	Differences in the *frequency of Sexual Acts* between *US over 40 and US under 40* are a result of chance.	Accepted
4	Differences in the *frequency of Sexual Acts* between *AU over 40 and AU under 40* are a result of chance.	Rejected (weak)

In this case the younger Australians in this corpus clearly used terms for Sexual Acts significantly more frequently than the other participants, but once again we can see that all of the groups have in fact been documented making use of the category. It is important to give similarities and differences equal emphasis because it is all too easy to fall in line with an existing cognitive bias in corpus research towards finding patterns and difference (Taylor 2013) and thus relegating findings of similarity to 'the bottom drawer' (cf. Baker 2010). Although it is definitely noteworthy (and perhaps worthy of further investigation) that there are differences in frequency, what is much more interesting to me is that members of every participant category can be found using either word category from time to time. The question then arises of what practices these markers are entailed in, and this will be the focus of the subsequent section. But first a word about what this word category frequency analysis has offered us.

We see that online sex talk forms part of the repertoire of chatter in these rooms regardless of users' age or whether they are in Australia or the USA. This presence of sexual language in public online chat rooms for gay men might or might not match the expectations of various readers, but at least the case can be made that it is not used only by a few individual participants or by one type of participant. By undertaking this counting process, one which demands a large investment of time and effort, the researcher can indeed manage to 'query "the who" plus "the when" and "the how often" on a larger scale than purely qualitative studies allow' (King 2009: 305). As stated earlier in the chapter, however, the purpose here is not so much to claim greater critical *objectivity*, but rather to enable the researcher to see the data at a *deeper subjective level*, thus enabling greater critical insight. Also, to stop at this point would be to risk reifying these researcher-compiled word categories. These findings conceal the fact that numerous highly specific terms are bundled into each word category and although it is useful for one purpose, this bundling erases each term's specific nuances of usage. It also tells us nothing about what 'work' this language is doing during social interaction as part of certain practices. Therefore, to be maximally useful, frequency counts of word categories must be combined with an analysis of how words are used in practice. It is at this stage of analysis that CADA truly reveals its affordances as a tool for critical insight.

Investigating act(ion)s and practices

The corpus-assisted investigation of practices is an important step towards even more fine-grained discourse analysis in which discourse in use can be analysed. As a first step towards identifying practices, a coding scheme was created using hypothesis testing (Hunston 2002), in which the corpus researcher views a small set of randomly selected lines in order to hypothesise about larger patterns and subsequently test those hypotheses. Sinclair

(1999) advocates selecting thirty random concordance lines, observing the patterns in them, and then doing it again until no new patterns emerge. During the process of hypothesis testing, it began to become clear that the two word categories were not in fact entailed in 'sexual' practices for the most part. Instead, the coding scheme that emerged contained a wide variety of other kinds of practices that I grouped into eight codes. Table 9.5 is a summary of the coding scheme with examples from the source texts.

Some of these practices entail *discourse prosodies* (Baker 2010), that is they contain elements which show connections of *attitude* between language and social actors (Baker 2005: 33; Stubbs 2002: 65). Attitudes and connotations are often built up over large sections of interaction and can be put into words in many ways. We intuitively recognise practices (e.g. compliments) because of the entailed lower level actions which make up the nexus of practices 'complimenting' (Scollon 2001) and in fact it is because I, as analyst, have internalised these entailed actions that I am able to identify a practice as a compliment. Once again, this identification was thus a subjective process, but as Hunston (2002: 23) observes, intuition is invariably called upon in corpus study and it is this continual interpretive need that has prompted the realisation that CADA is most useful to me as a tool for getting a particular *subjective* view of data as opposed to an objective one.

In this particular analysis I randomly selected 120 incidences of each word category per group and used these markers as the basis for examining

Table 9.5 Sexual Parts/Acts – practice coding scheme

	Practice codes	Examples
1	Joking & Horseplay	'With all this talk of cocks and balls, I'll never be able to sleep!'
		***john1764 jumps *southjock* and rips his shirt from his hot chest
2	Discussing Habits & Preferences	'I like hairy butts myself'
		'I usually prefer being top myself but flexible for the right man'
3	Sexual Soliciting & Offering	'Bi guy downtown, hot bod, seeks stud with hot ass 4 fun'
		'Since retirin I havnt fucked but in your case I'd make an exception'
4	Greetings	'Hey john, what's up' (gives john a wet kiss and a gentle grope)
5	Complimenting & Flattering	'Man, you have a great ass, my friend … WOOF … nice photo!'
6	Gossiping & Griping	'He rejected me but then I found out he hasn't even got 3 inches'
		'I had a threesome this weekend, yusss'
7	Insulting & Attacking	'Gotta grow your cock 5 inches b4 u can talk, you skank.'
8	Fantasy/Story Sharing	'I wanna walk up to a guy in the gym and touch his ass'

*** This kind of 'stage direction' shows motion, and is often accompanied by asterisks (Werry 2004).

which practices each category was entailed in. As can be seen in Table 9.6, this approach permits the analyst to view and compare the *proportions* of each practice for each variable. The raw frequency counting and statistical analysis used in the previous section cannot be fruitfully applied here because of the very small numbers involved, but this alternative approach still affords some insight into who is doing what and how often. This is important because these counts further demonstrate that the vast majority of tokens of these sexual word categories are entailed in practices that

Table 9.6 Sexual Parts/Acts – actions by corpus (raw counts)

Sexual Parts

US+40	US-40	AU+40	AU-40
Joking & Horseplay (38)	Joking & Horseplay (62)	Joking & Horseplay (46)	Joking & Horseplay (58)
Compliments/ Flattery (35)	Compliments/ Flattery (14)	Fantasy/Story Sharing (26)	Compliments/Flattery (19)
Discussing Habits/ Preferences (18)	Soliciting/Offering (12)	Compliments/ Flattery (19)	Fantasy/Story Sharing (16)
Soliciting/Offering (13)	Discussing Habits/ Preferences (9)	Discussing Habits/ Preferences (11)	Soliciting/Offering (13)
Greeting (5)	Insulting/Attacking (9)	Soliciting/ Advertising (8)	Greeting (7)
Fantasy/Story Sharing (4)	Fantasy/Story Sharing (5)	Greeting (3)	Discussing Habits/ Preferences (3)
Gossiping/Griping (1)	Greeting (4)	Gossiping/Griping (3)	Gossiping/Griping (1)
Insulting/Attacking (0)	Gossiping/Griping (1)	Insulting/Attacking (1)	Insulting/Attacking (1)

Sexual Acts

US+40	US-40	AU+40	AU-40
Joking & Horseplay (58)	Joking & Horseplay (48)	Joking & Horseplay (42)	Joking & Horseplay (43)
Discussing Habits/ Preferences (25)	Discussing Habits/ Preferences (26)	Discussing Habits/ Preferences (33)	Discussing Habits/ Preferences (23)
Soliciting/Offering (15)	Gossiping/Griping (20)	Soliciting/Offering (12)	Soliciting/Offering (21)
Greeting (9)	Soliciting/Offering (11)	Gossiping/Griping (11)	Gossiping/Griping (13)
Compliments/ Flattery (7)	Compliments/ Flattery (6)	Greeting (11)	Fantasy/Story Sharing (9)
Gossiping/Griping (6)	Greeting (5)	Fantasy/Story Sharing (9)	Greeting (5)
Fantasy/Story Sharing (0)	Fantasy/Story Sharing (4)	Compliments/ Flattery (2)	Insulting/Attacking (5)
Insulting/Attacking (0)	Insulting/Attacking (0)	Insulting/Attacking (0)	Compliments/Flattery (1)

are not particularly sexual but rather more general social practices such as joking and 'horsing around' (see King 2011), flattering each other, and giving compliments.

Once again, similarity is the most notable pattern here. Sexual Part terms are used across participant categories to flatter and compliment, and Sexual Act terms are likewise widely used when discussing sexual habits and preferences and to solicit sex from others (or offer it) but not in an overtly joking way. Moving one's eyes down each list reveals that for the most part there is little variation in the counts or the sequence. Two possible exceptions are Sexual Part terms as part of fantasy/story sharing for younger Australian participants and Sexual Act terms as used in gossiping and griping for the younger Americans. Closer examination of the transcripts would perhaps reveal explanations for this difference. However, most importantly, the results suggest that although sexualised practices are part of the mix, these 'public' chat rooms are predominantly places to socialise rather than places to take part in cyber-sex. They are places where talk *about* sex occurs now and then, accompanied by flirtations and advances, but for the most part the sexualised terms identified in the first stage of the study serve as aspects of relational practices. A more fine-grained analysis of transcripts would be the logical next step, and in fact some closer discourse analysis has been done of these actions as part of other studies (see King 2011, 2012).

Conclusion

To summarise, the word categories for this study and the practices they are deployed in were found through a combination of computer analysis and researcher observation. This approach allowed for the fruitful grouping of rare (and less rare) words into categories that perform similar functions in the data. It also allowed for the observation of actions and discursive patterns that neither the computer software nor a human observer could easily have reached independently (see also Baker 2014). Having identified some specific digital practices that the identified word categories were being used to perform, the analyst can undertake a more fine-grained analysis to learn more about precisely how these practices are done using language. So although digital data forces considerable adaptation of corpus-assisted methods (in order to deal with cyber-orthography and the particular ethical concerns of cyber-research), its tools combine well with discourse analysis for the examination of online chat.

I prefaced this chapter with a quotation from Stephen Ramsay in which he emphasises that computer algorithms, as a critical analysis tool, need not index objectivity and positivism. Speaking of the use of computer algorithms as a tool in literary criticism, Ramsay (2003: 173) further states that one would not ask how the ends of interpretation were or were not justified by means of the algorithms imposed, but rather, how successful the algorithms were in provoking thought and allowing insight.

I interpret this to mean that computer-assisted analysis should not strive to empirically *validate* critical analysis done by the human analyst (and thus mediated by other means such as language). I would like to argue that this same observation can apply to CADA, for social constructionist inspired discourse analysis aims to gain insight into social practices through considered *impressions* of data, not through 'proofs' of one right answer or a set of them (Baker 2009). Thus I hope that this study has begun to engage with the challenge in CADA of 'rethinking digital tools on basic principles of the humanities' (Drucker 2011) as opposed to suspending what we know about the sociology of knowledge production.

Thus it follows that the CA (i.e. corpus-assisted) can sit comfortably with the DA (i.e. discourse analysis) when CADA is framed as a set of research practices that works towards critical insight via 'deepened subjectivity' as much as (or perhaps more than) objectivity. I would like to propose that the case explored in this chapter is an instructive example of how to use corpus-assisted analysis to gain deeper qualitative critical insights into digital practices. By starting with a word list that produced items which caught my attention as sexual, CADA methodology permitted me to recall the vast majority of these items from the corpus and thereby to see the array of practices such terms were entailed in and the relative frequencies of each one in the corpus. As observed earlier, few of these practices were in fact 'sexual practices' in the end. What has been achieved here via CADA is arguably not centrally an objective result; rather it is a deeper subjective insight into language practices in these digital chat rooms, a fruitful result for scholars committed to critical social constructionist investigation.

References

Al-Sa' Di, R. A. and Hamdan, J. M. (2005) '"Synchronous online chat" English: computer-mediated communication', *World Englishes*, 24(4): 409–424.
Baker, P. (2004) 'Querying keywords: questions of difference, frequency and sense in keywords analysis', *Journal of English Linguistics*, 32(4): 346–359.
Baker, P. (2005) *Public Discourses of Gay Men*, New York: Routledge.
Baker, P. (2006) *Using Corpora in Discourse Analysis*, London: Continuum.
Baker, P. (2009) 'Issues arising when teaching corpus-assisted (critical) discourse analysis', in L. Lombardo (ed.) *Using Corpora to Learn about Language and Discourse*, 73–98, Bern: Peter Lang.
Baker, P. (2010) *Sociolinguistics and Corpus Linguistics*, Edinburgh: Edinburgh University Press.
Baker, P. (2014) *Using Corpora to Analyze Gender*, London: Bloomsbury.

Bassett, E. H. and O'Riordan, K. (2002) 'Ethics of internet research: contesting the human subjects research model', *Ethics and Information Technology*, 4(2): 233–247.

Chen, S. L. S, Hall, G. J. and Johns, M. D. (2004) 'Research paparazzi in cyberspace: the voices of the researched', in M. D. Johns, S. L. S. Chen and G. J. Hall (eds) *Online Social Research: Methods, Issues, and Ethics*, 157–175, New York: Peter Lang.

D'Arcy, A. and Young, T. M. (2012) 'Ethics and social media: implications for sociolinguistics in the networked public', *Journal of Sociolinguistics*, 16(4): 532–546.

Drucker, J. (2011) 'Humanities approaches to graphical display', *Digital Humanities Quarterly*, 5(1): n.p.

Dunning, T. (1993) 'Accurate methods for the statistics of surprise and coincidence', *Computational Linguistics*, 19(1): 61–74.

Gee, J. P. (1999) *An Introduction to Discourse Analysis: theory and method*, London: Routledge.

Gee, J. P., Hull, G. and Lankshear, C. (1996) *The New Work Order: behind the language of the new capitalism*, Boulder, CO: Westview Press.

Hunston, S. (2002) *Corpora in Applied Linguistics*, Cambridge: Cambridge University Press.

Jones, R. H. (2013) 'Discourse in action', in C. A. Chapelle (ed.) *Encyclopedia of Applied Linguistics*, London: Wiley-Blackwell.

Kennedy, G. (1998) *An Introduction to Corpus Linguistics*, London: Longman.

King, B. W. (2009) 'Building and analysing corpora of computer-mediated communication', in P. Baker (ed.) *Contemporary Corpus Linguistics*, 301–320, London: Continuum.

King, B. W. (2011) 'Language, sexuality and place: the view from cyberspace', *Gender and Language*, 5(1): 1–30.

King, B. W. (2012) 'Location, lore and language: an erotic triangle', *Journal of Language and Sexuality*, 1(1): 106–125.

Lawson, D. (2004) 'Blurring the boundaries: ethical considerations for online research using synchronous CMC forums', in E. R. Buchanan (ed.) *Readings in Virtual Research Ethics: issues and controversies*, 80–100, Hershey, PA: Information Science Publishing.

Meyer, C. F. (2002) *English Corpus Linguistics: an introduction*, Cambridge: Cambridge University Press.

Nissenbaum, H. (2009) *Privacy in Context: technology, policy, and the integrity of social life*, Stanford, CA: Stanford University Press.

Norris, S. (2011) *Identity in (Inter)action: introducing multimodal interaction analysis*, Berlin: Mouton de Gruyter.

Norris, S. and Jones, R. H. (2005) *Discourse in Action*, London: Routledge.

Oakes, M. P. (1998) *Statistics for Corpus Linguistics*, Edinburgh: Edinburgh University Press.

Ramsay, S. (2003) 'Toward an algorithmic criticism', *Literary and Linguistic Computing*, 18(2): 167–174.

Rayson, P. (2008) 'Log-likelihood calculator', *UCREL web server*. Online. Available HTTP: <http://ucrel.lancs.ac.uk/llwizard.html> (accessed 4 May 2014).

Reynolds, R. (2002) *From Camp to Queer: remaking the Australian homosexual*, Carlton South, Australia: Melbourne University Press.

Scollon, R. (2001) 'Action and text: towards an integrated understanding of the place of text in social (inter)action, mediated discourse analysis and the problem of social action', in R. Wodak and M. Meyer (eds) *Methods of Critical Discourse Analysis*, 139–183, London: Sage.

Sinclair, J. (1999) 'A way with common words', in H. Hasselgard and S. Oksefjell (eds) *Out of Corpora: studies in honour of Stig Johansson*, 157–179, Amsterdam: Rodopi.

Stubbs, M. (2002) *Words and Phrases*, Oxford: Blackwell.

Taylor, C. (2013) 'Searching for similarity using corpus-assisted discourse studies', *Corpora*, 8(1): 81–113.

Werry, C. C. (2004) 'Linguistic and interactional features of internet relay chat', in G, Sampson and D. McCarthy (eds) *Corpus Linguistics: readings in a widening discipline*, 340–352, London: Continuum.

Zimmer, M. (2010) '"But the data is already public": on the ethics of research on Facebook', *Ethics and Information Technology*, 12(4): 313–325.

Chapter 10

Apps, adults and young children

Researching digital literacy practices in context

Guy Merchant

The widespread availability of portable digital devices, such as the iPad, has led to the tablet outstripping earlier technologies in terms of its impact on early childhood. In many households, iPads have become the device of choice for family entertainment, being used, amongst other things, for on-demand TV, games and interactive stories. Early literacy practices have fallen under the sway of the iPad, which appeals to young children because of its size, weight, portability and intuitive touch screen interface (Merchant 2014). As a result of this, and a whole host of other environmental factors, literacy development for many children born in the twenty-first century has come to be infused with digital technology. This raises important issues for parents, carers and educators. For a start the commercial and economic stakes are high. But also there are some crucially important questions about learning and development that educators are only just beginning to consider. Indeed, early childhood literacy is beginning to look rather different from how it did in the past, and since various forms of semiotic representation and patterns of interaction are distinctive to new media, there may well be a need to re-draw our maps of literacy development.

How we think about technologically mediated literacy practices and how we go about investigating them are pressing questions in an era typified by the rapid diffusion of mobile devices. Observing the ways in which the mobile is 'subtly insinuating itself into the capillaries of everyday life' (Gergen 2003: 103) draws attention to how social groups and communities take up the affordances of the technology and make them work to fulfil their diverse needs and purposes, whether this takes the form of new expressions of activism (McCaughey and Ayers 2013), social enterprise (Donner 2006), or financial transaction (Morawczynski 2009). And the same is true for the everyday social interactions between partners and friends, parents and siblings, families and interest groups which are often, to a greater or lesser extent, transacted through digital media such as Facebook, Instagram, Skype and instant messaging. As a result, the ways in which literacy, technology and everyday social practice are interwoven is deserving of attention in the current climate of rapid change.

Early experiences of literacy are embedded in this wider context, and in what follows I sketch out some of the theoretical and methodological concerns that emerge from a study of the use of iPad apps conducted in two early education centres in the north of England. In doing this I work at the intersection between literacy studies and educational practice, producing an account of how we might make sense of the embodied, material, and situated experiences that are produced when hardware and software with 'global' circulation is taken up in particular local settings as part of the day-to-day lives of young children and their adult carers. This account reaches down into the detail of young children's lives and literacies, but also up into the broader context of changing literacies – changes that have involved shifts in the object of study, as these literacies themselves mutate and diversify. As we know, how we describe and define literacy, and ultimately what counts as literate behaviour is inseparable from its context – and that context, as outlined above, is rapidly changing. Furthermore, marked changes in the communicative context suggest that literacies are increasingly multiple, multimodal, mobile, and mediated by new technology.

In beginning to develop productive accounts of literacy practices in this changing situation it quickly becomes apparent that existing approaches, such as those informed by ethnography, multimodal discourse analysis and media studies, provide tools that need to be combined, recombined and creatively deployed in order to capture the richness of digital communication (Flewitt 2011). If this endeavour is to be successful, research approaches need to be sensitive to key areas that relate to specific contexts, technologies and practices.

The approach I adopt begins with a descriptive narrative approach that accounts for some of the wider influences that frame the interactions observed. This acknowledges the complex and multiple forces associated with the distribution of the technologies themselves and the texts they mediate (touch screen devices, popular children's stories, games and so on). Embedded within this is a finer grain analysis of how apps, adults and infants work together as the iPad enters what Schatzki (2005) refers to as the mesh of practices and material arrangements that constitute the institutional setting. To construct a microanalysis of these interactions I draw on the literature on gesture, touch and pointing (e.g. Clark 2003; Kendon 2004; McNeill 2000), and recent work on haptics (Minogue and Jones 2006) in order to underscore the ways in which the iPad is positioned within adult–child interaction as a 'thing in use', thus becoming absorbed into routines of educational practice.

Building on the ways in which early years researchers such as Flewitt et al. (2009), Wohlwend (2009) and Taylor (2010) have used multimodal discourse analysis, my approach highlights the material interactions that take place between people and things, by identifying the ways in which the smallest of actions contribute to the ways in which meaning is created through action in social settings (Scollon 2001). In some ways this has parallels with the work of Norris (2012) who describes how modal hierarchies fluctuate within everyday interactions. So, for example, in Norris's data, a painting is moved (object-handling mode), pointed at (deictic gestural mode) and then talked about (spoken language mode), and the hierarchical position of the modes shifts from one moment to the next as meaning is produced. This sort of analysis goes some of the way towards accounting for material interactions but, in Norris's example, the object remains silent, as a mute accompaniment to human interaction. When scripted material objects – like iPads – are so deeply woven into activity, a broader perspective is needed, one which shows how technologies can generate, initiate, and participate in action. Accordingly I use Latour's term *actants* to describe the agency of iPads and iPad apps, in illustrating how objects are 'participants in courses of action' (Latour 2005: 70) and the meanings that are created and recreated.

Technology, materiality and practice

To assert that communicative contexts are changing, and that hardware and software have global circulation suggests a smooth, homogeneous kind of universalism. Recent research and writing challenge this view. For example, Auld's (2007) study of technology-mediated indigenous storytelling in Northern Australia and Lemphane and Prinsloo's (2014) work with mobile technologies in two communities in South Africa both serve to illustrate how socio-economic forces and cultural values pattern local responses to global resources.

Technologies travel as multinational corporations seek out new markets for their products, but the role that they play in everyday life is always subject to the particularities of the local (Prinsloo 2005). In fact, to say that new technologies have global circulation is an unchallenged assumption in much of the literature on new literacies. Although major corporations, such as Apple, are built on a model of production and distribution, which reaches across national boundaries, the notion of 'the global' should be approached with some care. When used in a contemporary context, the global is often used as shorthand for universalism, connectivity, and the 'inevitable' state of late capitalism (Law 2004a).

Instead of global we might do better to place our emphasis on an idea like 'translocal assemblages' (McFarlane 2009), which is suggestive of the ways in which complex and multiple forces coalesce as place-based events – events that are partly constituted by the exchange of 'ideas, knowledge, practices, materials and resources across sites' (McFarlane 2009: 561). This counters ideas of homogeneity, as it becomes clear that local interpretation always determines how ideas and things are understood, interpreted and how they interact with other forces. To put it another way, we might replace the idea of 'the global' as an undifferentiated universal space with an understanding that 'the global is situated, specific and materially constructed in the practices which make each specificity' (Law 2004b: 24).

In the light of this, it may be more helpful to view technologies, such as iPads, as 'placed resources' (Prinsloo 2005), and to recognise that their use is always flavoured by the local as instantiated in routines, relationships and day-to-day operations, as well as by the beliefs, understandings and experiences of participants. Such a perspective underlines the idea that 'people and the material things they use are inextricably bound together' in everyday practices (Merchant 2014: 28). In other words, looking at either humans or the technologies they use in isolation provides a somewhat impoverished account. This is what Ihde implies in referring to the 'active relational pair, human-technology' (1993: 34). Based on this perspective it is evident that 'the things in use' – in this instance the incorporation of touch screen devices in early years educational practice – have to be of central concern, and this in turn necessitates developing an analytical approach that includes the materiality of the iPad, its technological affordances, and how it is positioned in adult–child interaction. By extension it must also be recognised that the relationship between iPads, adults and children does not take place in isolation – in a sort of social vacuum; it is situated in a larger context, constituted amongst other things by the discourses and practices of mobile technology use (Caron and Caronia 2007), and of adult–child relationships in the context of school literacy practices.

Recognition of the active role that technologies play in our lives, owes a lot to the insights developed by Latour who argued that what we do is co-shaped by the things we use (cf. Latour 2005). In this two-way relationship, technologies 'evoke certain kinds of behaviour' and through their scripted design they help to 'shape the actions of their users' (Verbeek 2006: 362). This is not only illustrated by the multitasking gestures of tapping, swiping and pinching that have rapidly become normalised in the use of touch screens, but also in the way in which hands and fingers are choreographed in the operation of specific apps, and how these apps then take their place in adult–child interactions. In these and other ways the material and the representational inter-weave as adults and children make meaning from digital texts. The material continually conjures the immaterial, which in its turn relies on material experience for its significance. This reflexive and recursive relationship between the material and immaterial has been referred to elsewhere as (im)materiality (Burnett et al. 2014).

These considerations are important to bear in mind when approaching the use of iPads in educational settings. Although they may be applicable to analogous digital practices in other contexts, my concern here is to develop some operating principles to inform how we might describe the use of touch screens in early literacy education. To summarise:

1   The uses of technology such as the iPad are part of complex assemblages that contribute to the construction of place-based practices that are both situated and translocal.
2   Adults, children and the material things they use in educational settings are inextricably bound together and held within wider discourses and practices.
3   Technologies are active in helping to shape both physical and social actions of their users – physical actions and representations are interwoven in acts of meaning making.

These perspectives suggest the need for a methodology that accounts for the detail of the active relationships between humans and technology, the subjective experience of texts and textual practices, and the ways in which these are embedded in broader historical, economic, political, and cultural flows (Burnett et al. 2014).

iPads in the early years

The empirical work under consideration here is drawn from a larger project which sought to investigate how young children respond to iPad stories in early educational settings, the types of interactions that they have with them, and the sorts of comparisons that might then be made with what we already know about the use of print texts. The research team wanted to identify the affordances of the iPad for supporting young children's early literacy development, both with and without adult support. We were therefore guided by two overarching aims:

•   to examine the interactions of young children when accessing books on iPads;
•   to identify the ways in which the technology might support early literacy development.

Research was conducted in two early years settings both of which cater for babies and toddlers, and are located in an urban area in the north of England. The research team observed babies and toddlers under three years of age as they used iPads to access interactive stories and related apps. Ethical practice was ensured at all times, the project adhered strictly to university ethical guidelines, and parental consent for filming was agreed beforehand. iPad encounters were video-recorded by members of the research team for subsequent analysis from two different points of view in an attempt to capture touch screen interactions and proxemics.

In the following extract I look at a single episode from the data gathered by my colleague and co-researcher Karen Daniels, which focuses on adult–child interactions around a familiar traditional story mediated by the iPad (pseudonyms are used in identifying the individuals involved). This is chosen to highlight some key methodological and interpretative issues associated with iPad technology in the context of research into literacy education, and in so doing brings into sharp focus key questions for future work. As described above, particular emphasis is given to the materiality of the technology. Focusing on the physical interactions that are involved sheds light on how the weight, portability and touch screen interface of the iPad take on significance with young children, sometimes scripting their interactions and at others leading to more unpredictable behaviours – or actions that are harder to account for.

Observing young children with iPads

A preliminary viewing of the video data highlighted the significant work done by the body and hands when sharing and using iPads. This led to the development of a basic taxonomy to classify the different functions they perform. Here I distinguish between 1) *stabilising movements*, responses to the weight and shape of the iPad – movements that are necessary to steady the device in order that participants can focus on the screen and then work at the interface; 2) *control movements* which are necessary for basic operations such as accessing apps, and the more complex work of navigating texts on screen; and 3) *deictic movements* that are used to draw attention to the screen or to point out specific features. More detail is given in Table 10.1. It should, perhaps, be noted at this point that although there are many other possible movements (common multitasking gestures such as pinching and enlarging) these are not referred to here because they were not present in the data.

Table 10.1 Hand movements used in the iPad study

1. Stablilising movements

Holding – *using one or both hands to support the tablet (as one might hold a tray).*

Holding and resting – *as above but using legs/knees for additional support (often only one hand is used).*

2. Control movements

General tapping – *using three or four fingers in a slapping motion (commonly used by the young children).*

Precision tapping – *using the forefinger (like the pointing gesture) or with the hand palm downwards slightly lowering one of the first three fingers so that it activates the screen.*

Swiping – *hand palm downward using one or more fingers to drag across the screen whilst maintaining contact.*

Thumb pressing – *using the thumb to tap, swipe or operate the home button.*

3. Deictic movements

Pointing, nodding and other gestures – *directing attention to the iPad, the screen, or visual items framed by the screen.*

One adult, two children and three little pigs

Setting the scene

In this episode the adult, Hannah, is sharing an iPad story app with two children: Iona and Kenny. Iona is fourteen months old, and throughout the story she sits on Hannah's lap. Hannah is sitting on the floor, resting against a wall in the book area (Figure 10.1). Kenny, who is eighteen months, sits next to them – although as time goes on, as we shall see, he appears to lose interest and moves away. Although iPads had not featured in this setting before the research began, it is easy to see how their use as a device for accessing story apps is accommodated within the mesh of practices and material arrangements that work together to constitute this setting as a space for early education. Schatzki's notion of 'site ontologies' is useful here as a way of conceptualising how a small shift in material provision, such as the introduction of a mobile device, leads to modifications in some practices and continuities in others (Schatzki 2005: 476). In some ways then, the iPad substitutes for a book and is fairly readily absorbed into the routine of story-sharing – a routine which is already deeply embedded in the history of early years practice, valorised by professional educators, enshrined in policy and curriculum documentation, and privileged within

Figure 10.1 Sharing the iPad

early literacy research (e.g. Flood 1977; Hammett et al. 2003; Levy 2010). These broader discourses flow through the material arrangements, and are observable in Hannah's choice to use the book area, and to invite Iona (and to a lesser extent Kenny) into an intimate and relaxed bodily relationship in which a shared focus on the screen is tacitly accepted.

At the same time the iPad, the knowledge and actions required to operate it, and the particular ways in which it mediates story content produces some turbulence, as both adult and children work on what is required of them to make use of it in this particular setting (what Schatzki refers to as modification to the site ontology). Although Hannah is familiar with what touch screens do from her own use of the mobile phone, the iPad is different and it takes on a different function in an educational setting. Similarly, even though we did not profile the children's home experiences of technology, we can safely assume that the same factors are at play for them. They draw on other experiences of technology, such as TVs, computers and mobile phones and how they are used in other settings, and these experiences form part of the assemblage that constitutes this episode.

The story app that is being shared is *The Three Little Pigs*, a traditional tale redesigned for the iPad by a new UK-based start-up Nosy Crow, who specialise in book and app development. *The Three Little Pigs* has a range of interactive features that include tapping to open the app, swiping to move characters and to turn pages, and blowing into the built-in microphone to 'help' the wolf. The story and characters of *The Three Little Pigs* are, of course, deeply embedded in children's culture, in that they are popular and familiar, and available in a wide range of media and hence part of a global mediascape (Appadurai 1996). It is likely that the narrative already has a place in the particularities of these children's lives – lives that are singular and situated, but also highly connected through this mediascape.

Microanalysis

At the beginning of the episode Iona is cradled in Hannah's arms, as we see in Figure 10.1. Hannah, who is seated on the floor, leans forward slightly as if to adjust to the infant's gaze. They are both attending to the screen, and Hannah holds the iPad in both hands. We can see clear parallels here with the proxemic conventions of story-sharing in the context of early education (Golden and Gerber 1990). In the lead up to the transcribed extract Hannah has been showing Iona how to turn pages on screen, using the swiping gesture, and Iona's index figure appears to be poised in readiness. Hannah has demonstrated page turning with a combination of deictic and control movements.

The screen display, how Hannah speaks to Iona, and the movements she makes are tightly woven together in an interaction in which action, representation and meaning making coalesce. After the book title is announced by the app, a screen providing options is displayed ('Read it yourself' and 'Read it to me'). In explaining this, Hannah's deictic gesture is an integral part of the 'You can read it' utterance. Her hand in prone position with index finger extended is synchronised with the word 'read' (see Kendon 2004). Then she draws her hand back towards her body, gently brushing Iona's hand in passing, as if transmitting a haptic learning point (Minogue and Jones 2006). Hannah extends her hand once again, this time in a slightly exaggerated or theatrical way as if to demonstrate the gesture, then taps the screen to enable the story to play in 'Read it to me' mode. As can be seen in Table 10.2, this all happens in less than two seconds, but it serves to illustrate a basic pedagogical move in which gesture plays a key role.

The story begins, with the familiar opening 'Once upon a time there were three little pigs', and this attracts the attention of Kenny, who soon makes his presence known. While Iona is happy to observe, using the index finger of her left hand poised to point (Figure 10.2), Kenny is immediately keen to exert control. It is impossible to understand his intentions but it does seem that he is more interested in the actions of pointing or tapping than listening to *The Three Little Pigs*. In the following sequence, Kenny dominates the interaction, successfully capturing Hannah's attention and her approval of his attempts to control the app (Table 10.3). Why he looks underneath the device is unclear. Similarly, one can only guess why Iona looks up at Hannah, although it is tempting to think that she is working to re-establish the intimacy of one-to-one story-sharing and resisting Kenny's attempts to dominate.

After this, Kenny appears to lose interest, crawling behind Hannah and then kneeling at a nearby book trolley. As Iona and Hannah continue with the story, he holds up a board book, which slips from his grip and turns upside down in his hands. He then tries to open it before it

Table 10.2 iPad app-sharing

Time	Speech	Movement	Actants
		Hannah is sitting on the floor and Iona is on her knee.	H and I with iPad
00:03	Snort- snort! The Three Little Pigs	Hannah's arms are encircling her and *holding* the iPad with both hands so they can both see the screen (*stablilising movement*).	
00:06	H:'You can <u>read</u> it'		H and I with iPad
00:08	Once upon a time there were three little pigs	Hannah *points* to the 'Read it to me' icon, and touches Iona's hand. Hannah *taps* the screen with her index finger. (*deictic → control movement*)	app

Figure 10.2 Preparing to tap

slides through his clasped hands and drops to the floor. Hannah and Iona resolutely continue to look at the iPad, listening to *The Three Little Pigs*. With careful support from Hannah, Iona gradually builds the confidence to turn pages herself. Only some of her efforts meet with success. In Figure 10.2 we can see Iona practising her page turning; Kenny clutching a rail with his left hand looks somewhat dejected. Throughout this he maintains contact with Hannah, applying firm pressure with his right shoe, to ensure that she cannot ignore his presence (Figure 10.2). Perhaps as a result of this, Hannah looks across at Kenny to re-engage his attention. It seems to work and Iona shifts to the right as Kenny approaches from the left.

Although Hannah tries to keep the narrative going with Iona there is now competition for her attention. As Kenny kneels down he extends his index finger to tap the screen, and Hannah angles the iPad in his direction. Kenny changes his gesture at the last minute so that when his hand makes contact with the iPad the thumb comes to rest on the home button, which he presses decisively (see Figure 10.3). The story comes to an abrupt end and Kenny looks up at the camera grinning mischievously. At the same time he levers himself up into a standing position with one hand pressing down on Hannah's forearm and the other on the book trolley.

Table 10.3 Kenny and the iPad

T-code	Speech	Movement	Actants
00:21	H:'Do you want to look at . . . ?'	All look towards the screen.	H to K
00:25	H:'The three little pigs.'	Kenny places his index finger on the	iPad app H,
00:30	It was time to leave their home . . .	screen – he could be either *pointing* or *touching* (deictic/control movement).	I and K
00:34	H:'One little pig.' The first little pig	Kenny repeats the finger movement (*deictic/control movement*).	K and iPad app
		Hannah *points* at the screen (deictic movement).	H to K
00:44	H:'Good boy!' H:'You press just there look.' The first little pig decided to make a house . . . .. H:'Watch this little pig.'	Kenny bends down to look underneath the iPad. Iona looks up at Hannah. Their faces are only about six inches apart.	iPad app K and iPad
00:47		Kenny grabs Hannah's hand to prevent any movement, and *taps* the screen with his index finger (*deictic/control movement*).	I and K
00:58		Kenny holds up his finger, with pride.	K, H and iPad app K

Figure 10.3 Kenny finds the home button

Making sense of iPads and apps in context

In the data presented a number of themes come to the fore. To some extent these illustrate the continuities and discontinuities with the story-sharing routines that are part of the mesh of practices and material arrangements that constitute literacy work in the early years. For instance, the proxemic arrangement of adult and children and text hold a lot in common with the story-sharing behaviour associated with print media. The physical prox-imity of Hannah and Iona and the way the device is held in both hands at a comfortable viewing distance by the adult is almost identical to book-sharing. Even Kenny's attempts to join in, take over or disrupt (depending, of course, on one's interpretation) are also to be found in informal story work in early years settings, and although it is tempting to read this as gen-dered behaviour, judgement should, perhaps, be reserved.

As we saw above, Hannah also makes some simple pedagogical moves – moves that are analogous to those found in print book practices. For instance, she directs attention to the text, she encourages page turning, albeit on screen, and she gives feedback. But these moves are also subtly different to those involved in book-sharing, and they would appear to be new to both Iona and Kenny. These functions depend on quite specific control movements on the flat touch screen surface of the iPad – there is a narrow margin of error. A particular kind of kinaesthetic control is needed, and it is different to that required when turning the pages of a print book. Kenny's behaviour deserves further comment, too. His engagement with the iPad seems to be more anchored to its materiality, the actions he can make and the control that he can exert, than to the story that the device mediates. Is it a mere accident that his first response is to make control movements, that he moves away when successful, and returns only to end the story before it is complete?

This isolated example of app interaction in an early years setting has focused on the analytical tools that are necessary for building an under-standing of digital literacies in context. This has been based upon three orientations. Firstly, I have argued that we need to develop detailed descrip-tions of how working with mobile technology is part of a translocal assem-blage in which ideas, practices and material resources from diverse sources coalesce as a space for meaning making. In doing this they jostle for space within the institutional site ontology of the educational setting, creating continuities and discontinuities with existing practices. Secondly, I have illustrated the need for an approach, which takes into account the mate-riality of the technology – not only in terms of the size, weight and rigidity of the tablet device, but also its specific operative functions. These char-acteristics establish distinctive ways in which meanings are made, how the stories themselves are experienced, how readers navigate a route through the text – and, of course, by implication and extension, how texts are then shared. Thirdly, I have suggested that technologies are active in helping to shape both physical and social actions of their users. The iPad is no exception as it requires specific gestures, control movements and physical adjustments to its material and technological affordances.

Both iPads and apps are located in the global mediascape of contemporary childhood and in this sense they contribute to the everyday experience and popular culture of toddlers and young children just as much as booksharing, TV and related media play. So although print literacies still have an important role to play, the new literacies of digital technology are now making significant inroads into early childhood, and it seems that portable touch screens, such as the iPad, have a key role to play in educational provision at home and in early years settings. Literacy education now needs to draw upon and develop methodologies that provide us with insights into how culture, technology and meaning-making practices are intertwined if we are to capitalise on their learning potential.

Acknowledgements

I am indebted to my co-researchers Julia Bishop, Karen Daniels, Jackie Marsh, Jools Page and Dylan Yamada-Rice for this work, which was funded by Sheffield Hallam University and The University of Sheffield under the Collaboration Sheffield initiative.

References

Appadurai, A. (1996) *Modernity at Large: cultural dimensions of globalization*, Minneapolis, MN: Minnesota University Press.

Auld, G. (2007) 'Talking books for children's home use in a minority indigenous Australian language context', *Australian Journal of Educational Technology*, 23(1): 48–67.

Burnett, C., Merchant, G., Pahl, K. and Rowsell, J. (2014) 'The (im)materiality of literacy: the significance of subjectivity to new literacies research', *Discourse: Studies in the Cultural Politics of Education*, 35(1): 90–103.

Caron, A. H. and Caronia, L. (2007) *Moving Cultures: mobile communication in everyday life*, Montreal: McGill-Queens University Press.

Clark, H. (2003) 'Pointing and placing', in S. Kitta (ed.) *Pointing: where language, culture, and cognition meet*, 243–268, Hillsdale, NJ: Erlbaum.

Donner, J. (2006) 'The use of mobile phones by microentrepreneurs in Kigali, Rwanda: changes to social and business networks', *Information Technologies and International Development*, 3(2): 3–19.

Flewitt, R. (2011) 'Bringing ethnography to a multimodal investigation of early literacy in a digital age', *Qualitative Research*, 11(3): 293–310.

Flewitt, R., Nind, M. and Payler, J. (2009) '"If she's left with books she'll just eat them": considering inclusive multimodal practices', *Journal of Early Childhood Literacy*, 9(2): 211–233.

Flood, J. (1977) 'Parental styles in reading episodes with young children', *The Reading Teacher*, 30: 864–867.

Gergen, K. (2003) 'Self and community in the new floating worlds', in K. Nyiri (ed.) *Mobile Democracy, Essays on Society, Self and Politics*, 103–114, Vienna: Passagen.

Golden, J. and Gerber, A. (1990) 'A semiotic perspective of text: the picture story book event', *Journal of Literacy Research*, 22(3): 203–219.

Hammett, L., Van Kleeck, A. and Huberty, C. (2003) 'Patterns of parents' extratextual interactions during book sharing with preschool children: a cluster analysis study', *Reading Research Quarterly*, 38: 442–468.

Ihde, D. (1993) *Postphenomenology: essays in the postmodern context*, Evanston, IL: Northwestern University Press.

Kendon, A. (2004) *Gesture: visible action as utterance*, Cambridge: Cambridge University Press.

Latour, B. (2005) *Reassembling the Social: an introduction to actor-network theory*, Oxford: Oxford University Press.

Law, J. (2004a) *After Method: mess in social science research*, London: Routledge.

Law, J. (2004b) 'And if the global were small and non-coherent? Method, complexity and the baroque', *Society and Space*, 22: 13–26.

Lemphane, P. and Prinsloo, M. (2014) 'Global forms and assemblages: children's digital literacy practices in unequal South African settings', in C. Burnett, J. Davies, G. Merchant and J. Rowsell (eds) *New Literacies across the Globe*, 14–32, London: Routledge.

Levy, R. (2010) *Young Children Reading at Home and at School*, London: Sage.

McCaughey, M. and Ayers, M. (2013) *Cyberactivism: online activism in theory and practice*, London: Routledge.

McFarlane, C. (2009) 'Translocal assemblages: space, power and social movements', *Geoforum*, 40(4): 561–567.

McNeill, D. (ed.) (2000) *Language and Gesture*, Cambridge: Cambridge University Press.

Merchant, G. (2014) 'Keep taking the tablets, iPads, story apps and early literacy', *Australian Journal of Language and Literacy*, forthcoming.

Minogue, J. and Jones, M. (2006) 'Haptics in education: exploring an untapped sensory modality', *Review of Educational Research*, 76(3): 317–348.

Morawczynski, O. (2009) 'Exploring the usage and impact of "transformational" mobile financial services: the case of M-PESA in Kenya', *Journal of Eastern African Studies*, 3(3): 509–525.

Norris, S. (2012) 'Three hierarchical positions of deictic gesture in relation to spoken language: a multimodal interaction analysis', *Visual Communication*, 10(2): 129–147.

Prinsloo, M. (2005) 'The new literacies as placed resources', *Perspectives in Education*, 23(4): 87–98.

Schatzki, T. R. (2005) 'Peripheral vision: the sites of organizations', *Organization Studies*, 26(3): 465–484.

Scollon, R. (2001) *Mediated Discourse Analysis: the nexus of practice*, London: Routledge.

Taylor, R. (2010) 'Messing about with metaphor: multimodal aspects to children's creative meaning making', *Literacy*, 46(3): 156–166.

Verbeek, P. (2006) 'Materializing morality: design ethics and technological mediation', *Science, Technology & Human Values*, 31(3): 361–380.

Wohlwend, K. (2009) 'Early adopters: playing new literacies and pretending new technologies in print-centric classrooms', *Journal of Early Childhood Literacy*, 9(2): 117–140.

Chapter 11

'It's changed my life'

iPhone as technological artefact

Victoria Carrington

This chapter is positioned in the new literacy studies (Street 1984, 1995) and it views literacies as multiple and changing social practices and identities around a diversity of textual forms. From this vantage point, it is interested in developing a sociomaterial understanding of the ways in which mobile phones are impacting on the ways in which young people conceptualise their engagements with the everyday and develop and deploy a range of identity and textual practices. It builds an object ethnography (Carrington and Dowdall 2013; Fowles 2006) in relation to a technological artefact – an iPhone – owned and used by Roxie, a sixteen-year-old Anglo-European adolescent living in a large European city, and draws from Ihde (1990, 1993, 2009) and Verbeek's (2005, 2006b) work around a postphenomenology of technology to sketch the broader implications of Roxie's close involvement with her iPhone. Roxie was interviewed as part of a larger study of young people from twelve to nineteen years of age and their phone use; however, the chapter argues that her particular engagement with her iPhone draws attention to interesting issues related to discourses of identity, technology and space and, as a corollary, the contexts in which young people develop a range of literate practices.

Object ethnographies take note of Miller's views of the important role of 'stuff' in the shaping of individuals and the structures of their lives (2009) while locating these relationships within broader framings that drawn on Appadurai's (1988) arguments about the 'social biography' of things as well the power of larger narratives or mythologies to transform an object into a universal sign (Barthes 1972). This layered framing allows an artefact to be considered as a material object with a biography or social history of its own as well as in consort with the user/s who interact with it, providing a 'commentary on issues of identity, meaning, structure, social critique, materiality' (Fowles 2006) within the broader cultural, technological and political currents in which artefact and use take on meaning.

In this instance, the analysis begins with an object, an iPhone, focusing on its particular design features and materialities. It then shifts focus to the role of the object in Roxie's everyday life, in this case using interview data of Roxie's discourses about the phone to understand the relationship that Roxie has constructed with it. Finally, the design and functionality of the object, along with the relationship established between user and object are located within broader social and cultural narratives around cultures of technology, ubiquity, and reconfigurations of space and time. In essence, the chapter builds a layered sociomaterial analysis that draws on the philosophy of technology to focus specifically on the interaction of an object and user in the construction of everyday life. The chapter further argues that this exploration of Roxie and her iPhone can potentially add a layer of richness to discussions of young people in relation to their use of communications technologies and textual practices, as well as opening up a discussion of the role of technological artefacts in the perception of everyday realities and our actions within them.

In locating this paper and the research underpinning it, it is clear that Roxie's cultural and geographic location bestows a range of benefits and advantages. She is a dual language speaker, currently living with her middle class family in a large European city, has access to multiple technologies and travels independently around her urban environment on public transport or via bicycle to attend school and meet up with friends. While privileged in comparison to many young people around the globe, Roxie is not unique within her own context. She is just one of many, many young people, who can be observed going about their everyday lives in large urban contexts, mobile phone in hand. While the focus of this paper is Roxie's relationship with her iPhone, the interview reported here was conducted with Roxie and her school friend Andreas. Andreas and Roxie share many of the same classes at their school. They live in different parts of the city but travel to the same school each day. Andreas – seventeen at the time of the interview – speaks four languages and his family form part of the large expatriate community of professionals working across European cities. While this chapter and analysis focus most specifically on Roxie, the interaction between Roxie and Andreas on the subject of their phones provides an interesting layer of richness to Roxie's engagement with the artefact, the ways in which they navigate their polymedia context, and their shared perception of the cultural status of the iPhone.

Roxie and her iPhone

When it was introduced in 2007, the Apple iPhone was ground breaking in its design and functionality. It was the first mass-market smartphone with touch screen capability and it quickly became an iconic design and model of functionality that has continued to dominate the appearance and function of all smartphones that followed. Utterback (1996) coined the term 'dominant design' to describe the way that some innovations became market leaders, noting that the 'dominant design' is: 'The one that wins the allegiance of the marketplace, the one that competitors and innovators must adhere to if they hope to command significant market following' (24).

The iPhone was also emblematic of global production and distribution: Schuman (2011) notes that the iPhone is constructed in China from parts created by companies located in China, South Korea, Taiwan, Japan and the United States and then shipped to eager consumers in all parts of the world. It is truly a product of globalisation, both as a manufactured product and object of consumer desire. Akrich (1992) argued that every artefact comes with an instructional message about intended use, the script, that is then interpreted by the user. The designers' prescriptions for the ways in which iPhones will be used, the script, are clear to see. The artefact itself is hand-sized and haptic-smooth and glossy, inviting and requiring touch to operate. It is small enough to fit in one hand, operated by using fingers on the full glass touch screen interface, the first ever released onto the market. The device cannot be used without the interaction of touch, screen, applications and user. Moreover, the iPhone exists symbiotically with the Apple App and Music online stores (App Store and iTunes) where applications, music, videos/movies, games and books are purchased and downloaded.

By the time of the interview, Roxie was on her fifth mobile phone while Andreas had owned four. Andreas was using a prepaid Samsung smartphone while Roxie had an iPhone 3G. Roxie's phone at this time was one of the earliest versions of the hugely successful Apple touch screen iPhones and therefore not new. In fact, it was so old in technology terms that it was unable to update to the latest software version – and has been jail-broken (which removes the pre-installed limitations of iOS and therefore enables the installation of applications (apps), games, extensions and themes not made available through the Apple store) and unlocked from a network so that she could use it. This also meant that she was able to operate the phone as a prepaid, at a time when iPhones were contractually locked to a limited number of service providers. The iPhone was unique in providing a software platform for developers to create games and apps that could be made available to consumers via the online stores.

This is the commercial ecology that Roxie's jail-breaking of the iPhone provider disrupted. The combination of cultural distinction that in Roxie's view attached to iPhones and her own accomplishment in jail-breaking the phone had led to a strong sense of connection.

As the interview unfolded, their discourse revealed a number of interesting aspects of their relationship with their phones. Andreas claimed no connection to his phone beyond his use of it for simple texting. This particular phone and its capacities were not, he claimed, central to his everyday life and instead were 'just in case'. The just-in-case-ness of the phone is reflected in how his mother and his dependence on her for money played out. His mother gave him money to top up his phone: 'Sometimes, it's like, "I need to put some money on my phone". (mimicking his mother) "Oh yeah, here's 20 euros, go top it up" . . . So I have money on my phone *just in case.*' Andreas had no games on his Samsung prepaid phone, no music, thought the camera was 'not that good', and he did not have internet access on it at the time of the interview. It seemed shocking to Roxie that someone would bother with a phone that had no internet access: 'His phone doesn't do the internet!' This view was shared by thirty-six out of the forty-one survey respondents in the study who all stated that the internet, apps and messaging were the most useful aspects of their phone.

Roxie, on the other hand, demonstrated a deep emotional as well as instrumental connection to her iPhone. In the interview, Roxie used a range of emotive terms to describe her sense of attachment to this specific artefact:

'I love my phone'
'Just having an Apple is special'
'I would never put a sticker on the Apple phone'
'It doesn't need to look any prettier'
'Everything sort of makes it your own'

Unlike Andreas' more detached relationship with the phone, Roxie had entirely personalised it. The jail-broken status of the phone allows Roxie to customise the app icon display and the selection and arrangement of apps is in no way random. The apps were purposefully selected and displayed on the screen in an arrangement selected by Roxie to foreground particular, important phone functions and connectivity. Ten years ago, young people routinely customised the physical appearance and contours of mobile phones to reflect their own identities. It was not unusual to see stickers, diamantes and multiple hanging ornaments and small toys attached to phones to customise them. Roxie, for instance, talks about her customisation of the outer shell of previous phones. The cultural status of smartphones, and the iPhone in particular, is evident in both Andreas and Roxie's view that this particular device requires no exterior customisation; that the Apple logo is too valuable to cover up or tamper with. While stickers and decorations would not interfere with the function of the device, it almost seemed that interfering with the Apple logo or disguising the smartphone would risk reducing its cultural value. She noted, 'It's a look. It's a look you go for.' At the time of the interview Roxie was unaware of the availability of attachments and decorations for iPhones and other smartphones; however, she very actively customised the other available 'surfaces' of the phone, the screen displays and selection and arrangement of applications.

The two young people demonstrated an awareness of their differing relationships to their phones:

I: You and Andreas have two different phones and you seem to use them quite differently.

R: Oh yeah. I love my phone.

I: Is it about the phone, or is it about you're just two different people who would use it differently?

A: I never really use my phone. For anything. When I was in Germany before and I had 20 euros on my phone network it lasted like half a year.

I: When you get your iPhone for Christmas do you think you will become more like Roxie and have all your life on your phone?

A: I'm not sure. Maybe. (laughs)

I: What are you looking forward most to using when you get it?

A: Well, the apps. Probably the internet, I guess.

I: Are the apps the big difference between the other phones and the iPhone?

A: Yes, yeah.

Andreas' phone use and his possession of a prepaid Samsung phone are measured against their shared high valuation of the iPhone. Andreas is hoping to receive a new iPhone for Christmas, looking forward particularly to the apps.

I: And do you personalise and customise your phone?

R: Yep.

I: What do you do to it?

R: Put backgrounds. You can change the themes. I down . . . I get different rings. You know how you can . . . you know how iPhone has that one ring. That old phone ring? I download my own ringtones . . . Um, photos. Everything sort of makes it your own.

The ability to mix and match apps to ensure that the phone reflected Roxie's particular interests and needs amplified this sense of personal connection.

While Andreas' current phone was not central to his everyday life, Roxie's phone very clearly mediated her everyday life and the ways in which she understood and interacted with her world; the ways in which she created, controlled and accessed information; and the ways in which she displayed, interpreted and enacted social relations. The iPhone was Roxie's constant companion. The script of the phone encouraged this action as well as the perception of closeness it facilitates. As Roxie notes, 'It's for holding something. It's holding the person you had to call if something, something happened. Holding them. It's also quite solid.' Of all the devices to which Roxie has access, the iPhone takes precedence: 'It has everything in one. It is the iTouch, iPad, laptop and phone. It's the transformer of all electronics.'

A polymedia world

Madianou and Miller (2011, 2012, 2013) argue that the increasing accessibility of communications technologies means that many of us live and interact in what they describe as a *polymedia* context. This useful description differentiates the contemporary context from notions of convergence (Jenkins 2006) or a view of media use as an interdependent ecology (Ito et al. 2010). Madianou and Miller's account of polymedia centres around the availability of internet supported platforms for communication such as email, instant messaging, Skype and social networking. They argue that in a contemporary context where there is a relatively equal selection of multiple media through which to communicate, the choice of medium becomes

> the idiom through which people express distinctions in the form and purpose of communication itself . . . media are not simply the means of transmission for content; rather they become the idiom of expressive intent.
>
> (2012: 125–126)

Individuals select the media which best serves their social purpose and this choice, in itself, forms part of the message: email for instance is a quite different way to communicate from Twitter and requires a different engagement by the recipient. Each of these systems positions sender and receiver quite differently. Madianou and Miller (2012) do not distinguish between 'technology, medium, platform and application' noting that platforms and apps can be accessed from more than one device. They argue that, 'convergence makes it difficult to retain categorical distinctions such as those between technologies, media and platforms given that all these continue to hybridise and overlap' (2012: 104).

Andreas and Roxie's everyday lives are characterised by their polymedia context (Madianou and Miller 2012, 2013). They each own and have relatively unrestricted access to multiple technologies and multiple media forms. They both have laptops of their own, can access laptops and desktop computers at their school and in their homes, have Wi-Fi at home and school (although this is limited to some extent by school firewalls/internet security protocols), and have iPods and iTouches and various gaming consoles. Many of these separate media have internet capacity, allowing access to a series of social networking sites, email, instant messaging and Voice over Internet Protocol (VoIP) voice communication. Reflecting Jenkins' (2006) arguments about convergence, it is no longer the case that each device does different, specialised things and it is no longer even the case that the technologies have converged their distinct capacities: increasingly they each allow access to all of these avenues for interaction and communication. Almost all of these varied devices afford access to the internet, which in turn opens up a world of communication and social options.

Figure 11.1 shows a mapping – constructed out of interview data and in collaboration with Roxie – of Roxie's polymedia context as it existed when the data for this paper was collected. In a sense, this is a mapping of her history as a participant in the many discourses around technology in the twenty-first century and her increasing independence as she grows older and the affordances of the technologies shift. An early shift from a shared desktop through a series of increasingly sleek laptops as broadband and then Wi-Fi access became available in her home can be seen. This movement could also be interpreted to parallel her growing independence as a computer user and the changing needs of homework and research as Roxie moved through school levels. The various gaming consoles are also listed, and evolution over time from older to newer models can be identified. By

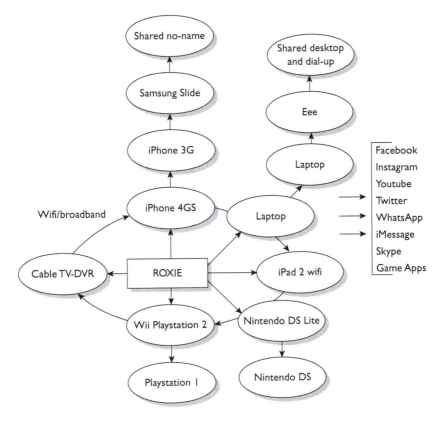

Figure 11.1 Roxie's polymedia context

the time of the mapping, Roxie had seemingly lost interest in the larger games consoles but continued to use the Nintendo and was an avid player of a range of games on the phone. The map also chronicles the shift from a first shared mobile phone – a phone that had a capacity for voice calls and Short Message Service (SMS) messages – through various upgrades and access to a phone of her own, and finally a shift to Apple smartphones. Capturing the rapid turnover in devices, the map indicates that during the period in which Roxie participated in the research she upgraded her iPhone from the 3G discussed in the research interviews to a 4GS (on a plan) prior to the context mapping discussion that took place only three weeks later. The polymedia context is, as Roxie's mapping shows, ever shifting.

The inner ring, which includes iPhone 4GS, laptop, iPad 2, represents Roxie's most recent access to multiple technologies, with the outer rings showing the historical progression of devices. Following Madianou and Miller's (2013: 172) argument that polymedia 'is not simply the environment; it is how users exploit these affordances in order to manage their emotions and their relationships', Roxie's media environment is one of multiple communication opportunities and affordances. As the map shows, many of the devices are internet enabled, allowing Roxie to access and use the many apps – including Facebook, Instagram, iMessage, WhatsApp and Skype – that feature in her polymedia context. The devices provide access to the internet where these apps facilitate various forms of communication, displays of identity, information gathering/sharing, and socialising.

The combination of the polymedia mapping and Roxie's discourse about the ways in which the phone works to enable a particular way of life is interesting. Roxie clearly lives in the polymedia context described by Madianou and Miller (2012, 2013) and the iPhone is a clear example of the type of convergence of capacity that both they and Jenkins (2006) noted. However, a sociomaterial analysis requires that we pay attention to the artefact alongside the communicative and social practices it enables. The iPhone is not a neutral carrier of Roxie's communications; instead, it clearly encourages particular practices such as holding, physical proximity, touching and her close relationship with the phone, which comes through clearly in her discourse.

Co-constructing everyday life: iPhone as a technological artefact

Drawing from the philosophy of technology outlined by Verbeek (2005, 2006b) and Nouri Esfahani and Carrington (2015), this close interaction between Roxie and a key technological artefact – her iPhone – takes on a new significance. Peter Paul Verbeek's postphenomenological philosophy of technology and artefacts is particularly useful in understanding the role of this particular technological artefact in Roxie's world. His framework builds from Ihde's (1990, 1993, 2009) repositioning of phenomenology in the context of the twenty-first century, 'a deliberate adaptation or change in phenomenology that reflects historical changes in the twenty-first century' (Ihde 2009: 5) which brings with it a focus on the particularities of specific technological artefacts and their mediations of lived reality, rather than on producing generalisations about technology as a category. Extending Ihde's (1990) positing of a contemporary *post*phenomenology and Latour's (2007) networks of material and semiotic relationships, Verbeek argues that technological artefacts or objects co-shape both human action and human perception, that they effectively 'mediate' how we see the world around us and how we act within and on it.

It is self-evident that an artefact is designed to fulfil a function. Verbeek (2005), however, suggests that while technological artefacts have an obvious functionality, they also have what has been termed 'intentionality'. Intentionality speaks to the non-neutrality of an artefact, suggesting that rather than being inert beyond the scope of pre-set functionality, technological artefacts play an active role in the relationship between humans and the world they live in and 'actively co-shape people's being in the world: their perceptions and actions, experience, and existence' (Ihde 1990: 364). Following Akrich (1992), Latour describes this influence in terms of 'scripts', with his interest focused on the impact of the material object on user action. While the work of Latour (1992, 1994) offers an analysis of the ways in which artefacts mediate action, arguing that, 'actions are the result not only of individual intentions and the social structures in which human beings find themselves ... but also of people's material environment' (Verbeek 2006a: 60), Verbeek's framework incorporates the mediation of *both* action and perception. He suggests that,

> artefacts mediate perception by means of technological intentionalities: the active and intentional influence of technologies. They mediate action by means of scripts, which prescribe how to act when using the artefact.

Technological artefacts are mediating technologies: they *mediate* how the user perceives the world and how s/he acts upon it by suggesting some actions while discouraging others. Verbeek goes further, suggesting that these artefacts work to 'amplify specific aspects of reality while reducing other aspects' (2006b: 365).

In this view, the iPhone owned and described by Roxie is a mediating technological artefact that exhibits intentionality. As a consequence, its various affordances – scripts – will work to amplify some aspects of Roxie's everyday life and interactions, while reducing the significance of others. It will consequently mediate how she perceives and acts within the worlds around her. Thus, while Madianou and Miller's (2013) notions of polymedia provide us with a sense of the social context of use and the intentions of the user, Verbeek's postphenomenology offers insight into the role of the artefact in the construction of these same contexts.

Given her polymedia context and the multiple devices available, her selection and integration of this particular device is telling. Verbeek's philosophy of technology shows us that a mediating technology, a technological artefact, such as an iPhone, has a significant impact on Roxie's perception of the world around her and her actions within it. Following Verbeek, we see that the phone is a non-neutral artefact, an artefact with its own intentionality, which works to mediate Roxie's relationship with the world around her.

As a technological artefact, the phone demonstrates an intentionality and a script that prescribes use and, in so doing, has the effect of amplifying or diminishing some aspects of Roxie's perception and action. The amplifications of the script encourage her to use the phone to create and access digital texts and images in social networking sites, to gather and distribute information, to build social networks and practices that cut across on/offline spaces, allowing her to exist in an integrated space (Carrington 2012). The mediation on action and perception performed by the artefact is reflected in her discourse. Roxie is very familiar with, and used to, the notion of upgrades and software updates. This shapes her perceptions and understandings of how technology operates and the cycle of non-stop change:

R: iPhones have a fancy thing now.
I: What's the 'fancy thing'?
R: New iOS5.
I: What does it do?
R: It's the Apple operating system . . . it's got this thing where you can pull the keyboard apart. And the thing where you can close the apps, open the apps. It's just, it's an upgrade.

Andreas and Roxie seemingly live within the polymedia context described by Madianou and Miller (2012). As Andreas' differing engagement with his phone described in the interview shows, not every phone artefact becomes as deeply embedded in the everyday life of a user. While both young people's everydays are characterised by the polymedia context described by Madianou and Miller (2012) with the capacity to select from a range of media and ways of communicating, it seems that Roxie embeds one material artefact into her everyday life as well as its communicative potential. This interaction between an artefact and user has, as Verbeek points out, significant implications for perception and action that stretch out beyond, and influence, the social and moral choices Madianou and Miller identified as a feature of emerging polymedia communicative contexts.

The larger narrative: always on and living in

While the iPhone as a technological artefact can be seen, following Verbeek, to co-construct Roxie's perceptions of the world and her actions, how do we account for the strong desire to have one? Roxie and Andreas' high levels of desire for iPhones can be understood in relation to connected narratives around Apple Inc., the neo-liberal focus on individualisation, and the growing economic and narrative power of a so-called 'creative class' (Carrington 2012). Nested within these larger cultural mythologies are other narratives-of-the-everyday around how we now live in a world saturated in internet enabled technologies – 'always on' and 'living in' – that influence how Roxie views her use of the iPhone.

According to Deuze et al. (2012: 1),

> the whole of the world and our lived experience in it can and perhaps should be seen as framed by, mitigated through, and made immediate by pervasive and ubiquitous media.

They make the case that there has been a sufficient ontological shift around the use of media that we can now talk about living 'in' media rather than 'with'. They argue that communications media is so pervasive that it is rendered invisible in the fabric of our everyday lives and that the young, in particular, do not think about getting 'on' line as a distinct type of activity set apart from any other: 'I don't look at it as "getting on the internet". The internet is part of life' (Deuze et al. 2012: 3). Elsewhere, Miller (2011) has talked about the social power of 'always-on'. Based on families and friends separated by migration, Miller describes the sense of dissatisfaction and disconnection that attach to having to find a computer and log on in order to stay in contact and update social networking sites. The dissemination of smartphones has made constant access and being 'always on' accessible and the intentionality of the devices amplifies this practice and the perception of access. He notes the power of this, especially for young women, as it 'establishes a kind of constant co-presence that may not involve any communication but rather than awareness that other people can always be present when you want them to be' (2011: 10). Miller terms this 'ambient intimacy'. Reichelt (2007) first used the term 'ambient intimacy' to describe

> being able to keep in touch with people with a level of regularity and intimacy that you wouldn't usually have access to, because time and space conspire to make it impossible.

For Roxie's generation, there is no sense of 'that you wouldn't usually have access to'. This reflects the earlier work of Ito (2005) who speaks of the Japanese context and the use of mobile phone technologies to form an 'intimate technosocial tethering' that works to create a 'constant, lightweight, and mundane presence in everyday life' (1). Roxie's sense of being always connected and the power of being mobile can be understood as nested within broader cultural economies. Wilken (2009) noted that the practices of 'networked mobility' are one of the defining features of contemporary life and to have access is to acquire both functional advantage and social status. Roxie is mirroring these values, embedding them in identity and her perception of the world and how to interact with it.

Ownership of the iPhone device and access to the apps that it enables and encourages gives Roxie the opportunity to participate in what she views as a valued cultural narrative and to maintain an 'ambient intimacy' of the type described by Miller. Her easy use of technological terms and her narration of herself as mobile but connected reflect this. Importantly, in this reading, the phone is not a neutral object in how Roxie understands this world and how she engages in it. To understand Roxie's world, we need to understand the interplay of user and artefact as well as the implications of the social fields and discourses in which Roxie engages. The script of the phone, its intentionality, amplifies the sense of 'always on' and Roxie's perception of the ambient intimacy that is enabled. These, in turn, work to shift Roxie's experience of space.

Mobile spaces and text

Notions of space have implications for the production, distribution and use of text. For one thing, Fairclough (2008: 134) observed that, 'changing communication technologies and associated semiotic regimes change semiotic affordances, potential and constraints in ways which impact upon orders of discourse'. He explicitly linked changes in communications technologies with shifts in our understandings of space, noting that 're-spatialisation is constituted through change in communication technologies' (2008: 136). In the contemporary context, discourses of mobility, network connectedness and technology have become culturally valued at the same time that they have impacted on the ways in which we experience and narrate our movements through space. Following Fairclough (2006), we might imagine that this re-spatialisation, alongside a discourse order – arguably located within, and shaded by, a much larger neo-liberal discourse – that gives value to discourses of mobility and technology, will influence the ways and purposes of text production. This has significance for understanding the full implications of Roxie's embedded iPhone and the practices it affords. While her discourses are shaded with terms invoking mobility, technology, networks and connection and her own expertise in relation to these things, the communications technologies that constitute Roxie's polymedia context have effectively re-spatialised her practices and perceptions. Roxie lives in this re-spatialised everyday, a space strongly mediated by the materiality of the device as well as its affordances.

She notes, for instance, the usefulness of the *Map App* on her phone for when 'like I get lost'. The *Map App* on the phone has altered how position in space is perceived and navigated:

> The *Map App* on my phone, complemented by the 3G SatNav aspect allows me to find my way to somewhere new without worry. I don't need to take a map with me, just the address. After typing the address, I click 'direct from current location' and it leads me on the way, showing my progress in the form of a little blue moving dot!
>
> (Questionnaire respondent, aged eighteen)

Speed (2011) argues that Global Positioning System (GPS) mapping apps have changed not only our understanding of ourselves in relation to space as we see our movement in real time on a screen, but also our notions of time. In Speed's view, time and movement through space have been melded more closely in our perception. He suggests that this new sense of being *in* the map suggests that, 'locative media offers a synthesis of time and space through the social and environmental networks to which we connect' (243). But to be *in* the map requires that we view the space through a screen, conceptualise ourselves and our movement in that space, and engage it visually and via touch. The smartphone, as a technological artefact, is influencing – mediating – how we understand and interpret the world around us as well as how we act within it.

This re-spatialisation amid a new order of discourse has implications for the purposes of text as well as the ways in which it is produced and disseminated. While this chapter is not specifically focused on the texts that are produced and accessed by Roxie, there are more general observations about text production and use as a socially situated practice that can be made. As new literacy study researchers we have focused particularly on social interactions, the multimodal texts, constructions and displays of identity, and the creative and participatory practices of young people in the emerging communications technology landscapes. The technologies involved have, in the main, been seen as enablers and/or carriers of these innovations. Krippendorff, for instance, allocates technological artefacts to the role of carrier of text 'into its future' (2011: 4), forming part of its material base, while Pahl and Rowsell (2010) alert us to the narratives and literacy practices that attach to objects in family sites. As Bryant (2012) has argued,

> the dominant tendency of contemporary critical theory or social and political theory is to see nonhuman entities as but blank slates upon which humans project meanings. Things are reduced to mere carriers or vehicles of human power and meaning, without any serious attention devoted to the differences that nonhumans contribute to social assemblages.
>
> (4)

However, drawing from the emerging philosophy of technology and from the data presented in this chapter, it must be argued that the technological artefact itself is more than a neutral access portal.

Texts, digital or otherwise, are produced for social purposes (Pahl and Rowsell 2006; Street 1984). In Roxie's case, I would argue that these everyday practices with text and identity should not be interpreted outside the mediating role of her iPhone and the valuation of particular discourses and practices associated with mobility, embedded mobile–personal technologies and the maintenance of intimate–ubiquitous networks. For Roxie, the social purposes that drive the production, distribution and consumption of these texts are often embedded in the networks she establishes, understands and acts upon via the internet and her iPhone. She is making Facebook comments, taking and annotating images before uploading them onto Instagram, inserting text into a mapping application in order to retrieve and interpret directions and then reading herself into the spaces of the map. Roxie's production and distribution of forms of text – her textual practices – cannot be seen in isolation from the mediated and co-constructed reality in which she and her iPhone – her central communication technology – operate.

The iPhone is not, in this account, a neutral technological blank slate that creates digital text. As Verbeek noted, her perceptions and understandings of how the world around her works and her position within it, alongside the ways in which she acts on and within it are bound up to a certain extent with the mediations of this one technological artefact. While this object ethnography is focused on the particular iPhone in Roxie's possession at the time of the study, it should be noted that this is one of a long series of technological artefacts, each with complementary or possibly, competing, scripts and intentionalities that Roxie will embed in her everyday lifeworld over the course of her life. This means, logically, that her perceptions and actions evolve and change over time and across technologies. These perceptions are also positioned within broader cultural narratives. Her perception of 'always on' and 'living in' and her maintenance of an ambient intimacy are co-constructed via the various amplifications and reductions of the technological artefact. Her everyday conversations are shaded with terms drawn from discourses of 'always on' and endless upgrades, software and apps. Her practices and perceptions are, additionally, linked to the scripts embedded in the design and functioning of the artefact. And as Ihde reminds us, there is an 'intimate connection between technology and culture' (1993: 6) and an ongoing relationship between perception and physical action.

This is a story about Roxie and her iPhone. As noted at the outset, Roxie and her network of friends live in a large European city and have enough access to multiple forms of media to justify Madianou and Miller's claims to a polymedia context. This is clearly not the case for all young people in all parts of the world. As always seems to be the way of things, the social advantages that accrue are distributed unevenly. However, mobile phone ownership around the world continues to grow rapidly, delivering a technological artefact with all of the potential mediating influence and intentionality that accompanies it into the pockets of immense numbers of young people. This perspective on text, technological artefacts and their embedding in the everyday provides us with a potentially rich understanding of Roxie's – and by extension other young people's – social relationships, perceptions of the world, and understandings of what text is and does.

References

Akrich, M. (1992) 'The de-scription of technological objects', in W. Bijker and J. Law (eds) *Shaping Technology/Building Society: studies in sociotechnical change*, New York: MIT Press.

Appadurai, A. (ed.) (1988) *The Social Life of Things: commodities in cultural perspective*, New York: NYU Press.

Barthes, R. (1972) *Mythologies*, New York: Hill and Wang.

Bryant, L. (2012) 'The gravity of things: an introduction to onto-cartography', Invited Lecture Collin College, University of Dundee, 12 September 2012. Online. Available HTTP: <http://larvalsubjects.wordpress.com/2012/09/04/the-gravity-of-things-an-introduction-to-onto-cartography> (accessed 13 April 2013).

Carrington, V. (2012) 'There's no going back. Roxie's iPhone: an object ethnography', *Language and Literacy*, 14(2): 27–40.

Carrington, V. and Dowdall, C. (2013) 'This is a job for Hazmat Guy! Global media cultures and children's everyday lives', in C. Hall, T. Cremen, B. Comber and L. Moll (eds) *International Handbook of Research in Children's Literacy, Learning and Culture*, 96–107, London: Wiley-Blackwell.

Deuze, M., Blank, P. and Speers, L. (2012) 'A life lived in media', *Digital Humanities Quarterly*, 6(1). Online. Available HTTP: <http://digitalhumanities.org/dhq/vol/6/1/000110/000110.html> (accessed 11 March 2013).

Fairclough, N. (2006) *Language and Globalization*, London and New York: Routledge.

Fairclough, N. (2008) 'Global capitalism and change in higher education: dialectics of language and practice, technology, ideology', in M. Edwardes (ed.) proceedings of the BAAL Conference, London, 2007, 131–140, Scitsuignil Press: London.

Fowles, S. (2006) *Thing Theory, Syllabus Outline*, Columbia University. Online. Available HTTP: <http://www.columbia.edu/~sf2220/Thing/web-content/Pages/Syllabus.html> (accessed 15 November 2012).

Ihde, D. (1990) *Technology and the Lifeworld: from garden to earth*, Bloomington, IN: Indiana University Press.

Ihde, D. (1993) *Postphenomenology: essays in the postmodern context*, Evanston, IL: Northwestern University Press.

Ihde, D. (2009) *Post-phenomenology and Technoscience: the Peking University lectures*, New York: SUNY Press.

Ito, M. (2005) 'Introduction: personal, portable, pedestrian', in M. Ito, D. Okabe, and M. Matsuda (eds) *Personal, Portable, Pedestrian: mobile phones in Japanese life*, 1–16, Cambridge: MIT Press.

Ito, M., Baumer, S., Bittanti, M., boyd, d., Cody, R. and Herr-Stephenson, B. et al. (with Antin, J., Finn, M., Law, A., Manion, A., Mitnick, S., Scholssberg, D. and Yardi, S.) (2010) *Hanging Out, Messing Around, and Geeking Out*. Online. Available HTTP: <http://digitalyouth.ischool.berkeley.edu/report> (accessed 5 April 2013).

Jenkins, H. (2006) *Convergence Culture: where old and new media collide*, New York: NYU Press.

Krippendorff, K. (2011) 'Discourse and the materiality of its artifacts', in Timothy R. Kuhn (ed.) *Matters of Communication: political, cultural, and technological challenges to communication theorizing*, New York: Hampton Press.

Latour, B. (1992) 'Where are the missing masses? The sociology of a few mundane artifacts', in W. E. Bijker and J. Law (eds) *Shaping Technology/Building Society*, 225–258, Cambridge: MIT Press.

Latour, B. (1994) 'On technical mediation: philosophy, sociology, genealogy', *Common Knowledge*, 3: 29–64.

Latour, B. (2007) *Reassembling the Social: an introduction to Actor-Network-Theory*, Oxford: Oxford University Press.

Madianou, M. and Miller, D. (2011) 'Mobile phone parenting: reconfiguring relationships between Filipina migrant mothers and their left-behind children', *New Media & Society*, 13(3): 457–470.

Madianou, M. and Miller, D. (2012) *Migration and New Media: transnational families and population*, London: Routledge.

Madianou, M. and Miller, D. (2013) 'Polymedia: towards a new theory of digital media in interpersonal communication', *International Journal of Cultural Studies*, 16: 169–187.

Miller, D. (2009) *Stuff*, London: Polity.

Miller, D. (2011) 'Transnationalism in the age of Facebook', paper presented at Migrations, ICTS and the Transformation of Transnational Family Life Conference, Centre for Research and Analysis of Migration (CReAM), London, 6 April 2011.

Nouri Esfahani, N. and Carrington, V. (2015) '(Re)scripting Barbie: post-phenomenology and everyday artifacts', S. Poyntz and J. Kenelly (eds) *Phenomenology of Youth Cultures and Globalization: lifeworlds and surplus meaning in changing times*, London: Taylor & Francis.

Pahl, K. and Rowsell, J. (eds) (2006) *Travel Notes from the New Literacy Studies*, New York: Multilingual Matters Ltd.

Pahl, K. and Rowsell, J. (2010) *Artifactual Literacies: every object tells a story*, New York: Teacher College Press

Reichelt, L. (2007) *Ambient Intimacy*. Online. Available HTTP: <http://www.disambiguity.com/ambient-intimacy> (accessed 17 March 2013).

Schuman, M. (2011) 'Is the iPhone bad for the American economy?', Time Blogs. Online. Available HTTP: <http://curiouscapitalist.blogs.time.com/2011/01/11/is-the-iphone-bad-for-the-american-economy/> (accessed 11 January 2011).

Speed, C. (2011) 'Kissing and making up: time, space and locative media', *Digital Creativity*, 22(4): 235–246.

Street, B. (1984) *Literacy in Theory and Practice*, Cambridge: Cambridge University Press.

Street, B. (1995) *Social Literacies*, London: Longman

Utterback, J. (1996) *Mastering the Dynamics of Innovation*, New York: Harvard Business Review Press.

Verbeek, P. (2005) *What Things Do: philosophical reflections on technology, agency, and design*, trans. R. Crease, Philadelphia, PA: Pennsylvania State University Press.

Verbeek, P. (2006a) 'Acting artifacts: the technological mediation of action', in P. Verbeek and A. Slob (eds) *User Behavior and Technology Development: shaping sustainable relations between consumers and technologies*, 60, Dordrecht, Netherlands: Springer.

Verbeek, P. (2006b) 'Materializing morality: design ethics and technological mediation', *Science, Technology and Human Values*, 31(3): 361–380.

Wilken, R. (2009) 'From stabilitas Loci to mobilitas Loci: networked mobility and the transformation of place', *Fibreculture*, Issue 6 - *Mobility, New Social Intensities and the Coordinates of Digital Networks*. Online. Available HTTP: <http://journal.fibreculture.org/issue6/issue6_wilken.html> (accessed June 15 2014).

Chapter 12

Digital discourse@public space

Flows of language online and offline

Carmen Lee

4 UR Convenience
See U again @ apm
THNK B4 U DRNK

These texts are not messages from the mobile phone or online chatting. They are printed texts found in public 'offline' spaces. '4 UR Convenience' is the name of a convenience store in London; the second example 'See U again @ apm' is a sign located at the exit of the shopping centre, apm, in Hong Kong, whereas 'THNK B4 U DRNK' is a warning sign found in a supermarket in New Zealand. A few initial observations can be made about these texts. First, the designers of these texts have 'stylised' some words by playing with the typography and orthography in English. '4 UR' is homophonous with the words 'for' and 'your'. 'U' stands for the pronoun 'you', and @ replaces the locational preposition 'at'. Similarly, word reduction is also employed in the third example, which could have been written as 'Think Before You Drink'. Because these unconventional forms of spelling and symbols are popular in computer-mediated communication (CMC), they are often referred to by the public or news media as features of 'chatspeak' or 'textspeak'. In addition, these texts are all located in public, commercial spaces in cosmopolitan cities and urban areas. This chapter focuses on the increasing presence of what has been considered 'internet-specific' language in physical public spaces, and how meanings of digital discourse are reconstructed and recontextualised in offline public spaces. Rather than assuming one static variety of language of the internet, this chapter takes a broad view of terms such as 'Netspeak', 'chatspeak', 'e-grammar', or even 'digital discourse' to refer to features of language on the internet that have been discursively constructed by the general public, news media, and academic research. The use of the terms 'online' and 'offline' in this chapter is also one of convenience. By 'online' I mean computer-mediated contexts, and by 'offline' I mean physical contexts beyond the screen. However, this distinction is still problematic as some of my examples will demonstrate.

The chapter first outlines how discourse and language use in digital communication have been conceptualised in the literature of linguistics and digital literacies, showing that previous studies have attributed these linguistic features as characteristic of exclusively 'online' activities. What follows is a description and discussion of a study that examines how digital linguistic practices have travelled offline and are given new social meanings in public spaces in Hong Kong. In analysing public texts, I draw on methodological approaches in linguistic landscape research and ideas in Scollon and Scollon's (2003) geosemiotics. I argue that the presence of internet language in offline spaces is not just a sign of public awareness of Netspeak features. Rather, it contributes to the enregisterment of internet language (Squires 2010), a process that is evident in both commercial and institutional discourses in Hong Kong.

Public and academic discursive construction of internet-specific language

Ever since the popularity and domestication of digital technologies, people have relied on written communication over the internet, from email to instant messaging, and more recently, mobile chatting (e.g. WhatsApp) and social network sites (e.g. Facebook). This has given rise to increasing public and mass media awareness about the linguistic features and styles frequently used in online communication. Labels such as 'chatspeak' and 'textspeak' have been used to refer to language containing such features as abbreviations and symbols used in Short Message System (SMS) texting and online chatting, and the everydayness of online communication has resulted in moral panics, centred around how young people's 'addiction' to the internet may negatively affect their literacy skills and even threaten the English language itself (see Thurlow 2007 for a more detailed discussion of media representations of internet language). Such fears about the negative impact of technology on language are largely rooted in people's standard language ideologies, that is beliefs that value correctness and grammatical rules of language (Lippi-Green 1997; Squires 2010; Woolard and Schieffelin 1994). Any change and deviation from standard language norms would then lead to worries about 'falling' standards of language. In turn, these ideologies reinforce public constructions of a specific online language variety, or what is referred to as the *enregisterment* of internet language.

Enregisterment is the process through which 'a linguistic repertoire becomes differentiable within a language as a socially recognised register of forms' (Agha 2003: 231). In investigating 'Pittsburgese', a local speech associated with Pittsburgh, Pennsylvania, Johnstone (2009) argues that one precondition for the enregisterment of Pittsburgese is that certain Pittsburgese features are frequently correlated with speakers' sociodemographic identities such as region or gender. This process is referred to as 'first-order indexicality' (Johnstone 2009; Silverstein 2003;). In the case of Netspeak, however, there is no evidence for such first-order enregisterment. Linguists may have drawn up lists of Netspeak or e-grammar features but these do not contribute to public awareness of an internet language 'variety'. As Squires (2010) argues, the enregisterment of Netspeak is based largely on language ideologies. Media reports and the frequent use of labels mentioned before such as 'textspeak' also reinforce people's shared conception of a recognisable and emerging internet language. This language is thought to be very different from other more 'standard' language forms that are already in use. While Squires' arguments are supported by her observations of online forums and academic discourses, my discussion in this chapter suggests that another emerging practice that contributes to the enregisterment of internet language is public *displays* of Netspeak.

Linguists and new media researchers have also contributed to the enregisterment of internet language by providing more descriptive depictions of online language and practices, from David Crystal's notion of Netspeak (Crystal 2006) to Susan Herring's 'computer-mediated discourse' (Herring 2001) and 'e-grammar' (Herring 2012). Such research aims to identify and document features of orthography, typography, morphology and syntax in CMC, but mentions social factors and individual differences only in passing. Also providing a list of features of internet language, Blommaert (2011) argues that 'mobile texting codes' have become a 'supervernacular', 'semiotic forms that circulate in networks driven, largely, by new technologies' (2). More importantly, Blommaert adds that the 'mini-language' of texting codes is associated with sociolinguistic rules; for instance, it is often found in young people's communication and is discouraged in formal education. It is some of these values that shape the recontextualisation of internet language in public spaces.

Any instance of language use, whether taking place online or offline, is situated in people's everyday social practices. A situated approach to language online (Barton and Lee 2013) is relevant to the present study as its ethnographic traditions help unfold the social meanings of digital discourse in public spaces. The framework of literacy studies (Barton 2007 [1994]; Gee 2000) provides an orienting theory to understand what roles the so-called Netspeak plays in people's lives, whether it is used on the screen to facilitate informal communication or off the screen in the form of public signs and advertisements. This overall approach, together with concepts from Scollon and Scollon's (2003) geosemiotics and a contextualised approach to linguistic landscape research (Leeman and Modan 2009), provide a powerful analytical framework for my understanding of the situated meanings of internet language in offline spaces.

Digital discourse and linguistic landscape research

Herring (2012) has noted that features of e-grammar have begun to emerge in offline spaces such as the use of 'lolspeak' in advertisements. When online language features move off the screen and are publicly displayed, they become public texts. Written language in the public sphere such as signage and advertising has been studied widely in traditional sociolinguistics and language for specific purposes, though few have foregrounded the significance of locations and situational contexts. *Linguistic landscapes* is an emergent research area that is concerned with 'language in its written form in the public sphere' (Gorter 2006: 2). Researchers of linguistic landscapes are interested in studying written language on display in public. This includes, according to Landry and Bourhis (1997: 25), 'public road signs, advertising billboards, street names, place names, commercial shop signs, and public signs on government buildings'. More recent research has expanded this scope of data to T-shirts, magazines, and graffiti, etc. (e.g. Papen 2012)

The locations in which public texts are situated are crucial, as the meanings of language are often dependent on the practices associated with these spaces. In their book *Discourses in Place*, Scollon and Scollon (2003) draw on public texts in Hong Kong, focusing particularly on the meanings of signs and discourses in relation to where they are located and how people take actions with the signs, an approach which they call *geosemiotics*. In addition to the situatedness of public texts, Scollon and Scollon also point out that language use on a sign may or may not offer a hint to the actual language used in a particular geographical location. This is why they make the useful distinction between the *indexical* and the *symbolic* meanings of language. For example, the presence of English in a Starbucks café in China does not necessarily index a group of English speakers – it may only serve as a symbol of globalisation or project an image of being 'western'. Although the boundary between indexicality and symbolism may be unclear in some cases, as the Scollons have also pointed out, the distinction is still useful in understanding the role of Netspeak features in some unexpected locations (such as shop signs, as will be discussed later). Other researchers have made similar observations, leading Leeman and Modan (2009) to call for a 'contextualised interdisciplinary approach' to linguistic landscape research, which enables the researcher to account for the meaning of signs through not just the spatial contexts but also political and economic factors that shape the design of the sign.

The majority of linguistic landscape research investigates public texts in the offline physical world, and few studies have explicitly considered the internet as part of the linguistic landscape of a particular locale. With the domestication of digital media, however, technologies and their related linguistic practices are so embedded in people's everyday lives that the opportunities for texts and their associated styles and practices to flow between online and offline domains has dramatically increased. In view of these initial observations and conceptual framings, this chapter discusses findings from a study that explores a) traces of online language features in the offline public sphere in Hong Kong, and b) the social meanings these internet-referential public texts may present for their audiences.

The study: data and methods

Following the tradition of linguistic landscape research, the study collected photographic evidence of public spaces where internet-specific language features are evident. Photographic records have proved fruitful in linguistic landscape research and geosemiotics as they can capture not only the text but also its design and surrounding environment that give it additional meanings. Photographs are also a manageable unit of analysis as they can be categorised and quantified. Unlike the majority of linguistic landscape studies which have particular locations as their starting point, photographs in the present study were taken around a given theme, that is internet-referential written texts in public spaces. In addition to the author, who was the principal investigator (PI) of an eighteen-month project (January 2012–May 2013), the photographers were selected through purposeful sampling – five undergraduate students who were all regular users of internet communication technologies. That way, they were able to make use of their own knowledge of frequently occurring internet-specific language when selecting what was to be captured. In this regard, the researcher is also a kind of viewer/audience who takes on a particular reading path and stance towards the research site and data (Barton and Lee 2013).

The student researchers were instructed to ensure that each photo captured the text and its surroundings. In addition to language features, they also took field notes about the location of the text. The photos in the broader study were collected from Hong Kong and other cities of the world including Bangkok, Singapore, London, and Berlin but this chapter focuses on the Hong Kong subset, which contains a total of 243 photos. The student researchers were requested to upload their photos onto the photo-sharing site Flickr (http://www.flickr.com/photos/onofflineproject/). Flickr provides many useful functions for the research team to categorise the photographs. For example, 'sets' were used to organise the photos by theme; tags or keywords were given to each photo for easy retrieval of photos with specific features; for each photo, a title and a description were added as the photos were being uploaded. These captions could then act as field notes for each photo. The photo album was publicly available and the student researchers could interact with one another and the PI through the comments function. The Flickr smartphone app also allowed the student researchers to upload their photos and write captions on the spot. What makes Flickr a suitable site for linguistic landscape research is that the location of each photo can be tagged (geotagged). After collecting and reviewing the photos, the data were coded according to their location, language, and internet-specific language features. The linguistic features identified and their corresponding frequency are summarised in Table 12.1.

The photos were then divided into two major domains: commercial/business (e.g. commercial ads, shop names, signs) and institutional/official (government slogans, banners in schools, street signs). In this study, about 83 per cent of the signs were of commercial/business nature; that means they were found in shops, shopping centres, and restaurants. A smaller number of texts (15 per cent) fall into the category of 'institutional/ official' (such as a banner for a government campaign), and their locations range from the exterior of a school to street railings. Some texts were coded 'mobile', meaning that they appeared on mobile surfaces such as T-shirts and trains.

The last piece of data to be highlighted here is the language choice of the texts, which is primarily categorised into three main types – bilingual, English only, and Chinese only (see Table 12.2).

The languages of the texts, on the one hand, reflect the city's sociolinguistic situation. Under the influence of the former British colony and the

Table 12.1 Internet-specific language features in offline public spaces in Hong Kong

Feature	Example texts	N (%)
Email @	• MENU@Level 7 (direction sign in a shopping centre) • English@CUHK (logo of an academic department)	106 (43.6%)
Heart symbol <3	• Gap <3 U (a slogan of a fashion store) • Dad I <3 U (poster of a bakery's father's day special)	37 (15.2%)
Facebook 'Like'	• 水果齊齊 LIKE (a slogan for the Hong Kong government's 'Fruit, We Like' campaign • 至 Like 推介 (printed on a vending machine)	29 (11.9%)
Letter homophones (e.g. U for 'you')	• Miss U (name of a clothing shop) • Y? Y? Y? 點可以有 Wi-Fi? (a Hong Kong Broadband ad)	26 (10.7%)
Emoticons	• a car plate featuring a smiling face xvx, • a smiling face :> accompanying bilingual texts on a shopping bag	20 (8.2%)
Number homophones (e.g. 2 for 'to', 4 for 'for')	• Looking 4 myself (on a CD cover) • GR8 (name of a clothing shop)	5 (2%)
Abbreviations (e.g. LOL for laugh out loud)	• OMG on a mug for sale • LOL, OMG, BFF on a T-shirt	3 (1.2%)
Others	• Reference to Golden Forum slang such as 'push' on a price tag, '巴打' (brother) in an MTR ad	17 (7%)

Table 12.2 Language choice in internet-referential public texts

Language(s)	N (%)
Bilingual (English + Chinese/Cantonese)	118 (49%)
English only	99 (41%)
Chinese only (including Cantonese)	26 (10%)

'biliterate and trilingual' language policy (reading and writing in Chinese and English and speaking in Cantonese, Putonghua and English), many official signs are required to be bilingual. In everyday communication, it is not uncommon for Hongkongers to code-switch between Cantonese/Chinese and English in both spoken and written contexts (Li 2002). Table 12.2 also shows that English is still highly visible in the public texts collected (either in the form of monolingual English or Chinese–English code-switching).

Readers' perceptions

Social meanings of signs are not easy to be 'read off' simply from looking at the symbols and icons on the signs. They have to be informed by ethnographic data (Blommaert 2013; Scollon and Scollon 2003). Part of achieving this in my study was to elicit viewers' perceptions of the use of internet language in public texts in the form of interviews. The student researchers successfully interviewed a total of twenty passers-by. These interviewees, aged between sixteen and sixty-five, came from all walks of life, including students, clerk, driver, and hotel staff. Most importantly, the interviews were conducted at the locations where the signs were found. This allowed us to elicit viewers' contextualised interpretations of the meanings of the texts, and, at the same time, prompted viewers to reflect upon their own linguistic practices online as well as their beliefs about internet language.

Internet language on display: commodifying and indexing a global register

Linguist David Crystal once argued that texting abbreviations 'were designed to suit a medium where there is a technological limit on what can be communicated' and that 'they have no place in a medium where such limitations do not exist' (Crystal 2005). This is apparently an overstatement as my data demonstrate that public spaces are gradually becoming infiltrated with internet-specific language. However, when used offline, Netspeak is no longer just the Netspeak found in online interaction or texting. In offline public spaces, internet language is often *on display* with new situated meanings.

The public displaying of Netspeak features can take many forms, from shop signs to print advertisements and even car plates. I use *display* here to mean that when internet language appears offline, it is not to be read or taken literally, but to be 'looked at' (Jaworski 2013b). An example in point is the name of a relatively low-end clothing shop 'GR8' (Figure 12.1). This small shop is located in Tsim Sha Tsui, one of the busiest and most commercialised districts in Hong Kong. The sign 'GR8', found above the entrance of the shop, is not to be read as a mobile text message 'great', but as an exophoric or situated indexing of where the sign appears (Scollon and Scollon 2003), pointing to the meaning: this shop is called GR8.

Figure 12.1 GR8

Another common example of 'displayed Netspeak' is the use of the email @ symbol, which is the most frequently occurring feature in my data. Direction signs in shopping centres often use @ to mark the floor of a certain area. For example, 'THE MENU@Level 7' (Figure 12.2), 'Luxury Brands @ Level 1 Ocean Centre'. Again, @ in these examples does not immediately index email or the internet at large. Clearly, @ here could have been replaced by the English preposition *at*. The question is: Why then is @ more preferred in these signs?

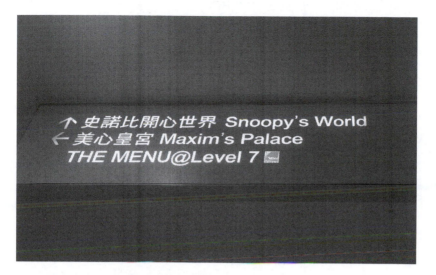

Figure 12.2 THE MENU@Level 7

In examining creative uses of punctuation marks in public spaces, Jaworski (2013a) argues that punctuation symbols have become a 'globalese' that is frequently employed in commercial discourse. One of his examples is the 'dot' as in EAT., which he argues has become an index to the 'internet-linked globalisation'. The GR8 shop sign and @ in direction signs mentioned above demonstrate exactly this. The @ is not expected to be read as a preposition. When asked to interpret the meanings of @ in direction signs in shopping centres, my interviewees immediately described the presence of @ as being 'cool', 'fun', 'youthful' and even 'cute'. These added values have been taken up widely by marketers and businesses. The locations of my data also suggest that selected features of Netspeak have developed into a commodified variety that serves as a symbol of global commerce. With few exceptions, the majority of my examples were found in shopping areas, especially upmarket shopping centres such as Festival Walk and Harbour City, as well as in popular tourist attractions such as the Star Ferry pier.

In fact, Netspeak itself has become 'sellable'. Abbreviations such as LOL and OMG have been printed on merchandises such as mugs, T-shirts, and postcards; emoticons are found on book covers and cushions. This phenomenon echoes Johnstone's (2009) observation of what has happened to Pittsburgese. According to Johnstone, stylising Pittsburgese words and printing them on T-shirts for sale is a way of connecting this local speech with social and economic values. Netspeak, like Pittsburgese, has certainly become part of the 'symbolic economy' (Zukin 1995), in which cultural symbols, including language, are used to 'enhance commodities' and 'become part of the marketplace' (Leeman and Modan 2009: 338).

The dominance of English in the data set, shown in Table 12.2, also indexes a language of global significance. Some linguistic practices of Netspeak that originate from English CMC (e.g. abbreviations, letter homophones, and emoticons) are used in computer-mediated discourses across the globe. The example at the beginning of the chapter 'See U again @ apm' (Figure 12.3), found at the exit of the shopping mall apm, is written in English only. There is no Chinese translation of the sign, which is unusual for an official sign at a shopping centre in Hong Kong. In this case, however, the use of English does not seem to be a pragmatic decision. Rather, Scollon and Scollon (2003) observe that the preference for English in some shopping centres in Hong Kong reflects the globalising economy. The use of English Netspeak at apm is also consistent with the shopping centre's overall marketing direction of promoting itself as a round-the-clock (as suggested by the name apm), 'play more sleep less' (an English slogan found on apm's website) location for young people to shop and hang out.

While most of the Netspeak features in the signs collected do not index the internet per se, the use of Facebook 'Like' is an exception. On Facebook, 'Like' is a button, usually accompanied by a 'thumbs up' symbol, that is intended for users to express their positive view towards a

Figure 12.3 See U again @ apm

post. Nowadays it is common for advertisers to include a Like button or a Facebook link in a print advertisement to point readers to their Fans page. At least 15 million businesses and companies now have a Facebook page. The strong presence of Facebook features in Hong Kong public texts is unsurprising, given there are over 4 million subscribers in the city (Internet World Stats 2013). The popularity of Facebook marketing also creates a culture of liking and sharing, and new meanings have been attached to the verb *like*. As Franzen (2011) suggests in the *New York Times*, the verb *like* has been transformed 'from a state of mind to an action that you perform with your computer mouse, from a feeling to an assertion of consumer choice'. In my data, about 12 per cent of the signs contain an expression in which

Figure 12.4 A poster for a fitness centre in Hong Kong

the word *like* has a reference to Facebook. The poster in Figure 12.4 is an advertisement of a fitness centre. The main slogan in the centre '一Like 即賞' asks potential customers to become a fan of the fitness centre by 'liking' its fans page on Facebook in exchange for a gift. The existence of the Like button in this poster immediately creates a highly complex nexus of practice (Scollon and Scollon 2004) – the Like button in the slogan, using Facebook's colour scheme and design, is intertextual to the Facebook website. Underneath the slogan, the smaller words refer readers to the fitness centre's Facebook page and give further details about what the reader can do to collect the gift. This design fits in well with Kress and van Leeuwen's (1996) visual grammar, that information at the bottom of a sign often indexes the 'real' action to be taken, that is clicking the Like button on this company's Facebook page.

In sum, the enregisterment of Netspeak is both a precondition and a result of the commodification of language (Heller 2010; Johnstone 2009). That is, both sign designers and readers have to be aware of internet language features (precondition) before they can recontextualise them in public spaces. At the same time, public displays of internet language also contribute to the ongoing process of enregisterment of Netspeak. Many examples in my study point to the commercial and economic values of internet-specific language, while others may create intertextual links to commercial spaces on the internet (e.g. Facebook Fans pages).

Language ideologies and the marketisation of institutional discourses

Netspeak has clearly become a popular, if not effective, branding and marketing strategy. This phenomenon is not confined to commercial contexts. In my data, the @ symbol, emoticons, and abbreviations are found in institutional discourses, for example, 'English@CUHK' on an academic department's note pad, and 'Discover & Innovate @ CityU' as part of the university's mission statement, printed on the wall of a covered walkway and elsewhere at the City University of Hong Kong. What is more interesting about institutional uses of Netspeak is the conflicting discourses that authorities themselves seem to have produced.

A banner on the exterior of a kindergarten in Hong Kong reads 'Fruit, We Like' and in Chinese translation, '水果齊齊LIKE'. It advertised the official 'Eat Smart' campaign by the Department of Health in 2012. The *like* in the slogan is suggestively Facebook-referential, given that it is accompanied by a blue thumbs up symbol as commonly seen on Facebook. The issue here is that the authority itself seems to have produced conflicting discourses. From time to time, teachers and government officials alike have reportedly complained about how the use of CMC may threaten students' literacy skills. In Hong Kong, code-switching, a linguistic phenomenon that is commonly found in students' online writing, is discouraged in formal education. A recent assessment report of public examinations in Hong Kong shows that technology-related words such as iPhone and iPad are considered inappropriate in oral examinations (*South China Morning Post* 2012). At the same time, internet language features and code-switching are increasingly adopted in official and institutional discourses. A similar case has been identified in the UK, where the London Grid for Learning, a consortium of London-based education authorities, produced a poster of ten tips on safe surfing for students (Boffey 2008). These tips, while being imperative, are all written in texting language (e.g. 'msgs u snd shd B respectful'). These incidents illustrate the way in which internet language has become a tool for authorities to exercise their power through informalisation or conversationalisation of public discourse (Fairclough 1992).

The tension between standard language ideologies and how internet language is actually used by young people in society is also evident in the interviews. For example, while a number of interviewees appreciated the aesthetics of Netspeak in public signs, a few young participants juxtaposed the use of internet language in public texts with their standard language ideologies, that is what they considered to be 'correct' and 'normal', as shown in the following opinions from three student interviewees:

> I think it (the use of @ in a shopping centre) is too confusing . . . Also, 'at' is easier to write and type than '@'. It's also more proper.
>
>> (Interviewee 1, male, student, twenty-one years old)

> The use of U in this ad makes it look lazy, unattractive. It would've been nicer if they wrote YOU with 3 letters.
>
>> (Interviewee 5, female, student, twenty-two years old)

> I never use it [an emoticon] in formal emails. That makes me feel like I'm not professional and have a casual tone.
>
>> (Interviewee 20, female, student, twenty years old)

Although these interviewees reported having incorporated Netspeak features into some of their online writing, they could not tolerate the presence of unconventional spellings beyond informal online interaction. Contrary to many public concerns and moral panics, however, the above ideas from the student interviewees also reveal that young people also have a clear idea about the contexts in which internet-specific language is or is not considered to be 'proper'. This lends support to Heller's (2010) argument that the commodification of language often presents tensions in society, particularly those between ideologies and linguistic practices. In the case of Netspeak, the tension between standard language ideology and linguistic creativity is evident.

Indexing the local

A final point to be made about the presence of internet language in Hong Kong offline spaces is that, while Netspeak seems to have been globalised into a supervernacular, it is also undergoing a process of *deglobalisation*, 'localisation of globally distributed resources' (Blommaert 2011). Looking through my data, only a small selection of Netspeak features have made their way to Hong Kong's offline spaces. 'See U again @ apm' could have been further shortened to 'CUA@apm'. It was perhaps the sign designer's pragmatic decision to retain the full form of some words to ensure a wider understanding of the sign by Hongkongers (and visitors from around the world) who know some English but may not be familiar with texting abbreviations.

A more obvious example of the deglobalisation of Netspeak is the insertion of English Netspeak into a Chinese or Cantonese utterance, as in 'Y? Y? Y? 點可以冇 Wi-Fi?' ('Why? Why? Why? No Wi-Fi here? No way!), as shown in Figure 12.5. This ad for a broadband company was found at various bus

Figure 12.5 Y? Y? Y?

stops, suggesting that commuters were the ad's target audience. The letter homophone Y for *Why* indexes a common texting code, thus symbolising the global internet. The bilingual advertising language style specifically indexes local Hong Kong Chinese internet users. Bilingual word play, such as Y rhyming with Wi-Fi in the code-mixed ad here, is a common linguistic strategy in advertisements in Hong Kong, as documented in research on code-switching in Hong Kong (Li 2002).

Apart from code-mixed signs in print-based texts, over the past few years, English Netspeak features have made their way to pop cultures in Hong Kong. A number of Canto-pop songs, for example, Louis Cheung's 火星文 (*Martian language*) and Charmaine Fong's 我 *LIKE* 你 (*I LIKE you*), contain notable Netspeak features such as 'XDD', 'BTW', 'R U', and 'Like' in the Facebook sense. This specific form of Chinese–English 'language mixing' may not serve any real communicative function in the songs, but they certainly contribute to the stylisation of the lyrics. These instances can also be seen as cases of 'polylanguaging' (Androutsopoulos 2013; Jørgensen 2008), realising an interplay between the globalised codes of Netspeak and the local deployment of them (Blommaert 2011).

Conclusions

Digital discourse, like any form of literacy, does not only stay in one spatial domain. It travels between domains of life and cuts across genres and spatial boundaries, as demonstrated by the examples discussed in this chapter. The infiltration of internet language in offline public spaces has brought about many interesting implications for digital discourse and literacies research.

Methodologically, this chapter has brought together ideas and research traditions in computer-mediated discourse, geosemiotics, and linguistic landscape research to understand better how digital discourse is recontextualised across spaces, showing that the internet is a salient linguistic landscape (Ivkovic and Lotherington 2009). While interviews were conducted, they were far from sufficient in providing a comprehensive understanding of the social meanings conveyed by online language in public spaces. Its actual meanings must be interpreted through further ethnographic work. Scholars including Leeman and Modan (2009) and Blommaert (2013) have called for a more historical approach to the study of public signs. This is particularly relevant to the present study as some aspects of internet language may become outdated quickly; a longitudinal study would allow researchers to trace changes in both forms and functions of Netspeak in public spaces over time.

The present study has also shed light on the relationship between discourse and space. Berry Wellman argues that '[t]he cyberspace-physical space comparison is a false dichotomy' (2001: 248). This is evident in a number of previous studies of CMC including Jones (2004) who also challenges existing concepts of context and space. In this chapter, I have demonstrated that linguistic practices are fluid and travel between online and offline communicative contexts. In the world of 'talk web culture' where online discourses are often reconstructed in offline contexts, the concept of space thus needs to be revisited in discourse analysis. The analysis in the present study takes into account digital discourse in both online and offline spaces, revealing conflicting discourses produced by authorities and even web users themselves with regard to language standards and the presence of online language in public texts.

From the point of view of literacy studies, this chapter serves as an example of the situated and changing nature of vernacular literacy practices. Language forms that are considered 'non-standard' in some contexts have become more visible and valued in public domains, be it commercial spaces or government campaigns. Although abbreviations and playful use of punctuation marks predate the internet, what seems to be happening now is that the indexical and symbolic values of online language have been enregistered by businesses and marketers to brand their products, and that digital discourse is gradually becoming a salient part of the sociolinguistic ecology in many commercialised cities around the world.

Acknowledgements

I thank the editors for their insightful comments on earlier versions of this chapter. I am also grateful to the participants at The Fifth International Roundtable on Discourse Analysis (2013) for their feedback on my presentation. The project reported in this chapter was funded by the Chinese University of Hong Kong's Direct Grant for Research (Ref. 2010372).

References

Agha, A. (2003) 'The social life of cultural value', *Language and Communication*, 23: 231–274.

Androutsopoulos, J. (2013) 'Networked multilingualism: some language practices on Facebook and their implications', *International Journal of Bilingualism*. Online. Available HTTP: <http://ijb.sagepub.com/content/early/2013/06/07/136700 6913489198.abstract> (accessed 9 April 2014).

Barton, D. (2007 [1994]) *Literacy*, Oxford: Blackwell.

Barton, D. and Lee, C. (2013) *Language Online: investigating digital texts and practices*, Abingdon: Routledge.

Blommaert, J. (2011) 'Supervernaculars and their dialects', *Working Papers in Urban Language & Literacies*, Paper 81. Online. Available HTTP: <http://www.kcl.ac.uk/innovation/groups/ldc/publications/workingpapers/WP81.pdf> (accessed 1 May 2012).

Blommaert, J. (2013) *Ethnography, Superdiversity and Linguistic Landscapes*, Bristol: Multilingual Matters.

Boffey, D. (2008) 'The £3,000 "txt-spk" poster that "undermines English teaching"', Online. Available HTTP: <http://goo.gl/LqF1HR> (accessed 9 April 2014).

Crystal, D. (2005) 'The scope of internet linguistics', Online. Available HTTP: <http://www.davidcrystal.com/DC_articles/Internet2.pdf> (accessed 9 April 2014).

Crystal, D. (2006) *Language and the Internet*, Cambridge: Cambridge University Press.

Fairclough, N. (1992) *Discourse and Social Change*, Oxford: Polity Press.

Franzen, J. (2011) 'Like is for cowards. Go for what hurts', *New York Times*, 28 May.

Gee, J. P. (2000) 'The new literacy studies: from "socially situated" to the work of the social', in D. Barton, M. Hamilton and R. Ivanic (eds) *Situated Literacies: reading and writing in context*, 180–196, London: Routledge.

Gorter, D. (2006) 'Introduction: the study of the linguistic landscape as a new approach to multilingualism', *International Journal of Multilingualism*, 3(1): 1–6.

Heller, M. (2010) 'The commodification of language', *Annual Review of Anthropology*, 39: 101–114.

Herring, S. C. (2001) 'Computer-mediated discourse', in D. Schiffrin, D. Tannen and H. Hamilton (eds) *The Handbook of Discourse Analysis*, 612–634, Oxford: Blackwell.

Herring, S. C. (2012) 'Grammar and electronic communication', in C. A. Chapelle (ed.) *The Encyclopedia of Applied Linguistics*, Hoboken, NJ: Wiley-Blackwell. Preprint Online. Available HTTP: <http://ella.slis.indiana.edu/~herring/e-grammar.pdf> (accessed 9 April 2014).

Internet World Stats. (2013) 'Asia marketing research, internet usage, population statistics and Facebook information', Online. Available HTTP: <http://www.internetworldstats.com/asia.htm> (accessed 9 April 2014).

Ivkovic, D. and Lotherington, H. (2009) 'Multilingualism in cyberspace: conceptualising the virtual linguistic landscape', *International Journal of Multilingualism*, 6(1): 17–36.

Jaworski, A. (2013a) 'Indexing the GLOBAL', *SemiotiX*. Online. Available HTTP: <http://semioticon.com/semiotix/2013/05/indexing-the-global/> (accessed 21 April 2014).

Jaworski, A. (2013b) 'Commentary: mobile language in mobile places', *International Journal of Bilingualism*. Online. Available HTTP: <https://www.academia.edu/4744692/Commentary_Mobile_language_in_mobile_places> (accessed 21 April 2014).

Johnstone, B. (2009) 'Pittsburghese shirts: commodification and the enregisterment of an urban dialect', *American Speech*, 84(2): 157–175.

Jones, R. H. (2004) 'The problem of context in computer-mediated communication', in P. LeVine and R. Scollon (eds) *Discourse and Technology: multimodal discourse analysis*, 20–33, Washington, DC: Georgetown University Press.

Jørgensen, J. N. (2008) 'Polylingual languaging around and among children and adolescents', *International Journal of Multilingualism*, 5(3): 161–176.

Kress, G. and van Leeuwen, T. (1996) *Reading Images: the grammar of visual design*, London: Routledge.

Landry, R. and Bourhis, R. Y. (1997) 'Linguistic landscape and ethnolinguistic vitality: an empirical study', *Journal of Language and Social Psychology*, 16(1): 23–49.

Leeman, J. and Modan, G. (2009) 'Commodified language in Chinatown: a contextualized approach to linguistic landscape', *Journal of Sociolinguistics*, 13(3): 332–362.

Li, D. C. S. (2002) 'Cantonese-English code-switching research in Hong Kong: a survey of recent research', in K. Bolton (ed.) *Hong Kong English: autonomy and creativity*, 79–99, Hong Kong: HKU Press.

Lippi-Green, R. (1997) *English with an Accent: language, ideology, and discrimination in the United States*, London: Routledge.

Papen, U. (2012) 'Commercial discourses, gentrification and citizens' protest: the linguistic landscape of Prenzlauer Berg', Berlin, *Journal of Sociolinguistics*, 16(1): 56–80.

Scollon, R. and Scollon, S. W. (2003) *Discourses in Place: language in the material world*, London: Routledge.

Scollon, R. and Scollon, S. W. (2004) *Nexus Analysis*, London: Routledge.

Silverstein, M. (2003) 'Indexical order and the dialectics of sociolinguistic life', *Language and Communication*, 23(3–4): 193–229.

South China Morning Post (2012) 'Pupils reminded to use only English or Chinese in exams', 2 November. Online. Available HTTP: <http://www.scmp.com/news/hong-kong/article/1074427/pupils-reminded-use-only-english-or-chinese-exams> (accessed 9 April 2014).

Squires, L. (2010) 'Enregistering internet language', *Language in Society*, 39(4): 457–492.

Thurlow, C. (2007) 'Fabricating youth: new media discourse and the technologization of young people', in S. Johnson and A. Ensslin (eds) *Language in the Media*, 213–233, London: Continuum.

Wellman, B. (2001) 'Physical place and cyberplace: rise of personalized networking', *International Journal of Urban and Regional Research*, 25(2): 227–252.

Woolard, K. and Schieffelin, B. B. (1994) 'Language ideology', *Annual Review of Anthropology*, 23: 55–82.

Zukin, S. (1995) *The Cultures of Cities*, Malden, MA: Blackwell.

Chapter 13

The discourses of celebrity in the fanvid ecology of Club Penguin machinima

Jackie Marsh

The growth of interest in 'fanvids' (Ito 2011), videos which are created by non-professionals for an audience interested in the subject/content of the video, can be discerned in a range of interest areas and include child audiences. This chapter considers videos created by children and young people who use the virtual world Club Penguin. The videos in question are 'Club Penguin Music Videos' (CPMVs) – which are machinima that are created in the virtual world and then posted to YouTube and other moving image media-sharing sites. The analysis focuses on the social practices embedded in the circulation and viewing of these machinima and considers the extent to which fandom practices are present in these online communities. A Foucaultian approach is taken to discourse analysis, which focuses on the discursive production of social practices in this particular fan culture. The chapter considers how discourse analysis can be undertaken of such digital practices and in particular reflects on the relationship between analysis at macro (focused on power relationships) and micro (focused on texts) levels. In the first part of the chapter, the nature of Club Penguin machinima are outlined before the discourses circulating the dissemination and viewing of these texts are analysed. The final section of the chapter considers the implications of this analysis for educators and researchers interested in the social practices of children in the digital age. It is argued that in these online worlds, discourses of recognition, status and competition circulate and serve to create celebrity–fan relationships that replicate those that operate outside of the peer-to-peer network.

Club Penguin machinima

Club Penguin is a virtual world that is aimed at children aged from six to fourteen, although younger children use it (see Marsh 2010). It was developed by a Canadian independent company and launched in 2005. In 2007, Disney acquired it for a reported 700 million dollars (Marr and Sanders 2007). It has grown in popularity since its launch, with an estimated 225 million registered accounts in 2014 (KZero 2014). It is popular in numerous countries in North and South America, Europe, Asia and Australasia. Club Penguin contains several features of virtual worlds aimed at this age group, including opportunities to dress up an avatar, to decorate a virtual home, to earn virtual money by playing games, to purchase items for avatars from virtual shops and to engage in chat with other users. These activities take place within an Arctic environment in which avatars are represented by penguins that live in igloos and can engage in a range of Arctic activities such as skiing and playing on icebergs. The environment features a range of spaces avatars can visit, such as a coffee shop, a nightclub, a pizza parlour, a theatre and shops. Users are also able to adopt puffles, which are virtual pets. The site also has some limited social networking functions, in that users are able to chat using text and can send each other postcards.

Previous studies of children's use of Club Penguin have examined the play, literacy activities and social interactions that take place in the virtual world, identifying the ways in which children's offline friendships, play artefacts, commercial practices and markers of capital (Bourdieu 1990) interface with their online practices (Marsh 2013, 2011; Wohlwend and Kargin 2013). This chapter extends this analysis by examining the music videos made in Club Penguin, which are machinima. Machinima is a word that combines 'machine' and 'cinema' to refer to films made in virtual worlds and computer games using screen capture software and editing software. Davis et al. (2013) suggest that because of the widely accessible software used to create the films, 'machinima has become a popular creative medium for hobbyists and novices while still retaining borrowed conventions from professional filmmaking'. The machinima created by children and young people are usually located within sets of social practices surrounding popular cultural texts and artefacts. Ito (2011), in a review of DIY films which circulate on the internet, suggests that machinima can be seen as part of a 'fanvid ecology' and argues that 'most are made in a celebratory mode, trafficking in geek-elite insider knowledge and reinterpretation of popular media' (52).

CPMV consist of a machinima that is normally made by capturing screen activity when the producer is using an avatar in the Club Penguin virtual world. The avatar is often filmed undertaking activities that relate to the lyrics of a song that is featured in the CPMV. The avatar is filmed saying the lyrics, which appear in a speech bubble above the penguin's head.[1] The CPMV producer then edits this footage so that is it synched with the soundtrack, to provide a karaoke-style depiction of the song. The songs that are used in CPMV are normally pop, rock, rap and Rhythm and Blues (R&B) songs that feature in the charts. CPMV producers are often keen to be the first to upload a machinima of the latest hit song.

Machinima made in Club Penguin started to appear regularly on YouTube from 2006, featuring various aspects of the site and being used to share cheats and so on, and by 2007 CPMV was well established as a sub-genre of these machinima. A recent (June 2014) search of YouTube using the phrase 'Club Penguin Music Video' found over 139,000 results, while the search term 'CPMV' identified 265,000 films, with some fan-made CPMVs enjoying almost 2 million views. Other popular genres include Club Penguin films, television programmes (talk shows, soap operas, comedies) and fashion shows. In this sense, CPMV can be seen as a 'sub-cultural' practice (Thornton 1996). While acknowledging the problematic nature of such a term, which appears to indicate the presence of cultural hierarchies, it usefully points to the way in which CPMVs nestle alongside closely related cultural practices (e.g. production of Club Penguin TV) that themselves are nested within a broader environment, in this case the Disney-produced virtual world. In addition to exploring the synchronic aspects of this phenomenon, the practices may be viewed diachronically. Examining the machinima created over the past five or six years indicates that early CPMVs were less complex in nature than contemporary CPMVs, which feature numerous special effects allowed by the software available, such as AVS video editor, iMovie, Sony Vegas and Windows Movie Maker.

CPMVs are located within what Steinkuehler (2007) identifies, in relation to the massively multiplayer online game (MMOG) *World of Warcraft*, as a 'constellation of literacy practices' which includes blogs, fanfiction websites and wikis that are related to MMOGs and games. I have discussed the nature and extent of the Club Penguin constellation previously (Marsh 2011) and so will not outline it here other than to signal that more recent developments include greater use of Twitter and Facebook by CPMV creators, the impact of which is discussed later in the chapter.

Increasingly, young children's musical practices involve social networking, with children aged from five to eleven in a previous study of their use of virtual worlds reporting regular use of online music sites such as Limewire, in addition to using YouTube to access music videos (Marsh 2014). CPMVs can be seen as one example of children and young people's creative digital activities with music; other practices include making films and adding soundtracks, uploading films of themselves and/or peers dancing to music or creating and circulating ringtones made from favourite songs. Small (1998) uses the term 'musicking' to characterise people's everyday engagement with music and these social networking practices can thus be characterised as vernacular digital musicking in which, as Woodruff (2009: 26) suggests is the case with many of the musical practices of children, there is a 'false binary between "artist" and "listener"', a point also made in the work of Bickford (2012) on children's encounters with the music industry.

There are a number of features of CPMV practice that can be characterised as constituting a 'fanvid ecology' as outlined by Ito, who suggests that:

> The socio-technical world of machinima embodies what I see as the key characteristics of a thriving amateur creative scene: accessible tools,

peer-based feedback and exchange, networked online distribution, spaces for participation for both beginners and experts, diverse exemplars (both creative work and people), and opportunities for competition, recognition and status.

(Ito 2011: 53)

The particular 'affinity space' (Gee 2005) of CPMVs embeds all of these characteristics; in the limited space available in this chapter, just three areas will be examined in order to illustrate this point in detail: the opportunities these online communities offer for competition, recognition and status and which thus construct a CPMV celebrity culture. In contrast to those who might seek to critique contemporary fascination with celebrity status (e.g. Ju Choi and Berger 2009), this analysis was undertaken in the light of Allen and Mendick's (2013) research which shows clearly that 'celebrity culture offers important sites of fantasy and investment for young people' (87) and provides opportunities for pleasure and community engagement.

Discourse analysis

The chapter focuses on the analysis of discourses embedded in the online musical practices of children and young people and engages in a review of issues of celebrity and fandom. The research question that underpinned the analysis of data as outlined in this chapter was, 'To what extent does a "discourse of celebrity" circulate the practices related to the production and consumption of Club Penguin Music Videos?' It is argued that questions such as this are important in developing an understanding of the nature of children and young people's online practices.

Given that some of the texts that are the focus for the discussion are multimodal, one might characterise the approach as constituting 'critical multimodal discourse analysis'. van Leeuwen (2012), however, notes that the use of such a term suggests a merger of the fields of critical discourse and multimodality but, he argues, such a merger has not taken place and it is more appropriate to examine multimodal work within the field of discourse analysis or examine criticality within the area of multimodality. More accurately, however, the analysis that takes place within this paper can be located in neither field, as the general focus is less on the texts themselves but on a broader review of the social practices that surround them. It therefore draws on a Foucaultian notion of discourse that analyses the way in which 'discursive practices' and 'discursive formations' (Foucault 1972) construct social practices and in turn are constructed and reinforced through social practices. The paper examines 'the economy of the discursive constellation' (Foucault 1972: 66) from which practices related to the production and consumption of music videos linked to the Disney virtual world Club Penguin draw. The discursive constellation informs the production of films related to Club Penguin that are publicly available on YouTube, comments posted about those films on YouTube and related exchanges on other social networking sites. The aim of the chapter is to examine some of the social practices surrounding the engagement with CPMV and to reflect on the ways in which these practices embed aspects of the fanvid ecology as outlined by Ito (2011), specifically recognition, status and competition, as these relate to celebrity culture.

The analytical approach undertaken in this chapter draws on Foucault's notion of discourse as a set of statements or 'enunciations' which are structured in specific ways according to the discursive practices that shaped their production. It also adopts the analytical steps proposed by Kendall and Wickham (1999) for a Foucaultian approach to discourse analysis, in which the body of statements which constitute a discourse are examined in terms of how they are created, what can be said and what cannot be said and how practices are both discursively and materially constructed. Because of Foucault's emphasis on the power/knowledge relationship in the production of discourse, it is not sufficient to undertake a solely linguistic or even multimodal analysis of discourse. Instead, other approaches need to be implemented and in the case of this study, a more ethnographic approach was undertaken that involved interviews with two key participants over a period of time, alongside observation of the cultural practices in which they were engaged (e.g. YouTube channels, Twitter stream). This enabled a macro analysis of power relationships, in addition to the knowledge of the processes involved in the constitution of celebrity status that it was possible to gain through a micro analysis of linguistic data (i.e. excerpts from online discourse).

Methodology

In order to explore the research question outlined above, I decided to attempt to contact popular CPMV producers, interview them about their practices and analyse their productions and comments left by their fans on their YouTube channels. It seemed appropriate to contact this category of producers, given that my interest was the extent to which a celebrity discourse circulated in this community of practice. While there are hundreds of CPMV creators, there is a small number who have such status. These CPMV creators produce machinima on a regular basis and amass a fan base.

I contacted fifteen of the more prolific CPMV producers through their YouTube accounts, directing them to a Facebook page (https://www.facebook.com/ CPMVResearch) which requested participation in an online survey and indicated the ethical consent process. Five producers responded; however, because four of the producers would not engage with the consent process as approved through the University of Sheffield's ethical review procedures (because it involved communication by email outside

YouTube), only one producer, QusonTheWolf,[2] was able to participate further. I had highlighted one of QusonTheWolf's CPMVs (http://www.youtube.com/watch?v=TK3Uo_-auLU) on the Facebook page as a particularly successful example of these machinima and was contacted by email by 'Wolfs', who thanked me for the 'props' on Facebook and who agreed to answer my questions, although refused to inform me about a/s/l (age, gender or location). Following several exchanges, Wolfs put me in touch with a friend of hers/his, XX (XX is a pseudonym of the second producer's Club Penguin name). XX agreed to participate in the study and was willing to comply with ethical procedures.

QusonTheWolf has a YouTube channel that contains fourteen CPMVs produced by her/him. The channel has 4,681 subscribers to date. XX has thirty-eight CPMVs on her/his YouTube channel and has 1,104 subscribers. XX also has a Twitter account that has over 2,700 followers. QusonTheWolf and XX have collaborated on the production of CPMVs. I undertook email interviews with both QusonTheWolf and XX, corresponding with them over several days. Data from both interviews are drawn upon in this chapter. I also undertook an analysis of the Club Penguin-related products, that is machinima, YouTube channel and Twitter stream, produced by both QusonTheWolf and XX.

The study consisted of the analysis of digital texts and practices and involved no face-to-face contact with participants at all. This has both strengths and limitations. The advantages of this approach are that it means that the location of participants does not limit their engagement in the study, nor do time differences in locations of the researcher and participants impact upon the process. Disadvantages of fully online methods have been well documented (Fielding et al. 2008) and include the inability to completely verify the identities of participants, although this can actually be positive when engaging in sensitive discussions (Hewson et al. 2003).

In terms of undertaking the kind of discourse analysis discussed above, it can be argued that there is little difference in the way this is approached in offline, blended or fully online contexts. This is because the approach involves examining the statements produced in a specific discourse and identifying how the social practices in a given context are discursively and materially produced, and as long as the material and ontological reality of specific contexts are taken into account, then the general approach taken to each context need be no different in nature – what is different is the nature of the data analysed in each case. In the case of the present study, the data analysed were: 1) CPMVs posted on YouTube; 2) responses to interview questions posed in emails to Wolfs and XX; 3) Wolfs' and XX's comments on YouTube; 4) comments posted on Wolfs' and XX's YouTube channels and the channel of a CPMV 'production company' they were involved in, by viewers of their CPMVs; and 5) XX's Twitter stream.

In the following discussion, issues relating to recognition, status and competition embedded within the CPMV fan sub-culture are considered. Given the points made above with regard to the similarities in analytical processes in offline, blended and online contexts, it would be entirely possible to consider matters relating to the circulation of celebrity discourses in non-digital contexts, given the importance of the categories of recognition, status and competition in interpersonal communication more generally. What the following discussion does is to highlight how such discursive practices take place within a digital space through the textual productions and social exchanges of this online community.

Recognition and status

Recognition and status are central tropes in celebrity culture. Both Wolfs and XX had attained celebrity status in the CPMV world. Wolfs had been a member of Club Penguin for a number of years and throughout this period had made CPMVs. He/she was self-taught and used Photoshop to create animations. I asked Wolfs if he/she knew anything about her/his fanbase: 'Often children, my videos involves blood and death, sad stuff really so they might be a little older, maybe 11-15.'

Previous research I have conducted on Club Penguin suggests that younger children search for CPMVs on YouTube (Marsh 2010), with children aged five and six reporting that they watch them. Wolfs stated that her/his rise in status as a CPMV producer happened suddenly and inexplicably:

> I animate a lot in my videos and it was very original, so people liked it. One day I had a breakthrough, I don't know why or what happened but one day my views rose to over 100k on one video!

Since that date, Wolfs has accrued CPMV legendary status. For example, he/she has YouTube playlists dedicated to her/his CPMVs, such as 'QusonTheWolf ROCKS' and 'best youtuber ever QusonTheWolf'. Another fan, DX, collected some of Wolfs's CPMV together and stated on the playlist:

> these songs are made by QUSONTHEWOLF NOT ME so do not put bad coments on my channel and plz like. P.S. qusonthewolf if you are reading this you are the best youtuber ever!

QusonTheWolf's channel has over 4,300 subscribers and comments are regularly posted on the channel by fans, indicating how much they like the CPMV produced by Wolfs:

> You have no idea how good your videos are!!! You don't know how much I want to be in one . . .

hey wolfs great job on that cpmv its the best cpmv you have done yet its epic :)

Hey wolfs! You have an epic channel and incredible videos! (:

Happy Bithrday Wolfs! You get better and even more awesome every-day that goes by in life! And that will happen even after the world ends when it does! Loads of us look up to you and so will the next genera-tions. Your existance has a true, wonderful meaning and to this very day, you have been loved by all. We are so happy to have you around and this message is from everyone who knows you

Regular requests are sent to Wolfs for particular productions:

Hai Quson! I know you probably don't do requests, but you should do Viva La Vida, or some Coldplay! Your Linkin Park music videos are pure beautiful, and I think Coldplay fits your style too :D

@QusonTheWolf, Do you think you can draw a picture of three pen-guins, under a uirl12mbrella in the rain? The penguins are me, GX, and sX. They are REALLY good friends and supported so I wanted to make a special CPMV on "Under My Umbrella" for them. I would appreciate it a LOT!!

In addition, fans request personal links with Wolfs:

Welcome! Could you please sub to me?? That made me soo happy that you replied! You are one of my favorite cpmvs makers of all time!

Hey Wolfs I`m glad you like linkin park! By the way I sent you a friend request on Club Penguin

Hey could we meet on club penguin sometime :)??

These are fan practices that are common on social networking sites with regard to music, film and television celebrities, with fans frequently contact-ing the celebrities directly with messages of praise or requests for specific actions, such as the offering of birthday greetings to fans or friends and family of fans. Iconic CPMV producers adopt strategies used by these main-stream celebrity groups to enhance their fame using social media. De Rijta et al. (2013), in an analysis of the social stratification of celebrity status in print media, suggest that self-reinforcing processes contribute to the conti-nuity of fame over time, in which 'every increase leads to a greater chance for recognition in the future' (268). This is a pattern that can also be seen in celebrity use of social media, with deliberate use of a variety of plat-forms that reinforce fame and together leverage higher visibility, such as the simultaneous and cross-referencing use of Twitter, Instagram/pic, and Facebook. Wolfs does not adopt these social media self-promotion practices, but other CPMV producers do, including XX.

XX is a prolific CPMV creator who has been using Club Penguin since 2008. She/he is a member of a CPMV production group that has many fans. XX also has a strong and loyal following, which means that XX's penguin sometimes gets mobbed in Club Penguin:

> I have been crowded by other penguins on CP after being recognized before, but since I don't want others around when I record, I go on empty servers to avoid that.

XX asserted that he/she did not actively cultivate fans:

> I don't really do anything to get more fans, but I do like to keep my fans happy. I know they like CPMVs so I will keep making those and I always keep up on my messages and comments daily on my channel. I make sure to let my fans know that I do appreciate them. They often make videos for me and I give them a shout out thanking them and I add the videos to a playlist I have for videos from fans.

While obtaining more fans might not be an overtly stated ambition here, an analysis of XX's practices does indicate a tendency for self-promotion. XX has a YouTube channel that links to a Twitter account named after the avatar used by XX in Club Penguin. The Twitter stream is used to reference XX's channel on YouTube and includes a tweet that provides a link to a film that offers evidence that XX's penguin avatar has been featured in the official *Club Penguin* magazine for the fifth time, thus indicating official Club Penguin celebrity status. XX also adopts some of the strategies used by music and film/television celebrities on their Twitter streams, including the following: 'shout outs' to fans that address them directly (e.g. 'you guys'); retweeting fans' tweets; tweeting messages that cite the fan's name alongside a message to that fan, often responding to a direct request/comment from the fan; retweets of the tweets of fans that praise XX and the avatar; tweets providing direct links to XX's productions on YouTube; tweets that link to photographs of XX's avatar activities in order to enable fans to have insights into her (in the case of the avatar) celebrity life and thus establish and maintain some kind of affinity and, finally, use of hashtags that may enhance XX's profile further because they link to hot, current topics. These are successful strategies, as XX has accrued over 2,000 Twitter followers and over 11,300 subscribers to her/his YouTube channel.

The experience of Wolfs and XX demonstrate how recognition and status operate in the CPMV community to confer celebrity status on some CPMV producers. Competition relates to recognition and status, as it is within a competitive and hierarchical arena that such discourses operate comfortably. In the next section, the construction of competition in this online word is considered.

Competition

Recognition and status are reinforced through membership of elite CPMV production crews, which are highly competitive to join. Wolfs is a member of 'Wicked Awesomeness Productions', which consists of experienced CPMV producers who create machinima badged as 'W.A.P. CPMV'. When someone leaves the collective, auditions are held for replacement members. Wolfs reported that W.A.P. receives 'About 20-25 entries each time when we have guy auditions. Girl auditions can get up to 30 entries.' W.A.P. set out specific requirements when recruiting new members which competitors have to meet, as in the example below, which was placed beneath the CPMV that had been posted as part of the audition process:

> W.A.P Requirements: 1) Yes, I am a boy =) 2) I have boxed all W.A.P Members, My youtube channel is active, I reply to messages and comments! 3) Yes, My CP account is a member. Sometimes I use a cpps to film numbers etc and the account name is the same! 4) Yes, I have a filming and editing programme : Hypercam 2 and Sony Vegas Pro 10. 5) I know all the basic knowledge of music video making. 6) I currently don't have an AIM account, But if I get into W.A.P. I will be making an AIM account! 7) I am not in any productions or crews. 8) I have good reputation in CP and Youtube - I dont start fights and I'm very kind! 9) As you can see my audition is a full cpmv and I use my penguin. 10) This video is a video response to http://www.youtube.com/watch?v=3lLy2f . . .
>
> Short paragraph of what WAP means to me: I would love to join WAP and have always been a fan of the music videos and love seeing everyones parts! I am a creative video editor and always get the job done. CPMVS are a passion of mine and I enjoy making them. I have auditioned once before and my good friend jx recomended that I should try out. So I hope you take my audition into consideration and I hope that you enjoyed it. I worked hard on it and took my time.

The list of rules indicates some of the cultural values and practices surrounding CPMV production. This competitor was not successful, but several attempts to get into W.A.P. are frequently made, as was the case with the above competitor, who provided an update at a later date: 'UPDATE : I did not make it into W.A.P. Maybe it will be a 3rd time lucky next time, who knows?'

Frequently, the unsuccessful competitors are sent supportive comments by CPMV fans, which may alleviate their disappointment somewhat:

> Beyond belief amazing, just amazing :0 Wow. That is just the best CPMV I have ever seen. It is so shocking you didn't win! Your so talented :D

> This is still really good! I can tell you and the winner were neck and neck, and I'm not just saying dat!!

Membership of elite CPMV production crews, therefore, leverages particularly high status for members and W.A.P. is frequently referred to by non-members as a mark of distinction. For example, a CPMV producer who was flamed in a YouTube discussion by another user posted the comment: 'dont be rude im getting in W.A.P.' One further mark of recognition in the CPMV circuit that deserves consideration here is the distinction of being selected to participate in collaborations, or what are frequently referred to as 'CPMV collabs', in which several producers work on the same CPMV. These begin with one person inviting participation and posting the collaboration rules, such as the following:

> Rules: Must have screen recorder and editors that will be accepted: Sony Vegas, AVS video editor and imovie, Please use lots of effects and make it flashy! Windows Movie Maker is accepted as long as you use lots of effects! c: Also you're allowed to choose up to 3 Parts!

The machinima above such messages outlining the rules for participation feature the chosen song for the collaboration, while specifying parts of the song that are numbered. Other producers then have to make a pitch to create a section for a specific numbered part. Some CPMV collab organisers insist that the contributors include a 'watermark' on their section (the signature of the producer), thus excluding those that are unable to perform this feat technically and distinguishing experienced producers from 'newbies'. Of course, the more famous CPMV producers can pick and choose which collabs they participate in, as XX notes:

> I didn't used to participate in collabs, I had a strict rule about only being in videos with my production group members but collabs got more and more popular and I saw how much it meant for fans to be in a video with "XX" so I reconsidered and I get a lot of offers, but just agree to the ones with songs I like or that I have time for. I feel bad to have to turn some people away but sometimes I'm busy with my own videos or my production group videos and I just don't have time. They are usually very understanding.

Collabs, therefore, appear to be useful for the less famous producers, with an understanding that the competitive aspect of these may lead to enhanced fame. A further element of competition is introduced by the holding of CPMV competitions themselves. For example, XX posted the following text underneath a machinima announcing a CPMV competition:

> Winner Prizes:
> Party Made For Them.
> 5 Or More Subs.
> Star In My Video.
> Runners Up Prizes:
> 2 Or More Subs.
> V.I.P's At Party.
> Give Ur CPMV As A Video Response - The Results Will Be Out On 18th June, Thankyou.

Being chosen to star in a CPMV is an accolade desired by many and therefore an attractive prize, as is being a VIP at the many parties that are hosted in igloos in the virtual world. Competition, therefore, can be seen to be linked to recognition and status in this context.

What is absent from this analysis of celebrity in the CPMV world is any notion of the relationship between 'celebrity culture and the regulation of classed and gendered selves within neoliberalism' (Allen and Mendick 2013: 78). Important as such an analysis would be, it is beyond the scope of this chapter, due to the constraints on establishing the gender and social class profiles of the featured CPMV producers. Given the way in which online capital relates to offline capital in children's virtual worlds, this kind of analysis would be useful to undertake in terms of identifying how far the more successful CPMV producers conform to or transgress normative expectations with regard to gender, social class and relationship to/with celebrity status in a digital environment.

Conclusion

This chapter has offered an analysis of three aspects of the fanvid ecology of CPMV – recognition, status and competition, as these relate to the construction and performance of a celebrity culture. These have been found to be key elements of the 'the economy of the discursive constellation' (Foucault 1972: 66) of CPMV. It would appear that the CPMV community meets many of the characteristics of 'a thriving amateur creative scene' as described by Ito (2011: 53) and this analysis points to the social function of celebrity in these users' practices.

The implications of the existence of this 'creative scene' for researchers and educators interested in the online digital activities of children in the new media age are numerous. First, I would argue that there is a high level of creativity embedded in the production of CPMVs. This should be recognised in formal educational contexts, as should the range of literacy practices embedded in the production and consumption of such machinima. In an analysis of the meaning-making practices surrounding the machinima *The Trashmaster*, Merchant (2013) makes a similar argument, suggesting that those who are adept at using technologies outside school might not thrive when focusing on print-based literacy in school and thus work which enables the two domains to connect may prove fruitful; conversely, those who are successful in schooled literacy practices may need support from teachers in developing digital literacy skills and knowledge. There is certainly an argument to be made, on viewing many CPMVs, that children and young people could be taught in formal settings how to make more effective transitions in their machinima and how to adopt a more judicious approach to the use of special effects.

Second, the social practices circulating the production and consumption of CPMV should be understood as an example of children's productive engagement with 'new media assemblages' (Carrington 2013) in which media artefacts, such as pop songs, cross with user-produced texts and artefacts in ways that challenge traditional notions of intellectual property rights. To this end, further research needs to be conducted into the way in which children and young people understand and navigate copyright in the music industry, with specific reference to the production of music machinima, and at the same time such studies should examine how the music and game industries respond to the current challenges in this area.

Third, this analysis of CPMVs has raised questions with regard to the extent to which children and young people are able to operate effectively within the social networking sites they use in order to leverage social and cultural capital (Bourdieu 1990). Some of the CPMV producers were able to do this in ways that suggested the use of deliberate strategies that garnered many viewers (and subsequent revenue from YouTube advertisements), while others languished in the comment streams of iconic CPMV creators, attempting to draw attention to their machinima but, ultimately, managing to attract only a few, if any, viewers. Given that engagement in online social networks might offer extended opportunities for individuals in terms of contacts and prospects for enhancing cultural (and perhaps economic) capital, it is important that all children and young people are able to develop strategies that might provide enhanced access to these opportunities. Further research could help to illuminate how children develop the relevant strategies and might identify what support could be offered for those who do not know how to navigate these aspects of online networks.

Further, there are implications for an understanding of children's peer-to-peer cultural practices. Machinima production and related practices are indicative of the rich range of literacy practices in which some children and young people participate in the new media age and which are becoming increasingly popular amongst peer groups. Machinima production might still be a minority activity, but engagement in the viewing of peer-produced texts is more widespread. Children, through their search on YouTube for films produced by other children and young people, whether that is a version of a popular meme that is child-focused (e.g. the *Harlem Shake* performed by soft toys [http://www.youtube.com/watch?v=pZBT5Ko09pM], or *Gangnam Style* danced to by a Furby [http://www.youtube.com/watch?v=U4CV9LebIa8]), a film made by children of their play with popular toys, such as *Thomas the Tank Engine* (Edwards 2013), or a clapping game performed by other children that they might copy in the playground (Marsh and Bishop 2014), are becoming avid consumers of peer-to-peer DIY online texts and artefacts. This can be seen in the growing popularity of 'unboxing' videos, in which children watch other children unpack commercial products, or in the launch of a new video sharing website, AwesomenessTV, which features over 70,000 YouTube channels created by children and young people and watched by this age group, with 1.2 billion views reported in August 2013 (Dunn 2013). This is a phenomenon that is only going to grow in the decades ahead and this brief analysis of CPMV offers some insights into how these peer-to-peer networks operate, but there is scope for more extensive study of this area.

Finally, the chapter has considered issues relating to undertaking discourse analysis in online spaces. Ultimately, the analysis offered here differs little from Foucaultian analyses of offline discourse in that the focus has been on identifying the social practices embedded in a particular space and examining the power and social identities that circulate in such spaces. This is not to suggest that this is always the case; there may be some instances in which discourse analysis in online sites is distinct in comparison to analysis of offline discourse. Nevertheless, given the way that the traditional dichotomy between online and offline practices is being challenged in contemporary societies in which children and young people move fluidly across these domains (see Burke and Marsh 2013), perhaps a future concern for discourse analysts should be related to developing methodological approaches that enable an understanding to be developed of the texts and practices that cross, challenge and dissolve the boundaries between digital and non-digital spaces.

Notes

1 See an example of a CPMV at: http://www.youtube.com/watch?v=TK3Uo_-auLU.
2 YouTube, Twitter and Club Penguin avatar names are only used in relation to QusonTheWolf/Wolfs because permission has been granted by that individual, otherwise they are anonymised throughout the paper. Wolfs read the chapter and had an opportunity to comment on it.

References

Allen, K. and Mendick, H. (2013) 'Young people's uses of celebrity: class, gender and "improper" celebrity', *Discourse: Studies in the Cultural Politics of Education*, 34(1): 77–93.

Bickford, T. (2012) 'The new "tween" music industry: the Disney Channel, Kidz Bop and an emerging childhood counterpublic', *Popular Music*, 31(3): 417–436.

Bourdieu, P. (1990) 'The logic of practice', trans. R. Nice, Cambridge: Polity Press.

Burke, A. and Marsh, J. (eds) (2013) *Children's Virtual Play Worlds: culture, learning and participation*, New York: Peter Lang.

Carrington, V. (2013) 'An argument for assemblage theory: integrated spaces, mobility and polycentricity', in A. Burke and J. Marsh (eds) *Children's Virtual Play Worlds: culture, learning and participation*, 200–216, New York: Peter Lang.

Davis, N., Zook, A., O'Neill, B., Headrick, B., Riedl, M., Grosz, A. and Nitsche, M. (2013) 'Creativity support for novice digital filmmaking', paper presented at Computer Human Interface 2013 Conference, 27 April–2 May 2013. Online. Available HTTP: <http://www.cc.gatech.edu/~riedl/pubs/chi13.pdf> (accessed February 2014).

De Rijta, V., Shorb, E., Ward, C. and Skiena, S. (2013) 'Only 15 minutes? The social stratification of fame in printed media', *American Sociological Review*, 78(2): 266–289.

Dunn, G. (2013) 'Meet the stars of the teen empire', *The Daily Dot*, 2 August. Online. Available HTTP: <http://www.dailydot.com/entertainment/awesomenesstv-youtube-stars-ingrid-nilson/> (accessed February 2014).

Edwards, S. (2013) 'Post-industrial play: understanding the relationship between traditional and converged forms of play in the early years', in A. Burke and J. Marsh (eds) *Children's Virtual Play Worlds: culture, learning and participation*, 10–25, New York: Peter Lang.

Fielding, N. G., Lee, R. G. and Blank, G. (eds) (2008) *The SAGE Handbook of Online Research Methods*, London: Sage.

Foucault, M. (1972) *The Archeology of Knowledge*, trans. R. Sheridan, London: Routledge.

Gee, J. P. (2005) 'Semiotic social spaces and affinity spaces: from the age of mythology to today's schools', in D. Barton and K. Tusting (eds) *Beyond Communities of Practice: language, power and social context*, 214–232, Cambridge: Cambridge University Press.

Hewson, C., Yule, P., Laurent, D. and Vogel, C. (2003) *Internet Research Methods*, London: Sage.

Ito, M. (2011) 'Machinima in a fanvid ecology,' *Journal of Visual Culture*, 10: 51–54.

Ju Choi, C. and Berger, R. (2009) 'Ethics of global internet, community and fame addiction', *Journal of Business Ethics*, 85: 193–200.

Kendall, G. and Wickham, G. (1999) *Using Foucault's Methods*, London: Sage.

KZero (2014) 'Slideshare presentation: KZero Universe Chart Q2 2014'. Online. Available HTTP: <http://www.kzero.co.uk/blog/category/universe-graph/> (accessed September 2014).

Marr, M. and Sanders, P. (2007) 'Disney buys kids' social-network site – WSJ.com', *Wall Street Journal*, 2 August. Online. Available HTTP: <http://online.wsj.com/news/articles/SB118599768804085026> (accessed February 2014).

Marsh, J. (2010) 'Young children's play in online virtual worlds', *Journal of Early Childhood Research*, 8(1): 23–39.

Marsh, J. (2011) 'Young children's literacy practices in a virtual world: establishing an online interaction order', *Reading Research Quarterly*, 46(2): 101–118.

Marsh, J. (2013) 'Breaking the ice: play, friendships and social identities in young children's use of virtual worlds', in A. Burke and J. Marsh (eds) *Children's Virtual Play Worlds: culture, learning and participation*, 59–79, New York: Peter Lang.

Marsh, J. (2014) 'The relationship between online and offline play', in A. Burn and C. Richards (eds) *Children's Games in the New Media Age: childlore, media and the playground*, London: Ashgate.

Marsh, J. and Bishop, J. C. (2014) *Changing Play: play, media and commercial culture from the 1950s to the present day*, Maidenhead, UK: Open University Press/McGrawHill.

Merchant, G. (2013) 'The Trashmaster: literacy and new media', *Language and Education*, 27(2): 144–160.

Small, C. (1998) *Musicking: the meanings of performing and listening*, Hanover, NH: University Press of New England.

Steinkuehler, C. (2007) 'Massively multiplayer online gaming as a constellation of literacy practices', *E-Learning*, 4: 297–318.

Thornton, S. (1996) *Club Cultures: music, media, and subcultural capital*, Oxford: Polity.

van Leeuwen, T. (2012) 'Critical analysis of multimodal discourse', *The Encyclopedia of Applied Linguistics*, published online, 5 November 2012, DOI: 10.1002/9781405198431.wbeal0269.

Wohlwend, K. and Kargin, T. (2013) '"Cause I know how to get friends—plus they like my dancing": (L)earning the nexus of practice in Club Penguin', in A. Burke and J. Marsh (eds) *Children's Virtual Play Worlds: culture, learning and participation*, 79–98, New York: Peter Lang.

Woodruff, J. A. (2009) 'Learning to listen, learning to be: African-American girls and hip-hop at a Durham, NC Boys and Girls Club', unpublished PhD thesis, Duke University.

Chapter 14

Discourses of 'curation' in digital times

Ilana Snyder

In 2010, Eliot van Buskirk announced in *Wired* that we live in the 'age of curation'. In this era of digital excess, he argued, we're surrounded by too much music, too much software, too many websites, too many feeds, too many people and too many opinions. Van Buskirk was onto something. In response to the deluge, curation has emerged as a significant social practice in online spaces, rapidly becoming fundamental to the way in which we view the world: Facebook curates the web, Spotify curates music, the Huffington Post curates the news, and the iPad curates functionality. Curating information is about helping people to find what they need. However, when viewed as a social practice, curation is far more complex: it is always ideological, always rhetorical and often political. This chapter examines the discourses and practices associated with curation in the multiple spaces of the internet. It begins by looking at the genealogy of the word with particular attention to its use in museum studies which continues to influence its application in digital contexts. Next, it explores the growing cultural cachet the notion of curation has experienced in digital marketing, online communication, education online and digital literacy studies. In marketing, online content curation focuses on identifying ways to maximise brand penetration. In online communication, the emphasis is on 'social curation'. In education online, discussions have turned to 'curated learning'. In digital literacy studies, researchers are exploring the notion of curation in relation to identity and multimodality. To conclude, the chapter considers the implications of new ways of thinking about curation in digital times for critical literacy education.

Critical discourse analysis and digital practices

My analysis of the discourses and practices associated with 'curation' in online contexts is informed by an understanding of critical discourse analysis (CDA) that integrates elements of the work of Fairclough (1995), Wodak (2001) and Gee (1996). Although CDA was conceptualised in the context of print texts, as a scholarly orientation it retains its potential to reveal the way power is diffused through the prevalence of various discourses on the internet. The tools of analysis provided by CDA are enduring, as useful in online contexts as they are in the world of print. A discourse is understood as a coherent way of making sense of the world or some aspects of it as reflected in human sign systems including verbal language (Locke 2004). It is a particular construction or version of reality. As Gee explains: 'Discourses are . . . "ways of being in the world"; they are "forms of life". They are, thus, always and everywhere *social* and products of social histories' (1996: viii). CDA is analytical, discourse-oriented and critical. Being 'critical' is understood as 'having distance to the data, embedding the data in the social, taking a political stance explicitly, and a focus on self-reflection as scholars doing research' (Wodak 2001: 9).

The analysis is also informed by the broad understanding of 'practices' integral to the field of literacy studies: 'regular and sustained socio-cultural activities, involving elements of knowledge, identity and being, that vary across social settings, resulting in different kinds of engagements with writing and artefacts of literacy' (Prinsloo and Baynham 2013: xxxi). Practices are passed on through interaction and activity and within them 'knowledge is constituted and social life is produced, maintained and changed' (xxxii). They are habits, dispositions, routines, customs and traditions that provide an account for how the social order is constrained, reproduced and modified.

In literacy studies, practices is used in at least two distinct ways. First, it refers to 'observable, collectable and/or documentable specific ethnographic detail of situated literacy events, involving real people, relationships, purposes, actions, places, times, circumstances, feelings, tools, resources'. Second, it refers to 'culturally recognisable patterns of behaviour' (Tusting et al. 2000: 213). Thinking about curation as a social practice provides a useful lens to examine how people engage with the different forms of curation available online: how they interact and how they construct knowledge.

The genealogy of 'curation'

A few comments about the genealogy of the term and its application in contemporary museum studies are apposite as traces of these meanings are evident in its reinvented forms elsewhere, particularly online. Early usage of 'curation' as a noun in the fourteenth century suggests 'healing' and 'taking care of' (Merriam-Webster Online Dictionary 2013). First used in 1909, 'curate' as a verb means 'to act as curator of (*curate* a museum or an exhibit *curated* by the museum's director)' (Free Dictionary Farlex 2013). The purpose of curation in a museum, but also in a gallery, library or archive, has traditionally involved tangible objects of some sort, whether it be artwork, collectables, historic items or scientific collections. However, these tangible objects are also increasingly available in digitised form. Curation involves content specialists who are responsible for an institution's collections and the interpretation of the material. In the context of museums, 'curation' denotes the selection, organisation, presentation and sharing of information by experts and professionals across a range of areas.

In the late 1960s, understandings of the role of curators in curating exhibitions in museums and galleries began to shift. The turn towards curating as well as the professionalisation of contemporary curating began to establish curatorial practice as a potential space for critique. By the 1990s, curating had emerged as a form of critical intervention into ways of understanding contemporary culture (O'Neill 2007). The new discourse around curatorial practice 'placed an emphasis on individual practice, the first-person narrative and curator self-positioning' as the curators mapped out 'a relatively bare field of discourse' (O'Neill 2007: 242). The 'new' curators attempted to distinguish between the activity of curating and artistic production. In museum studies, the role of the curator had begun to usurp the role of the critic (O'Neill 2007).

Today, exhibitions, especially group exhibitions, art fairs, temporary perennial shows and large-scale international art exhibitions, have become the main means through which contemporary art is mediated, experienced and historicised. At the same time, the respectability of the phenomenon of curating has been enhanced. The relatively recent appearance of the verb 'to curate' in museum studies where once there was just a noun indicates the growth of discussion around curatorial practice. The curator is no longer perceived as a carer but rather as someone who has a more creative and active part to play within the production of art (O'Neill 2007).

Curating is the medium through which the communication between the art and its audience takes place. Curating has become a form of individual creative practice and self-presentation in the processes of artistic production as curators select existing art objects to construct their own 'truths' about art in thematic exhibitions. But it is not a neutral medium. Exhibitions are 'contemporary forms of rhetoric, complex expressions of persuasion whose strategies aim to produce a prescribed set of values and social relations for their audiences' (O'Neill 2007: 244). As such, exhibitions are subjective political tools that uphold particular identities such as artistic, national, international, gender- or race-specific, avant-garde, regional, global etc.: they are always ideological. It follows that curating as a social practice, no matter the context, is always ideological (cf. Street 1984). These new ways of thinking about the exhibition, the curator and curating have important implications for thinking about the discourses and practices associated with curation in online spaces.

The fields of inquiry

Informed by a view of CDA as part of the ethnographic tradition of field research, I set out to find and analyse 'typical texts' that illustrated the discourses of curation evident on the internet (Myer 2006). I did not consider the selection of texts on the internet to be a specific phase that I needed to complete before I began the analysis. I collected some texts by searching for 'curation', analysed those texts finding indicators for particular concepts, expanded those concepts into categories and, on the basis of those results, collected more texts. I selected texts and sites by drawing on my knowledge of experts and key figures in thinking about curation, and their eminence as gauged by multiple references by others. My focus was on the dominant styles, genres and discourses associated with curation. I make no claims about the representativeness of the material I have included. I have dealt with only small corpora which I regard as typical of the discourses associated with curation.

The four categories or fields of inquiry I selected for consideration in this chapter are: digital marketing, online communication, education online and digital literacy studies. Although these fields are usefully distinctive, at the same time, the borders between them are blurred, reflecting as with all social and cultural categories their constructedness as discrete independent disciplines. As would be expected, there is much that is common to them all. Marketing is given the most attention because the influence of marketing discourses that reinforce ideologies like consumerism is pervasive across the other three fields.

The ubiquity of digital marketing

Although the internet is still valorised by some as a free source of information and services, the commercial nature of much online activity is widely acknowledged. Digital technologies bring with them infinite opportunities for profit-making at multiple intersections. The result is that many digital spaces are intrinsically commercial environments (Friesen and Lowe 2012; Snyder et al. 2011). Marketers target particular consumers through the advanced digital tracking and analytics used by companies such as Google and Facebook which then sell the eyeballs of their users to advertisers (Friesen and Lowe 2012). The presentation of interactive customised marketing content via digital channels of communication subtly changes the nature of the communication from overtly commercial advertising and promotion to individual news, comment and word of mouth from 'trusted' and 'credible' electronic sources and 'friends' (Gabbott and Jevons 2009).

For those working in online marketing, content curation represents an untapped reservoir for commercial endeavours. According to Rosenbaum (2010, 2011, 2012), it is vital for marketers (but I would argue also for educators) to understand how content curation differs from content creation and content aggregation. Content creation involves the development of newsworthy, educational and entertainment material for distribution over the internet or other electronic media (Rosenbaum 2011). It verifies the maxim that anyone can be a publisher on the internet, even though how many actually do publish is contested. Content creation includes creating a website and posting material to another site. The materials posted for sharing might be photos, artwork, writing or audio and video files. Wikipedia, 'the free encyclopaedia that anyone can edit', is the iconic example of content creation (Wikipedia 2014).

Around for more than a decade, with sites using algorithms to find and link to content, content aggregation involves the automatic gathering of links. The computerised processes include gathering, organising and filtering content. RSS (rich site summary) is a family of web feed formats used to publish frequently updated works such as blog entries, news headlines, audio and video in a standardised format. An RSS document, or a feed, includes full or summarised text. Users can subscribe to a feed which allows them to monitor and read the feed instead of visiting all the websites they're interested in (Wikipedia 2013). Google News is an example of an RSS feed: 'Comprehensive up-to-date news coverage, aggregated from sources all over the world by Google News' (Google News 2014).

By contrast, content curation or editorial curation, which involves human filtering and organising, is an expanding practice online in which people, the 'human element' (Rosenbaum 2010), add their work to that of the machines. Its antecedents are the weblogs of the late 1990s, which often involved weblinks, a kind of cataloguing of individuals' web browsing aiming to provide a record of useful sites for the bloggers and their communities (Blood 2002). Content curation is the gathering and dissemination of information, utilised by many, from small bloggers to aggregate news giants like the Huffington Post. The Huff, a highly successful example of content curation, is 'the destination for news, blogs and original content offering coverage of US politics, entertainment, style, world news, technology and comedy' (Huffington Post 2014).

Of course, content creation often involves marketing – take for example the use of Wikipedia for self, institutional and corporate promotion. Content aggregation can also involve marketing where just simple branding is evidence of marketing activity as on Google News. However, Rosenbaum argues that content curation has the most potential for people with something to sell. In *Curation Nation*, Rosenbaum (2011) presents an emerging model of how people will find, organise, share and ultimately consume content. With too much information available, content curators offer internet users help to locate what's worthwhile.

Using language that resonates with Rosenbaum's (2011) soft sell of content curation, Gunelius (2012) explains the notion in *Forbes*:

> a form of content marketing where a publisher . . . editorially collects the best content related to a specific niche and targeted to a specific audience then enhances that content by adding personal opinions and expertise. That enhanced content delivers added value to the target audience who consumes it after it's published.

What makes content curation different from the systematic aggregation and syndication of content and links is that it is 'editorially-selected, enhanced, and added value'. Says Gunelius, well-executed content curation is not just a regurgitation of content that was already published but rather 'a personalised retelling of a story. The human element of content curation is what makes curated content compelling.'

There has been intense polarised debate about the differences between content creators and content curators (see Benkler 2006; Lessig 2008). Content creators avoid intellectual property concerns by creating their own content, whereas content curators aggregate, validate and annotate existing content with its associated intellectual property claims. Central to the controversy are questions about the ethics of 'taking' the work of content creators and repurposing it. In the context of news reporting, critics argue that in repackaging other companies' news, some news aggregators are diverting readers and revenue from advertising and undercutting the incentive and also the capacity to spend money on original reporting.

In response to claims that hosting a content-aggregated site is vampirism, Rosenbaum (2011) argues that curation does not kill anything but rather adds a powerful new tool that makes content destinations 'more relevant, more robust, and more likely to attract and retain visitors'. Advertisers will embrace 'trusted places of trusted sources' and creators will have the ability to establish boundaries, both editorial and economic, around what they create and how it is repurposed. He believes that 'curation cannot exist without creation' so much so that it's impossible to imagine curators 'adding value' without a reasonable economic arrangement with content creators. However, the ethical issues around attribution, repurposing and editorialising about others' content are far from resolved.

Online communication

Online communication emerged as a field of study in the 1960s when US researchers first developed protocols that allowed the sending and receiving of messages via computers (Hafner and Lyon 1996). The ARPANET, launched in 1969 by a handful of research scientists, eventually evolved into the internet which in 2014 brings together approximately 2.5 billion people around the world, about a third of the total population. Online communication first became possible in education in the 1980s, following the development and spread of personal computers. Warschauer (2001) suggests dividing online communication into two distinct periods: the introduction of computer-mediated communication in education in the mid-1980s and the emergence of the World Wide Web in the mid-1990s. The popularisation of the term Web 2.0, used in the first decade of the 2000s to describe the transition from static web pages to a more dynamic web, represents a third period to add to Warschauer's earlier two. Although Berners-Lee (2006,

2013), the inventor of the web, has argued that Web 2.0 is not substantially different from earlier technologies, a distinguishing feature is that it allows users to interact and collaborate with each other in contrast to websites where users are limited to the passive viewing of content. Examples of Web 2.0 technologies include social networking sites, blogs, wikis, videosharing sites, hosted services, web applications, mashups and folksonomies.

In the context of Web 2.0, online communication is considered through a social lens. Through the use of Web 2.0 technologies, people create, organise, interpret and share pictures, video, music and opinions. In other words, they 'curate' stuff by engaging in the social practice of content curation, often now referred to as 'social curation'. Of course, this is not a new social phenomenon; the sharing of all sorts of things including media and news predates the internet. People have long shared information about the media content they have heard on radio, seen on television or read in a newspaper or magazine. However, in the online environment it is much easier to share the digital content, not just provide verbal descriptions of it (Villi 2012).

The cultural pervasion of the term curation is evident everywhere but particularly online. Borrelli (2013) discusses why curation, until recently, a job rarely claimed outside the marble halls of museums, has become 'a ubiquitous, quintessentially twenty-first century act'. The title 'curator' has flown from its ivory tower and become democratised connoting 'any thoughtful artisanal soul engaged in an activity that involves selecting, organising and discernment'. Some museum curators are up in arms protesting that the word has been diluted. However, Schlatter (2010), who is an art curator, argues that the practice of social curation complements rather than replaces the role of the professional curator. The real difference between what she calls 'curation 2.0' and museum curation is scholarship. The kind of expertise required to study objects and put together an exhibition for cultural and educational purposes is very different to the kind of curation going on in the context of Web 2.0: at one end of the continuum there is collaboration and participation with visitors and audience, and at the other a very scholarly level of expertise and experience.

Online curators are 'people who can separate quality from junk and put it together in creative ways' (Schlatter 2010). This is what curators have always done in a museum context but now the landscape is broader. If the word 'curation' is getting wider use beyond the art world, that is not necessarily a problem. It doesn't always water it down or devalue it. It takes the word from the rarefied context of the museum to new spaces. Social curation 'encourages the gathering of stories, sharing expertise and creating meaning within a community' (Schlatter 2010). Like Borrelli, Schlatter invokes a discourse long associated with the internet and the web, that Web 2.0 has 'democratised' the social practice of 'curation', adding that it has created the need for experts to identify the best and most relevant online content for people's different requirements.

Credited with coining the term 'virtual community' in the 1980s, Rheingold (2011) explains curation as:

> an act of self-interest that enriches the commons and benefits everybody. I need to search, scan, and select the best resources I can find for my own personal interests, and by making my choices available to others, I create a resource for many besides myself. Curation is also a signal to others who share my interests, people I probably would not have known or known about otherwise, who, in turn, suggest resources to me. I feed the networks of people who do me the honor of valuing my choices, and they feed me back. It's about knowing, learning, sharing, and teaching, all in one.

Echoing Rheingold's social politics about the importance of community, Shirky (2010) argues:

> Curation comes up when people realise that it isn't just about information seeking, it's also about synchronising a community . . . so that when they're all talking about the same thing at the same time, they can have a richer conversation than if everybody reads everything they like in a completely unsynchronised or uncoordinated way.

The practice of social curation comprises the networked distribution of content to which qualitative judgement, imbued with personal and social significance, is added (Villi 2012). What makes social curation a specifically social activity is that it entails communicative interactions and relationships between two or more individuals. Social curation is about people distributing and marketing content in their networks by making personal referrals and guiding their peers to consume content that they consider interesting and relevant. Social curation is involved in the shift from individualised and personalised content consumption towards consumption as a networked practice (Jenkins 2006).

For Villi (2012), social curators are knowledge brokers who interpret, publicise and endorse content so that there is always an aspect of recommendation involved. This links social curation with word-of-mouth communication but the difference between the two is that social curation is also about distribution, in that the access to the digital, internet-based content is often provided with the recommendation. Traces of Rosenbaum's (2011) marketing perspective on social curation are evident in Villi's comments which highlights the artificiality of discussing the different fields of inquiry as discrete categories.

That social curation is essentially ideological is demonstrated by juxtaposing the views of Rheingold, who sees the political possibilities of social curation for transforming cultures and communities, with a website advertising a marketing conference, the Social Curation Summit in Los Angeles (2012). The conference organisers also see value in social curation and the sharing of content, but for commercial purposes:

> Harnessing the power of social curation for marketing campaigns, product launches, promotions, events, and every-day projects is what Social Curation Summit is all about. Join us as we explore how the social graph is transforming from a network of who-knows-who into a dynamic interest graph of who-knows-what discovered through social curation.

It seems that the discourses of communication and marketing are constantly rubbing up against each other in the online world of social curation.

Education online

A common thread in writing and research about education, particularly school education, is the importance of developing skills for the twenty-first century. The focus is on 'producing effective citizens in a global economy' (Partnership for 21st Century Skills 2013). The Partnership for 21st Century Skills, a coalition of business people, education leaders and policy makers, was founded in 2002 to 'kickstart a national conversation' on the importance of twenty-first century skills for all K-12 students. It outlines the twenty-first century skills that must be mastered by K-12 students:

> Today's graduates need to be critical thinkers, problem solvers and effective communicators who are proficient in both core subjects and new, 21st century content and skills. These 21st century skills include learning and thinking skills, information and communications technology literacy skills, and life skills.

Using similar language and emphases, the Assessment and Teaching of 21st Century Skills (ATC21S) project (2013), led by the University of Melbourne, like its US counterpart, the Partnership for 21st Century Skills, supported by the IT industry, puts twenty-first century skills into four broad categories: ways of thinking – creativity, critical thinking, problem-solving, decision-making and learning; ways of working – communication and collaboration; tools for working – information and communications technology (ICT) and information literacy; skills for living in the world – citizenship, life and career, and personal and social responsibility.

Clearly, there is a high degree of consensus amongst educators world-wide about what twenty-first century skills comprise. Also noteworthy is that these educational policy and strategic directions are strongly linked to corporate interests and closely associated with standards and assessment.

Although none of the documents surveyed used the term curation, many active blogs and sites developed and maintained by educators draw attention to the important links between curation and twenty-first century education. The owners of these sites are often teacher librarians and educators, but also marketers of curation software, highlighting the porous border between business and education.

Take, for example, Barbara Bray (2011), a 'creative learning strategist' in California, who makes connections between twenty-first century skills and curation on her website and, at the same time, promotes Scoop-it curation software:

> A curator pulls together and oversees collections of materials. The Internet, Web 2.0 tools and social media have expanded the traditional role of publisher to almost anyone. The role of curator is changing too. Anyone can 'curate' online material, pulling together their own collections . . . I started a new Scoop-it 'Curate your Learning' and now I see why curating is important.

Some academics working in the field of education are using the term curation in their writing. A notable exponent is George Siemens (2008), a Canadian researcher who writes about learning, networks and technology in digital environments. Rather than twenty-first century skills, his focus is 'connected learning' but there is some resonance between the two. Siemens (2008) asks:

> What becomes of the teacher in these new times and spaces? How do the practices of the educator change in networked environments, where information is readily accessible? How do we design learning when learners may adopt multiple paths and approaches to content and curriculum? How can we achieve centralised learning aims in decentralised environments?

To answer these questions, he explores the shifting role of educators in networked learning, with particular emphasis on curatorial, atelier, concierge and networked roles of educators. He explains that these metaphors have been developed to help educators think about how they might assist learners 'in forming diverse personal learning networks for deep understanding of complex fields'. Siemens describes a curatorial teacher as one who,

> acknowledges the autonomy of learners, yet understands the frustration of exploring unknown territories without a map. A curator is an expert learner. Instead of dispensing knowledge, he creates spaces in which knowledge can be created, explored, and connected. While curators understand their field very well, they don't adhere to traditional

in-class teacher-centric power structures. A curator balances the freedom of individual learners with the thoughtful interpretation of the subject being explored. While learners are free to explore, they encounter displays, concepts, and artifacts representative of the discipline. Their freedom to explore is unbounded. But when they engage with subject matter, the key concepts of a discipline are transparently reflected through the curatorial actions of the teacher.

Siemens presents the teacher as curator as an appealing model for education 'in the twenty-first century': his discourse resonates with the language of student-centred approaches to teaching and learning in which the teacher plays an important role as guide and mentor, except that he has added the notion of curation.

Digital literacy studies

Within the field of literacy studies, recent thinking in identity studies and multimodality refers to curation. Although the use of the word is still rare, the notion is central to Potter's (2012) *Digital Media and Learner Identity: the new curatorship*. The book is informed by the idea that curatorship is a useful metaphor for understanding young people's learning both in and out of school. New digital media, he argues, provide new contexts for 'making the self' (43). With the impact of social media, many people have created a profile of some sort – a place to collect favourite videos, moments to share, maintain affiliations with friends, family etc. – a cultural space shaped by new media technologies. As Potter (2012: 5) explains:

> It is quite natural for those who choose and have the means to do so, to share a mediated and 'curated' version of their experience when they make, edit, and present media texts of various kinds from the online CV to the photo gallery, from the blog to the YouTube clip. Whereas in earlier times, apposite words to describe activities around publication may have been 'written,' 'edited,' and/or 'produced,' it is quite clear that they are inadequate to capture all the self-representational activities or practices in networked, digital culture. The word 'curated' does so by subsuming all of those practices and adding others that are possible in social media.

He defines curatorship as 'an active cultural and literacy practice in new media with its own ways of reading and writing the self, its own lexis and grammar'. Potter argues that curating is not only about writing or creating but also about collecting, distributing, assembling and disassembling. All of these activities are part of what people do in new media production – from posting a status on a social networking site through to making a short clip, sharing an online gallery, or any number of other activities. He describes it as an 'active practice' (Barton 1994) that is larger in its reach, scope and nature than the others but which contains and subsumes them. He explains curating as 'knowing how the different forms you are working with work together to make meaning intertextually and for which purposes and audiences they are successful' (Potter 2012: 5).

Appropriations and borrowings have always been enacted across the arts but those with access to digital technologies have the opportunity to take and remix content, to publish things they have made alongside things they created by others and to establish new relationships and thus new meanings but always with consideration of the complex ethical issues associated with using content created by others. These practices embody 'the curatorial nature of lived experience in the twenty-first century' (Potter 2012: 7). It is of interest to note that both Potter (2012) and Rosenbaum (2011) raise the same ethical issues related to the use of others' content.

Curation and critical literacy education

The term curation has moved from the rarefied context of museums and galleries to online spaces where it is used for a range of different purposes and audiences. In all the discourses associated with the term in online practices, traces of its century-old use in museum studies linger, suggesting that 'the objects have been chosen and presented by an expert equipped with the appropriate knowledge and experience . . . making selections and recommendations appealing' (Schlatter 2010). Fairclough's (1992) notion of 'interdiscursivity', the mixing of diverse genres or styles in a single text, is useful here to explain how understandings of curation in the gallery domain bleed into and affect other domains. Often seen as a special kind of intertextuality, interdiscursivity is where texts have the propensity to be full of snatches of other texts which may be 'explicitly demarcated or merged in, and which the text may assimilate, contradict, ironically echo, and so forth' (Fairclough 1992: 84). In this process, elements that were previously unique to a particular domain meet online, a meeting that has fundamental consequences for the discourses of curation as they become part of our 'remix culture' (Lessig 2008) and the wider processes of social change. But no matter the domain or field of inquiry, the use of the term is never neutral; it is always ideological. The curation of digital assets is a contemporary form of rhetorical persuasion aimed at producing a particular set of responses and interpretations amongst users. Users can resist such efforts to influence them but to varying degrees. These understandings have important implications for critical literacy education.

While young people's use of the internet is never naive, research has demonstrated that they are not easily able to appreciate the complex social, political and outright commercial practices and relationships that are integral to the new digital spaces (ACMA 2009; Buckingham 2009). As active participants in virtual worlds, they develop their digital literacy practices through different online pursuits. They learn new social practices, as well as applying and extending their existing knowledge to engage with online worlds. It is important that literacy educators develop a deep understanding of how young people learn to negotiate these worlds as the spaces in which they interact are saturated with cultural, political and commercial messages and influences (Chester and Montgomery 2007). Although pedagogical responses which provide young people with opportunities to learn a critical approach to the use of digital media have been called for (Potter 2012; Snyder et al. 2011), as yet not enough has been done to make it a reality.

Much of the discussion around the use of new media in literacy education has centred on the 'consumers versus producers' debate, a bifurcation that has never been very helpful. Views vary wildly about the number of people who actively produce content on the internet ranging from the '1% rule' to many, but it seems that the producers are far fewer in number than the consumers. A more useful approach might be to describe what people do on the internet, in other words their discourse practices (Fairclough 1992), in terms of the three categories identified in this chapter: content creators, content aggregators and content curators. Such an approach might generate a more nuanced account of the activities in which young people engage in the new media environment and how schools and teachers might use the knowledge to inform teaching and learning. All three are important but the one literacy educators know least about is curation. When broadly applied, curating suggests the functions of editing, aggregating, organising, culling, directing or conducting. But it can also involve trying, testing new attitudes, rethinking and pushing boundaries (Schlatter 2010). Literacy educators need to develop strategies to raise young people's critical awareness of the various forms of curation evident online in which the process of discourse naturalisation can make what is local, universal, what is partisan, neutral, and what is arbitrary, natural (Vázquez 2006). The implications for new directions in critical literacy education in digital times, aimed at producing more informed critical users of online spaces, are clear.

A critical literacy approach is underpinned by the view of the social world and its texts elaborated earlier: in CDA terms, the social world and its texts are neither natural nor neutral but constructed in ways that naturalise the operations of power and discrimination. A critical literacy approach offers education systems and teachers a powerful knowledge base to develop children and young people's social awareness and active, responsible citizenship by using effective classroom strategies (Lankshear and Knobel 2006; Luke 2000, 2012). In a critical literacy classroom, the aim is to enhance students' understanding of the constructed nature of the world they inhabit (Buckingham

2007). While critical literacy has often focused on the analysis of the texts students consume in the mass media, the rise of digital technologies has seen the emphasis shift to the texts they produce (Larson and Marsh 2005). The focus needs to move beyond seeing students as either consumers or producers of texts. The sophisticated discourses of curation demand attention.

By focusing on the ethical, cultural, environmental and societal implications of the changes to language and discourse evident on the internet, children and young people need to use a critical approach so that they begin to understand the complex relationships between language, power, social groups and social practices in the context of the internet. The enhancement of children and young people's *critical* capabilities in this domain has direct implications for their personal development and their future impact on society and the environment. Bernstein's (1990) notion of 'recontextualisation', the ideological process by which discourses are delocated, relocated and refocused, might be useful here to inform teachers' critical digital literacy pedagogies in the context of online curation practices. Students' attention needs to be drawn to how texts might be read differently when they are recontextualised on various online sites.

In an afterword to *Digital Media and Learner Identity*, Potter (2012: 177–181) presents nine principles in the form of a manifesto to inform teaching and learning in the twenty-first century. All of Potter's principles would be useful in efforts to elaborate the notion of critical literacy for digital times. But it is the last principle which is of particular relevance. Taking a little licence with the wording, it could read: 'Curation is a new literacy practice: think about how we can develop critical literacy education which recognises this.' Integral to the notion of 'newness' must be recognition that curation is aligned with aspects of older practices and forms, but in the context of digital technologies curation comprises creation, aggregation, organisation, interpretation and production of digital content and assets. Understanding curation in the context of the internet needs to be intrinsic to critical literacy education.

If indeed we are in the age of curation, literacy researchers and educators need to understand the different forms curation has assumed on the internet, the purposes for which it is used and the young audiences towards which it is often directed. Intrinsic to this analytic work is consideration of the discourses and practices associated with curation. Moreover, it is the tools of analysis offered by CDA which remain vital for contemporary critical literacy education.

Acknowledgements

Thanks to Denise Beale for her help with the library and online searches for relevant material and for her thoughtful comments about an early version. Thanks also to Julie Faulkner and Mastin Prinsloo for their generative responses to a draft.

References

ACMA (Australian Communication and Media Authority) (2009) 'Click and Connect 02: young Australians' use of online social media', Australian Media and Communication Authority, Canberra. Online. Available HTTP: <http://www.acma.gov.au/> (accessed 1 April 2010).

ATC21S (Assessment and Teaching of 21st Century Skills) (2013) 'What are 21st century skills'. Online. Available HTTP: <http://atc21s.org/index.php/about/what-are-21st-century-skills/> (accessed 9 April 2013).

Barton, D. (1994) *An Introduction to the Ecology of Written Language*, Oxford: Blackwell.

Benkler, Y. (2006) *The Wealth of Networks: how social production transforms markets and freedom*, New Haven, CT: Yale University Press.

Berners-Lee, T. (2006) 'IBM developer Works Interviews podcast'. Online. Available HTTP: <http://www.ibm.com/developerworks/podcast/dwi/cm-int082206.tx> (accessed 8 April 2013).

Berners-Lee, T. (2013) 'Tim Berners-Lee'. Online. Available HTTP: <http://www.w3.org/People/Berners-Lee/> (accessed 5 April 2013).

Bernstein, B. (1990) *The Structuring of Pedagogic Discourse*, London: Routledge.

Blood, R. (2002) *The Weblog Handbook: practical advice on creating and maintaining your blog*, New York: Perseus Books Group.

Borrelli, C. (2013) 'Everybody's a curator', *Chicago Tribune*, 4 October. Online. Available HTTP: <http://articles.chicagotribune.com/2013-10-04/entertainment/ct-ae-1006-borrelli-curation-20131004_1_curator-fake-shore-drive-kristin-cavallari> (accessed 22 December 2013).

Bray, B. (2011) 'Curation as a 21st century skill'. Online. Available HTTP: <http://barbarabray.net/2011/10/27/curation-as-a-21st-century-skill/> (accessed 9 April 2013).

Buckingham, D. (2007) 'Selling childhood? Children and consumer culture', *Journal of Children and Media*, 1(1): 15–24.

Buckingham, D. (2009) 'The impact of the commercial world on children's wellbeing', Report of an Independent Assessment, Nottingham: DCSF Publications. Online. Available HTTP: <http://publications.dcsf.gov.uk> (accessed 12 December 2009).

Chester, J. and Montgomery, K. (2007) 'Interactive food and beverage marketing: targeting children and youth in the digital age', Berkeley Media Studies Group. Online. Available HTTP: <http://digitalads.org/reports.php> (accessed 1 September 2010).

Fairclough, N. (1992) *Discourse and Social Change*, Cambridge: Polity Press.

Fairclough, N. (1995) *Critical Discourse Analysis*, London: Longman.

Free Dictionary Farlex (2013) 'Curate'. Online. Available HTTP: <http://www.thefreedictionary.com/curate> (accessed 1 April 2013).

Friesen, N. and Lowe, S. (2012) 'The questionable promise of social media for education: connective learning and the commercial imperative', *Journal of Computer Assisted Learning*, 28(3): 183–194.

Gabbott, M. and Jevons, C. (2009) 'Brand community in search of theory: an endless spiral of ambiguity', *Marketing Theory*, 9(1): 119–122.

Gee, J. P. (1996) *Social Linguistics and Literacies: ideology in discourses*, 2nd edn, London: Taylor and Francis.

Google News (2014) Online. Available HTTP: <http://news.google.com.au/> (accessed 21 February 2014).

Gunelius, S. (2012) '5 Ways to use content curation for marketing and tools to do it', *Forbes*. Online. Available HTTP: <http://www.forbes.com/sites/work-in-progress/2012/07/05/5-ways-to-use-content-curation-for-marketing-and-tools-to-do-it/> (accessed 3 April 2012).

Hafner, K. and Lyon, M. (1996) *Where Wizards Stay Up Late: the origins of the Internet*, New York: Simon & Schuster.

Huffington Post (2014) Online. Available HTTP: <http://www.huffingtonpost.com/> (accessed 21 February 2014).

Jenkins, H. (2006) *Convergence Culture*, New York: NYU Press.

Lankshear, C. and Knobel, M. (2006) *New Literacies: changing knowledge and classroom learning*, 2nd edn, Buckingham: Open University Press.

Larson, J. and Marsh, J. (2005) *Making Literacy Real: theories and practices for learning and teaching*, London: Sage.

Lessig, L. (2008) *Remix: making art and commerce thrive in the hybrid economy*, New York: Penguin.

Locke, T. (2004) *Critical Discourse Analysis*, London: Continuum.

Luke, A. (2000) 'Critical literacy in Australia', *Journal of Adolescent and Adult Literacy*, 43(5): 448–461.

Luke, A. (2012) 'Critical literacy: foundational notes', *Theory into Practice*, 51(1): 4–11.

Merriam-Webster Online Dictionary (2013) Online. Available HTTP: <http://www.merriam-webster.com/dictionary/curation> (accessed 1 April 2013).

Myer, M. (2006) 'Between theory, method, and politics: positioning of the approaches to CDA', in R. Wodak and M. Myer (eds) *Methods of Critical Discourse Analysis*, 14–31, first published in 2001, London: Sage.

O'Neill, P. (2007) 'The curatorial turn: from practice to discourse', in J. Rugg and M. Sedgwick (eds) *Issues in Curating Contemporary Art and Performance*, 240–259, Chicago, IL: Intellect Books and University of Chicago Press.

Partnership for 21st Century Skills (2013) Online. Available HTTP: <http://www.p21.org/> (accessed 9 April 2013).

Potter, J. (2012) *Digital Media and Learner Identity: the new curatorship*, New York: Palgrave MacMillan.

Prinsloo, M. and Baynham, M. (2013) 'Introduction: great divides and situated literacies', in M. Prinsloo and M. Baynham (eds) *Literacy Studies Vol 1: great divides and situated literacies*, xxiii–xxxv, London: Sage.

Rheingold, H. (2011) 'Lord of Curation series: Howard Rheingold', Online. Available HTTP: <http://blog.scoop.it/2011/09/13/lord-of-curation-series-howard-rheingold/> (accessed 12 April 2013).

Rosenbaum, S. (2010) 'Why content curation is here to stay', Online. Available HTTP: <http://mashable.com/2010/05/03/content-curation-creation/> (accessed 4 April 2010).

Rosenbaum, S. (2011) *Curation Nation*, New York: McGraw-Hill.

Rosenbaum, S. (2012) Huffington Post: MTV and the "curated me"', Online. Available HTTP: <http://www.mtvinsights.com/post/27497920659/huffington-post-mtv-and-the-curated-me> (accessed 10 April 2013).

Schlatter, N. E. (2010) 'A new spin: are DJs, rappers and bloggers "curators"?', *Museum*, 49–55, American Association of Museums, January/February.

Shirky, C. (2010) 'Talk about curation', Online. Available HTTP: <http://curation chronicles.magnify.net/video/Clay-Shirky-6#c=1RMHLF18HLLBQ6WK&t=Talk about Curation> (accessed 8 April 2010).

Siemens, G. (2008) 'Learning and knowing in networks: changing roles for educators and designers', ITFORUM for Discussion 27 January. Online. Available HTTP: <http://itforum.coe.uga.edu/Paper105/Siemens.pdf> (aaccessed 9 April 2013).

Snyder, I., Jevons, C., Henderson, M., Gabbott, M. and Beale, D. (2011) 'More than chatting online: children, marketing and the use of digital media', *English in Australia*, 46(3): 320–340.

Social Curation Summit: Visual communities and commerce (2012) Online. Available HTTP: <http://www.mediabistro.com/socialcurationsummit/> (accessed 7 April 2013).

Street, B. V. (1984) *Literacy in Theory and Practice*, Cambridge: Cambridge University Press.

Tusting, K. R., Ivanic, R. and Wilson, A. (2000) 'New literacy studies at the interchange', in D. Barton, M. Hamilton and R. Ivanic (eds) *Situated Literacies*, 210–218, London: Routledge.

van Buskirk, E. (2010) 'Overwhelmed? Welcome the age of curation', Wired. Online. Available HTTP: <http://www.wired.com/business/2010/05/feeling-overwhelmed-welcome-the-age-of-curation/> (accessed 20 April 2013).

Vázquez, G. P. (2006) 'The recycling of local discourses in the institutional talk: naturalization strategies, interactional control, and public local identities', *Estudios de Sociolingüística* 7(1), 55–82. Online. Available: HTTP: <file:///C:/Users/ilanas/Downloads/f185_a194_FD5JC.pdf> (accessed 8 April 2014).

Villi, M. (2012) 'Social curation in audience communities: UDC (user-distributed content) in the networked media ecosystem', *Journal of Audience and Reception Studies*, 9(2): 614–632.

Warschauer, M. (2001) 'Online communication', in R. Carter and D. Nunan (eds) *The Cambridge Guide to Teaching English to Speakers of Other Languages*, 207–212, Cambridge: Cambridge University Press.

Wikipedia. (2013) 'RSS', Online. Available HTTP: <http://en.wikipedia.org/wiki/RSS> (accessed 6 April 2013).

Wikipedia. (2014) Online. Available HTTP: <http://en.wikipedia.org/> (accessed 21 February 2014).

Wodak, R. (2001) 'What CDA is about – a summary of its history, important concepts and its developments', in R. Wodak and M. Meyer (eds) *Methods of Critical Discourse Analysis*, 1–13, London: Sage.

Chapter 15

The discursive construction of education in the digital age

Neil Selwyn

While digital technology and media now proliferate in contemporary society, the relationship between education and 'the digital' continues to be of particular interest to many academics. This reflects the significant but uneasy relationship between education and digital technology that has developed over the past three decades or so. On one hand, digital technology is now part of education in ways that would have been hard to imagine even a few years ago. Learners and educators have unprecedented access to information and communications through a variety of portable and personalised digital devices. Classrooms and other learning environments are awash with digital resources, and a growing amount of educational work is conducted on a 'virtual' basis. Yet the consequences and outcomes of these educational 'digitisations' have tended to be mixed. Indeed, it could be argued that digital technologies have promised much in the way of educational improvement and innovation over the past thirty years – but delivered much less. As such, it makes sense for us to approach digital education in problematic terms.

The digital practices and processes of contemporary education are therefore best understood as sites of struggle and intense conflict. These struggles take place across a number of fronts – from the allocation of resources and maximisation of profit, to concerns with epistemology or equality of educational opportunities. As such, many of the key issues underpinning education and digital technology would appear to be the fundamentally *political* questions that are asked continually of education and society – that is questions of what education is, and questions of what education should be. Developing a fuller sense of the educational application of digital technology could therefore be said to come from recognition of broader issues of power, control, conflict and resistance. Put bluntly, any account of digital technology use in education needs to be framed in explicit terms of societal conflict over the distribution of power.

This brings us to the focus of this chapter – that is approaching digital education as discourse. To extend Stuart Hall's (2003: 12) critique of education policy making, the discursive construction of digital education could be said to be 'critical to the whole venture' of educational technology. Aside from attempting to persuade relevant 'stakeholders' of the legitimacy, viability and value of digital products, processes and practices, these discourses play a subtle role in 'squaring circles' and rationalising often contradictory perspectives, motivations and goals – thus seeking to enrol the popular consent of often sceptical practitioners and the general public. Carefully studying the discourses that have been employed (and teasing out the contradictions, fault lines and recurring themes within) can therefore provide far richer insights into the growing place of digital technology and media within education than would be possible through analysis of educational practice alone (see for example Rudd 2013; Williamson 2013).

Problematising digital education through a critical analysis of discourse

This focus on politics and power has a clear bearing on how we might best analyse the discourses that surround digital education – pointing in particular towards the domain of critical discourse analysis (CDA). As has been reiterated throughout this book (see for example the chapters by Snyder and Marsh), the basic premise of CDA is that language use is not neutral but infused with issues of power, privilege, ideology and politics. Language use is therefore seen as a form of social practice that is entwined with social struggle and, it follows, is contested *and* contestable (Fairclough 1989; van Dijk 1993). On one hand, then, what is said about 'new' digital developments in education is clearly shaped by existing relations of power, ideological agendas and forms/conditions of dominance. However, what is said about digital technology also acts to shape ongoing educational conditions in terms of the knowledge, social relations and social identities that surround them. In this sense, discourse should be understood as a key element in the production of the social reality of contemporary digital education – how people understand 'the way things are' and (perhaps most importantly) 'the way things could be' when it comes to the use of digital technology in education. Indeed, as Thomas (1999: 42) reasons, 'each discourse embodies constraints on the meanings it makes possible'. CDA can therefore be used to ask questions of how certain meanings and understandings of digital education come to dominate over others, and how particular groups wield discursive power over others.

There is much, then, that a CDA approach can bring to the analysis of digital education – particularly in terms of unpacking the meaning making implicit in recent discussion of the implications of new technologies for changing the future arrangement of compulsory and post-compulsory education. The CDA approach suggests, for example, making a distinction between different dimensions of the digital education discourse (Fairclough 1989). These include the *contents* of the discourse – that is what is said (and not said) about digital technologies and education; the implicit social *relations* that the discourse assumes and helps establish between participants; and the *subject* positions which the discourse sets up – that is implicit power relations, social distance, authority claims and construction of oppositional groups. The CDA approach therefore draws attention to the question of how particular representations of the content, relations and subjects come to dominate popular understandings of digital education, and in particular come to be 'naturalised' as a generally unchallenged form of 'common sense' (Fairclough 1989). This is when the ideological character of a discourse is obscured – when 'received wisdom' works to obscure the vested interests, dominant agendas and power imbalances of any situation, especially the social relations and power hierarchies that exist between different actors and interests. In this sense (and the particular focus of this chapter) the CDA approach highlights the need to complement any concern with the contested notion of 'digital education' as technological form with concern with digital education as social form – that is through consideration of the social actors (individuals, institutions, vested interests) and social relations that are implicated in these changes.

With these thoughts in mind, this chapter will now go on to offer a brief account of how digital education has been constructed recently in political, professional, academic and commercial discursive arenas. The examples drawn upon are offered as an illustrative – rather than systematic – analysis of some of the most widely discussed and highest-profile examples of educational technology over the past thirty years. These examples will be examined to explore the role of discourse in the construction, consolidation, and reproduction of the 'reality' of education and digital technology (Fairclough 1995). In particular it will examine the various ways in which the topic of education and digital has been framed – that is the recurring rhetorical structures and argumentative structures that articulate seemingly diverse discourses 'together in a particular way' (Fairclough 2005: 37). It will also examine how various linguistic and rhetorical features – such as lexical strategies, propositions and presuppositions, metaphors, attribution, interpersonal functions and agency – have been mobilised to implement the argumentative and discursive strategies at play within ongoing debates over education and digital technology over the past thirty years or so. Using this analytic approach, therefore, we can now go on to ask just what are the wider philosophies, priorities and values that are shaping the ongoing drive towards digitisation throughout education? More importantly, how might we understand the potential gains and losses of what is being advanced?

Digital education and 'discourses of disruption'

Discourses of digital education have proliferated since the introduction of the first 'standalone' computers into university and high school classrooms in the 1960s. We have now long moved on from talk of the 'computer tutor', the 'mighty micro', 'computer-assisted instruction' and the like – yet the contemporary dominance of these now faded discourses should be remembered when making sense of more recent developments. Indeed, most recently a fresh set of educational discourses has accompanied the emergence of 'new' technologies such as social media, wireless connectivity and cloud data storage, and not least the seemingly unassailable rise of personalised and portable computing devices such as smartphones and tablets. Within educational circles, popular debate, commercial marketing, education policy texts and academic research are now replete with sets of phrases and slogans such as 'twenty-first century skills', 'flipped classrooms', 'self-organised learning environments', 'unschooling', an 'iPad for every student', 'massive online open courses' and so on. If we are to make sense of current forms of digital education, then it is necessary to consider the nature of *these* particular discourses.

As is common with matters relating to new technology, these discourses relate predominantly to notions of change and transformation. Common tropes here include notions of renewal, re-versioning (as evident in the suffixing of '2.0', '3.0', '4.0' and so on) and the antagonistic promise of 'disruption'. Indeed, the idea of 'disrupting old-fashioned practices' is a familiar element of the discourses surrounding the 'social' media and personalised digital devices of the past ten years or so (Poole 2012). Yet, while these arguments are applied to many areas of society – from the newspaper industry to high street retailing – they are particularly prevalent with regards to education. This is typified by Jeff Jarvis' (2009: 210) assertion that 'education is one of the institutions most deserving of disruption-and with the greatest opportunities to come of it'. To the unfamiliar, this is a highly provocative and deeply disconcerting proposition. Yet statements such as these are now being made with such frequency and force within technological circles that they tend to no longer register fully with those of us who work in and around the educational technology field. The idea of impending 'digital disruption' is beginning to pass into educational common sense.

While it is all too easy to concur unthinkingly with such rhetoric, blithe statements such as '*education is one of the institutions most deserving of disruption*' raise a host of important questions. For example:

- What meanings and understandings of education are being conveyed through these portrayals of digital disruptions, and in whose interests do they work?
- To what extent are these constructions of digital disruption situated within dominant structures of production and power?
- What freedoms and restrictions are being associated with such statements?

- How are these likely to be experienced by different individuals and social groups?
- How do these discourses frame the relationship between the individual and the commons, the public and the private?

As such, these discourses of educational change and disruption certainly merit further exploration and unpacking. This chapter will now present a brief review of some of these discourses that can be clustered into two loose categories that can be termed 'digital re-schooling' and 'digital de-schooling':

Discourses of digital 're-schooling'

This first category of digital 're-schooling' refers to descriptions of formal education provision being reoriented and recast into forms that reflect the individually centred, connected, fluid, creative qualities of the 'digital age'. Here the broad understanding is of a substantial reconstruction of educational institutions along digital lines – retaining the institutional notion of the 'school', 'college' and 'university', but as a reconfigured set of relations. These discourses celebrate the role of digital technology in breaking down barriers between and within institutional settings, facilitating new ways of participating/interacting, and allowing participants to 'bring in' their own vernacular practices. Within any educational institution, digital technologies are therefore seen to break down traditional barriers between time/space; experts/novices; production/consumption; single/simultaneous acts; and synchronous/asynchronous communications. In terms of what takes place within educational institutions, digital technologies are therefore seen to support a range of radically different learning practices and altered social relations.

Such 're-schooling' arguments were advanced throughout the 2000s via proposals for so-called 'School 2.0' – that is the development of digitally aligned modes of schooling that are built around the active communal creation of knowledge (rather than passive individual consumption and a 'one-size-fits-all' mentality), and imbued with a sense of play, expression, reflection and exploration. As Collins and Halverson (2009: 129) put it, this involves not only 'rethinking what is important to learn' but also 'rethinking learning'. This need to reconfigure the structures and processes of formal schools has perhaps been explored most thoroughly in terms of curriculum and pedagogy, as evidenced in the rash of proposals from enthusiastic academics and practitioners for the development of 'pedagogical mash-ups' and new pedagogies of social interaction. Growing numbers of authors have also pursued the likely nature and form of 'curriculum 2.0' – what Whitby (2013: 9–11) describes as a 'new model' of schooling based around 'openness to learning and masterful tech-savvy'.

These discourses are implicit in popular discourse surrounding the 'future of education' – from Ken Robinson's animated arguments for 'Changing Education Paradigms' to movements endorsing the 'flipped classroom' and 'open badges'. In a more tangible form, re-schooling discourses are now embodied in a number of high profile physical forms, such as Microsoft's 'High School of the Future' in Philadelphia, and Apple's long-running 'School of the Future' in New York. These ventures are imbued with familiar sets of descriptions – with digital technology seen to support 'community collaboration'; 'content creation and sharing content'; 'innovative education practices and new models for learning'; empowering 'learning community members' with a 'passionate, personal responsibility for learning' (Microsoft 2013). Similar projects have involved the embedding of game mechanics and 'interactive online design that plays on people's competitive instincts' (Quitney and Rainie 2012: 1) into the (re)development of public high schools in New York and Chicago. This so-called 'gamification' of education has involved the social organisation and physical architecture of these schools being based around a game-based learning model, with classrooms and curriculum designed to support students within inquiry-based activities of 'questing'. Under these conditions the school curriculum is divided into 'domains', with teaching and learning based around game principles involving secret 'discovery missions', students being 'levelled-up' in academic difficulty and so on. In this sense, gamification can be seen as striving to combine intrinsic motivation, competitive sentiment, performance measurement and metrics with the extrinsic rewards associated with play (Jones this volume; Nelson 2012). As Salen et al. (2011) conclude:

> Gaming and game design offer a promising new paradigm for curriculum and learning. The designers of Quest to Learn developed an approach to learning that draws from what games do best: drop kids into inquiry-based, complex problem spaces that are built to help players understand how they are doing, what they need to work on, and where to go next. Content is not treated as dry information but as a living resource; students are encouraged to interact with the larger world in ways that feel relevant, exciting, and empowering.

Perhaps the most pervasive example of these re-schooling discourses has been the notion of 'twenty-first century skills' – a recurring feature of educational technology debate around the world. 'Twenty-first century skills' is now an accepted description of the required skill sets, competencies, pedagogies, curricular and assessment reforms and systemic arrangements that are seen to necessitate education reform – quite simply a blueprint for education in a digital age. While descriptions of these 'twenty-first century skills' may vary, the underlying imperatives remain the same – that is changing the structures, processes and practices of schools, teachers and students along more high tech, networked and 'innovative' lines. These discourses have been evident throughout a number of key discursive sites. For example, the United Nations Educational, Scientific and Cultural Organization's (UNESCO's) ICT Competency Framework for Teachers had an explicit focus on 'twenty-first century skills'. Similarly, the Organisation for Economic Co-operation and Development's (OECD's) New Millennium Learners programme positioned so-called 'twenty-first century competencies' (defined as 'the skills and competencies that a knowledge economy requires') within the educational agenda for the Program for International Student Assessment (PISA) comparative educational indicators.

The normalisation of these discourses has been supported by the efforts of multinational technology corporations in facilitating research and development efforts to outline and promote the 'principles' of twenty-first century skills. One such initiative was the Apple Classrooms of Tomorrow–Today programme (ACOT^2), run during the 2000s with its aim of 'changing the conversation about teaching, technology and learning'. Notably, the first phase of the ACOT^2 study identified six design principles for the twenty-first century high school, including the reorientation of curriculum and content, assessment and the social/emotional environment of skills around the notion of 'twenty-first century skills and outcomes'. Similar agendas were subsequently pursued through Microsoft's Innovative Teaching and Learning global research programme with its focus on 'twenty-first-century learning outcomes' and 'innovative teaching practices' characterised by student-centred pedagogy, knowledge building, problem solving and innovation, skilled communication, collaboration, self-regulation, and use of technology for learning. Within the US legislative context, the Partnership for Twenty-first Century Skills has spent much time popularising the notion of 'the four Cs': that is critical thinking and problem solving; communication; collaboration; and creativity and innovation. All told, a complex of interests has put much effort into establishing these ideas and agenda in the general educational consciousness.

Discourses of digital 'de-schooling'

These discourses of digital re-schooling focus on the continuation of educational institutions – concerned primarily with 'remixing' the major structures and process of formal education while retaining the physical and spatial confines of educational institutions. Another increasingly popular set of discourses, however, is those concerned with more radical forms of de-institutionalisation – what contrastingly can be termed 'digital de-schooling'. From this perspective, digital technology is seen to completely usurp the educational institution. Key concepts here include self-determination, self-organisation, self-regulation, learner autonomy and control, and (in a neat twist on the notion of 'DIY') the idea of 'do-it-ourselves'.

As with other aspects of digital activity, education is therefore imagined as something that is now open to reprogramming, modification and 'hacking' to better suit one's individual needs. As Dale Stephens (2013: 9) reasons:

> The systems and institutions that we see around us–of schools, college and work–are being systematically dismantled . . . If you want to learn the skills required to navigate the world–the hustle, networking and creativity–you're going to have to hack your own education.

In these terms, digital technology is aligned readily with arguments for the encouragement of 'unlearning' – that is 'learning how to learn indepen-dently' (Chokr 2009: 6), and a general rejection of the institutionalised 'banking model' of accumulating 'knowledge content'. Instead, digital education is conceived along lines of supporting open discussion, open debate, radical questioning, continuous experimentation and the sharing of knowledge.

De-schooling discourses have long persisted within discussions of digital education. Indeed, a subtle rejectionist line of thinking is apparent through-out the arguments of Seymour Papert – perhaps *the* founding father of academic educational technology. Papert was fond of asserting along lines that 'the computer will blow up the school' (Papert 1984: 38), or new tech-nology will 'overthrow the accepted structure of school . . . and pretty well everything that the education establishment will defend to the bitter end' (Papert 1998). These bon mots have been repeated frequently and with much approval in educational technology circles, and over three decades on continue to be an accepted part of mainstream thinking about educa-tion and technology. Now, many commentators are willing to denounce formal educational institutions as 'anachronistic' relics of the industrial age that are now rendered obsolete by contemporary digital technology. As Suoranta and Vadén (2010: 16) conclude:

> in their current forms it might be that schools no longer belong to the order of things in the late modern era, and are about to vanish from the map of human affairs.

This oppositional framing of digital technology and educational institutions has been reflected in a number of high profile and much lauded educa-tion programmes. For instance, while ostensibly relying on national school systems as its means of distribution, Nicholas Negroponte's One Laptop Per Child (OLPC) programme was built around explicitly anti-institutional discourses. Through the production of a low-cost, low-specification but highly durable personal computing device that can be handed over to children and young people around the world, OLPC has been positioned deliberately around values of networked individualism and a belief in the self-determining power of the individual child. This sentiment was certainly evident in Negroponte's proposal at the Social Innovation Summit in New York for a mass airdrop of tablet computers into remote villages from helicopters (Bajak 2012). As such, OLPC has been conceived and executed as an 'educator-free' model of learning – as Negroponte has argued:

> There are about 100 million kids without schools, without access to literate adults, and I would like to explore a way to get tablets to them in a manner that does not need 'educators' to go to the village.
>
> (Negroponte, cited in Bajak 2012)

Similar discourses surround the similarly feted Hole in the Wall and School in the Cloud initiatives (recently the recipient of the annual $1 million TED prize). These programmes are built around an ethos of 'minimally invasive education' where children and young people can access digital technology at any time, and teach themselves how to use computers and the internet on an individually paced basis. The guiding ethos for the Hole-in-the-wall programme was to locate digital technologies in what Arora (2012) characterises as 'out-of-the-way, out-of-the-mind locations' rather than in formal settings such as schools or universities. Indeed, the programme's credo of 'minimally-invasive education' was an avowedly non-institutionalised one, with children expected to engage with the technology 'free of charge and free of any supervision' (Mitra 2010). The initiative has since been extended – with its latest School in the Cloud incarnation attempting to use online communications to allow older community members in high-income countries to act as mentors and 'friendly but not knowledgeable' mediators to young autonomous learners. As such the provision of such access and support is seen to underpin what the project team term 'self-organised learning environments' and 'self activated learning' – thus providing an alternative 'for those denied formal schooling' in low-income countries (Arora 2012).

Yet perhaps the most pertinent example of the de-schooling ethos was to be found in the original development of 'massive open online courses' (or 'MOOCs') throughout the late 2000s and early 2010s. Now, of course, MOOCs have become profoundly institutionalised – most notably through the development of large-scale programmes such as Coursera and edX. These are quasi-corporate ventures concerned with delivering university courses on a free-at-the-point-of-contact basis to mass audiences. Yet while these MOOCs are now multi-billion dollar businesses supporting many of the most prestigious global university 'brands', the MOOC concept was developed originally by a loose collective of radically minded university teachers and researchers with a shared interest in developing open courses in online environments. This led to the idea of individuals being encouraged to learn through their own choice of digital tools – what was termed 'personal learning networks' – the collective results of which could be aggregated by the course coordinators and shared with other learners. In this original form, then, the MOOC was a grass roots, counter-cultural attempt by technology-savvy educators to subvert the dominance of top-down models of traditional higher education provision. In contrast to the commercially led, for-profit MOOCs of today, this was not a model of learning designed to reap dividends for shareholders or reinforce the brand identity of the world's major-league universities. Instead, in its original state, the MOOC marked an audacious attempt to disrupt the problematic elements of institutionalised higher education, such as assessment, payment and an emphasis on mass instruction rather than individually directed discovery learning.

Unpacking the discursive construction of digital education

These are all powerful discourses that have certainly influenced the recent 'tone of the conversation' around educational technology-defining educational problems (i.e. the rigid 'industrial-era school') *and* defining their solutions (i.e. the 'innovative' use of digital technology). In Jones and Hafner's (2012) terms, these discourses contain a number of seductive and convincing propositions (i.e. statements about education and how it works); presuppositions (treating certain propositions as given); and interpersonal functions (how relationships between people are represented). While these discourses clearly vary in the degree to which they perceive the reformation of existing educational arrangements, they can be seen as forming a general common sense – if not orthodoxy – around the nature and form of what education in the digital age 'should be'. These discourses certainly bolster a general imperative for educational change. In these terms, the digital realignment and reconfiguration of education is inevitable – the only question concerns the extent of these changes.

While in many ways oppositional, the 're-schooling' and 'de-schooling' discourses can be seen to legitimise a number of common sense understandings of contemporary educational change. Take, for example, the common framing of such discourses – that is the rhetorical structure and argumentative structure of these descriptions 'within which diverse discourses are articulated together in a particular way' (Fairclough 2006: 57). Here we can see a common device of presenting a problem of outmoded 'fixed' educational systems somehow failing the needs of contemporary society, and a solution of more flexible modes of digital technology somehow offering an alternative. Accompanying this logic is a dominant framing of digital education in terms of digital *learning*. Indeed, with much contemporary debate, the discourses of education and digital technology would appear to be an area that is dominated by the language of 'learning'. As Gert Biesta (2013: 8) has argued, this posits learning as 'an entirely natural phenomenon . . . [and], in the end, there must be something wrong with you if you do not want to learn and seek to refuse the learner identity'. Throughout these discourses of digital education, the primacy of learning can be seen in the emphasis on the individual accumulation of knowledge, skills, values and disposition (what Biesta terms 'qualification'), and the corresponding silences on the wider educational domains of socialisation and subjectification (i.e. the role of education in an individual either becoming part of and/or resisting existing social, political and professional 'orders'). Indeed, throughout these discourses of digital technology the idea of social and power relations being 'flattened' and recast along non-hierarchical lines was prominent. For example, 'traditional' forms of knowledge, expertise and institutionalism were devalued from pre-digital terms of 'curriculum', 'teachers' and 'schools' to ideas of mentors that were 'friendly but not knowledgeable' and de-institutionalised 'non-locations' in the form of 'holes in the wall' and 'the cloud'.

Despite the potentially violent connotations of the notion of 'disruption', it was noteworthy how these shifts, changes and rearrangements were usually presented in benign and creative terms. For example, proposals for quite fundamental rearrangements and reconfigurations were described in playful, creative and non-threatening terms of 'flipping', 'mashing-up' and 'remixing'. These are terms that imply constructive rather than destructive action, drawing on language more reminiscent of the culinary arts or music production than systematic reform. In addition to these mis-directions, it was also noteworthy how these discourses of digital education often position changes in the urgent but nebulous language of technology development – drawing on terms that are too 'high tech' to retain a tangible meaning – such as the practice of 'hacking', the process of 'gamificiation' and the notion of re-versioning in the form of '2.0'

As a whole, discursive forms such as these do much to legitimise and rationalise the continued reshaping of education along digital lines in what could be seen as times of considerable economic, technological *and* demographic change. As such, the nature of digital education discourse is understandably nebulous, vague, ambiguous and contradictory. That said, it is also worth questioning what the underpinning values and agendas of these discursive currents might be. In particular, how should we understand the potential gains and losses of educational transformation and educational disruption along neo-liberal lines associated with the increased use of digital technology? Here, our analysis leads us to highlight the discursive role of digital 'disruption' in normalising (and perhaps even domesticating) new digital forms of content production and content consumption within the changing order of mainstream education – most notably along neo-liberal lines. These issues therefore merit consideration in the brief space that remains in this chapter.

Perhaps the most prominent values throughout the discursive construction of digital re-schooling and de-schooling relate to the *individualisation of practice and action.* All these discourses involve an increased responsibility of the individual in terms of making choices with regards to education, as well as dealing with the consequences of choice. All these forms of digital education therefore demand increased levels of self-dependence and entrepreneurial thinking on the part of the individual, with educational success dependent primarily on the individual's ability to self-direct their ongoing engagement with learning through various preferred forms of digital technology.

Alongside this individualisation of action is the notion of *education as an area of increased informalisation and risk.* In this way, digital technology is seen to support forms of learning that could be said to be indeterminate, fragmented, uncertain and risky. Moreover, this informality is usually assumed to work in favour of the individual and at the expense of self-interested formal institutions. Thus, unwittingly or not, digital education provides a ready means through which informalised and disorganised sensibilities are internalised as norms and values by individuals, groups and institutions.

Another prominent value is the reframing of *educational concerns along less collective lines.* Unencumbered by the need to learn with those in one's immediate context or locality, these forms of re-schooling and de-schooling certainly make it easier to interact and learn with other people of one's choosing. The 'communities' of learners established through these digital technologies differ considerably in terms of social diversity, obligation, solidarity and underlying structures of power.

These discourses also tend *to frame learning as a competitive endeavour.* This belies the presentation of digital education as allowing individuals to learn harmoniously alongside others. Instead, digital technology places individuals in 'personal formative cycles, occupied in unison within individual feedback-action loops. They learn to become industrious self-improvers, accepting and implementing external goals' (Allen 2011: 378; see also Jones this volume). Thus while a sense of achievement at the expense of others may not be immediately apparent, 'competition is humanised and disguised and therefore intensified by this formative technology' (Allen 2011: 378).

Another value underpinning the discourses of digital education reviewed in this chapter is the *promotion of free-market values and sensibilities as a preferred mechanism of educational organisation.* On one hand, many forms of digital re-schooling and de-schooling support rational market exchange as a dominant framework for organising and regulating educational interaction and exchange. On the other hand, some of these discourses also support the overt monetisation of education provision within commercial marketplaces.

As such, these discourses also promote the *reconfiguration of education into a commodity state* – that is framing education processes and practices into the 'market form' of something that has calculable and quantifiable value, and that is therefore exchangeable. It seems clear that one of the values implicit in these discourses of re-schooling and de-schooling is the reconfiguration of educational practices and relations into forms that can be quantified and exchanged.

These latter points raise *the increased valuing of privatisation* through the digitalisation of education. In particular, these discourses tend to implicate the enhanced importance of non-state and private actors as education providers. Indeed, one of the clear outcomes of the re-schooling and de-schooling described in this chapter is the reconstitution of education into forms that are reducible, quantifiable and ultimately contractible to various actors outside of the educational community.

All these discourses also imply an *increased expansion of education into unfamiliar areas of society and social life* – leading to an 'always-on' state of potential educational engagement. Indeed, all these discourses support the expansion of education and learning into domestic, community and work settings. There are clear parallels here with what Basil Bernstein (2001) identified as the 'total pedagogisation of society' – that is a modern society that ensures that pedagogy is integrated into all possible spheres of life.

All these points also relate to the correspondences between digital technology and *the altered emotional aspects of educational engagement.* In particular, the disaggregated forms of re-schooling and de-schooling could all be said to involve the education being experienced on less immediate, less intimate and perhaps more instrumental grounds. From this perspective, the partial, segmented, task-orientated, fragmented and discontinuous nature of digital education could be seen as a form of 'spiritual alienation' – that is alienation at the level of meaning, where 'conditions of good work' become detached from the 'conditions of good character' (Sennett 2012).

Conclusions

Whether one agrees with any of these interpretations or not, current understandings of digital education clearly disguise a number of significant conflicts and tensions that need to be fully acknowledged and addressed. Of course, these apparent contradictions should not be assumed automatically to be cause for concern. There are, after all, many people who will be advantaged by more individualised, elitist, competitive, market-driven, omnipresent and de-emotionalised forms of educational engagement. Yet, many of these values surely do not sit easily with the traditional values and desires of 'public education' – that is education as a public good rather than private interest. Certainly many of the forms of digital education implicit in the discourses of re-schooling and de-schooling align readily with the values and agendas of what has been noted elsewhere as a 'neo-liberal turn' within educational provision – that is based around values and agendas of profit, decreased state involvement, satisfying the requirement of post-industrial capitalism, and so on.

At best, then, current forms of 'digital education' appear to be doing little to challenge or disrupt the prevailing individualisation, commodification and privatisation of contemporary education. Conversely, there is far less that actively promotes 'positive' concerns of social justice, inequality and the notion of education as a collective public good. These tensions may – or may not – constitute a problem, but they at least deserve to be fore-grounded more readily within the dominant discourses about education and digital technology. While it is difficult to identify easy solutions to this predicament, there are some modest means through which these tensions might begin to be addressed. For example, ways need to be explored of stimulating vigorous ongoing public debate about education and digital technology – leading to the framing of digital education as a public contro-versy, and allowing current 'common sense' understandings of digital edu-cation to be challenged, contested, problematised and de-reified. Similarly, there is clearly scope for the continued problematising of digital educa-tion from within the academic community – engaging in discussions and debates that move beyond the celebratory nature of much scholarly work on digital media, and better demonstrates the links between the various types of dominance and inequality inherent in digital education. As Jones and Hafner (2012: 98) conclude, in this respect 'what we really mean by a critical stance is a *conscious* stance'. Above all, then, is the need to encour-age more people's interactions with digital education in conscious terms of power and ideological conflict. As Alexander Galloway (2012: vii) reminds us, 'digital media ask a question to which the political interpretation is the only coherent answer. In other words, digital media interpellate the politi-cal interpretation.'

References

Allen, A. (2011) 'Michael young's the rise of the meritocracy', *British Journal of Educational Studies*, 59(4): 367–382.

Arora, P. (2012) 'Typology of web 2.0 spheres', *Current Sociology*, 60(5): 599–618.

Bajak, F. (2012) 'Peru's ambitious laptop program gets mixed grades', *The Guardian*, 3 July.

Bernstein, B. (2001) 'From pedagogies to knowledges', in A. Morais, I. Neves, B. Davies and H. Daniels (eds) *Towards a Sociology of Pedagogy*, 363–368, New York: Peter Lang.

Biesta, G. (2013) 'Interrupting the politics of learning', *Power and Education*, 5(1): 4–15.

Chokr, N. (2009) *Unlearning: or how not to be governed?*, Exeter: Imprint Academic.

Collins, A. and Halverson, R. (2009) *Rethinking Education in the Age of Technology*, New York: Teachers College Press.

Fairclough, N. (1989) *Language and Power*, London: Longman.

Fairclough, N. (1995) *Critical Discourse Analysis*, London: Routledge.

Fairclough, N. (2005) 'Neo-liberalism – a discourse-analytical perspective', presentation to Conference on British and American Studies, Braşov. Online. Available HTTP: <http://cpd1.ufmt.br/meel/arquivos/artigos/4.pdf> (accessed 30 April 2014).

Fairclough, N. (2006) 'Discursive transition in Central and Eastern Europe', in X. Shi (ed.) *Discourse as Social Struggle*, 49–72, Hong Kong: Hong Kong University Press.

Galloway, A. (2012) *The Interface Effect*, Cambridge: Polity.

Hall, S. (2003) 'New labour's double-shuffle', *Soundings*, 24: 10–24.

Jarvis, J. (2009) *What Would Google Do?*, London: Collins.

Jones, R. H. and Hafner, C. A. (2012) *Understanding Digital Literacies*, London: Routledge.

Microsoft (2013) 'School of the future', Online. Available HTTP: <http://www.microsoft.com/education/schoolofthefuture/> (accessed 15 May 2013).

Mitra, S. (2010) 'Give them a laptop and a group of pupils will teach themselves', *The Guardian*, Educational Supplement, 19 October. Online. Available HTTP: <http://www.theguardian.com/education/2010/oct/18/sugata-mitra-slumdog-teach-self> (accessed 30 April 2014).

Nelson, M. (2012) 'Soviet and American precursors to the gamification of work', proceedings of the 16th International Academic MindTrek Conference. Online. Available HTTP: <http://ssrn.com/abstract=2115483> (accessed 30 June 2014).

Papert, S. (1984) 'Trying to predict the future', *Popular Computing*, 3(13): 30–44.

Papert, S. (1998) 'Does easy do it?' *Game Developer*, June/September, 88–92, Online. Available HTTP: <http://www.papert.org/articles/Doeseasydoit.html> (accessed 30 April 2014).

Poole, S. (2012) 'Invasion of the cyber-hustlers', *New Statesman*, 6 December. Online. Available HTTP: <http://www.newstatesman.com/sci-tech/internet/2012/12/jeff-jarvis-clay-shirky-jay-rosen-invasion-cyber-hustlers> (accessed 30 April 2014).

Quitney, J. and Rainie, L. (2012) *Gamification*, Washington, DC: Pew Internet and American Life Project.

Rudd, T. (2013) 'The ideological appropriation of digital technology in UK education', in N. Selwyn, and K. Facer (eds) *The Politics of Education and Technology*, 147–168, New York: Palgrave Macmillan.

Salen, K., Torres, R., Wolozin, L., Rufo-Tepper, R. and Shapiro, A. (2011) *Quest to Learn*, Chicago, IL: Macarthur Foundation. Online. Available HTTP: <https://mitpress.mit.edu/books/quest-learn> (accessed 30 June 2014).

Sennett, R. (2012) *Together*, London: Allen Lane.

Stephens, D. (2013) *Hacking Your Education*, London: Penguin.

Suoranta, J. and Vadén, T. (2010) *Wikiworld*, London: Pluto Press.

Thomas, S. (1999). 'Who speaks for education?', *Discourse: Studies in the Cultural Politics of Education*, 20(1): 41–56.

van Dijk, T. (1993) 'Principles of critical discourse analysis', *Discourse and Society*, 4(2): 249–283.

Whitby, G. (2013) *Educating Gen Wi-Fi*, Sydney: Harper Collins.

Williamson, B. (2013) 'Networked cosmopolitanism?' in N. Selwyn and K. Facer (eds) *The Politics of Education and Technology*, 39–62, New York: Palgrave Macmillan.

Index